The Cavalry Trilogy

John Ford, John Wayne, and the Making of Three Classic Westerns

Michael F. Blake

TWODOT®

ESSEX, CONNECTICUT
HELENA, MONTANA

A · TWODOT® · BOOK
An imprint of Globe Pequot, the trade division of
The Rowman & Littlefield Publishing Group, Inc.
4501 Forbes Blvd., Ste. 200
Lanham, MD 20706
www.rowman.com

Distributed by NATIONAL BOOK NETWORK

British Library Cataloguing in Publication Information available

Library of Congress Cataloging-in-Publication Data available

LCCN 2023042709
ISBN 9781493077069 (paperback)
ISBN 9781493077076 (epub)

∞™ The paper used in this publication meets the minimum requirements of American National Standard for Information Sciences—Permanence of Paper for Printed Library Materials, ANSI/NISO Z39.48-1992.

To

Kevin Brownlow

My inspiration to become a film historian

and my friend.

Contents

Preface

John Ford never planned to make a cavalry trilogy.

In many ways, Ford's cavalry trilogy did just what was expected of the cavalry in the movies: They came to his rescue.[1] The reason for directing *Fort Apache* and *She Wore a Yellow Ribbon* was to help relieve his company's heavy debt incurred by the box office failure of *The Fugitive*. *Rio Grande* was a means to an end to finally make his dream project, *The Quiet Man*.

John Ford dismissed his cavalry trilogy as potboilers; his only praise was the films made a lot of money. In his later years, Ford was brusque when critics hailed his films as works of art, stating that directing was just "a job of work." John Ford and his films have been dissected in lectures, scholarly papers, and books, with discussions ranging from camera angles to speculating about the director's meaning of a specific scene. Ford did not tolerate theoretical scrutiny, and when asked penetrating questions regarding his films, he claimed he had no idea what they were talking about.

When Orson Welles was asked which directors he admired, he replied the old masters appealed to him. "By that I mean John Ford, John Ford, John Ford. With Ford at his best, you feel that a movie has lived and breathed in a real world, even though it may have been written by Mother Machree." Before he ever shot a framc of *Citizen Kane*, Welles endlessly screened and studied Ford's *Stagecoach*. Welles was not the only director to be influenced by the work of John Ford, as David Lean, Akira Kurosawa, Martin Scorsese, Steven Spielberg, Walter Hill, and Christopher Nolan have all acknowledged the indelible impression Ford and his films left on them.

It is hard for anyone not to be influenced by a John Ford film. In some respects, anyone who watches a John Ford film can relate to his cinematic storytelling—whether it is standing up for others like Tom Joad in *The Grapes of Wrath*, marshaling a large group of people to make his widow feel better at her husband's wake in *The Last Hurrah*, the family dinners in *How Green Was My Valley*, or a man facing the end of a long career in *She Wore a Yellow Ribbon*. While the majority of viewers will never likely experience what a character does in a Ford film, there is *something* the director injects into those celluloid images that causes us all to relate.

Ford refused to accept accolades that he was a cinematic poet. In one of his last interviews, Ford stated to Walter Wagner, "You say someone's called me the greatest poet of the Western saga. I am not a poet, and I don't know what a Western saga is. I would say that is horseshit. I'm just a hard-nosed, hardworking, run-of-the-mill director."[2] (The closest Ford ever came to admitting artistic talent was saying he was "the best cameraman in the business.")

John Ford was a cinematic poet.

Whether in black-and-white or in color, Ford created scenes of beauty, sensitivity, and magic that defied description. He gave us memorable images, such as the shadows of the attacking Indians reflected against a train car (*The Iron Horse*), the wanted poster of his friend trailing behind Gypo Nolan in the fog-shrouded streets of Dublin (*The Informer*), Wyatt Earp walking down the rain-soaked boardwalk (*My Darling Clementine*), the cavalry making their way through a thunderstorm (*She Wore a Yellow Ribbon*), Ethan Edwards standing in the doorway (*The Searchers*), or the defeated political candidate walking alone in a park as his rival's victory parade passes by him (*The Last Hurrah*). Even though some of his efforts in his filmography are not as strong as others, the weakest John Ford film has something worth watching.

Starting in silent movies, Ford quickly learned to let the visual advance the story instead of dialogue. *Straight Shooting* (1917), his fifth film as a director, demonstrates Ford taking a different approach to a standard Western plot of a shoot-out, while *The Iron Horse* (1924), *Three Bad Men* (1926), and *Four Sons* and *Riley, the Cop* (both 1928) present a creative artist using the camera to enhance the narrative. During a UCLA retrospective in early 1964, Ford stated, "Pictures, not words, should tell the story."[3] With the birth of sound, Ford, like other filmmakers, had a learning curve, but the director quickly adapted to the new medium of talking pictures. Ford soon found his rhythm, impressively displayed in *The Lost Patrol* (1934) and *The Informer* (1935).

In so many of his films, Ford would have several actors, as well as extras, in a scene, but they never seemed crowded into a set, unless it was necessary, such as the passengers in *Stagecoach* or the sailors belowdecks in *The Long Voyage Home*. Ford moved his actors with tremendous grace in any sequence, making it appear so natural that one is unaware of the effort it took to coordinate such a scene. Examples can be found in the scene where York reports at an officers' dance that Cochise has agreed to talk in *Fort Apache*, or the Texas Rangers arriving at the Edwards cabin in *The Searchers*.

Ford was a master of the camera. It was rare to find him looking through the camera lens during his career. He instinctively knew where to place his camera, often working with the same cinematographers on many projects (Archie Stout, Winton Hoch, Bert Glennon, William Clothier) where they developed a "shorthand" communication. He once advised future filmmakers they should get a cinematographer "you know well and trust."

Ford always preferred to shoot in black-and-white versus color. Asked why, Ford replied, "You can get a guy off the street and he can shoot a picture in color. But it takes a real artist to do a black-and-white picture."[4] Ironically, three of his finest films were photographed in color (*She Wore a Yellow Ribbon*, *The Quiet Man*, and *The Searchers*), with the first two winning Oscars for Best Color Cinematography. However, had Ford photographed either *My Darling Clementine* or *The Man Who Shot Liberty Valance* in color, it would have seriously detracted from the emotional impact of the story. Many historians regret that *Fort Apache* and *Rio Grande* were not filmed in color, but, as the reader will see, the decision was economical.

While the main purpose for making the cavalry films was financial, Ford had been considering a film centered on a cavalry outpost in the

Western territories. "When in doubt, make a Western" is a quote credited to John Ford; although some question its veracity, that is exactly what he did with the trilogy.[5]

Ford had a strong love and admiration for the military, especially the US Navy. His love of the sea can be traced to his childhood in Maine, and carried into his adult life with the purchase of his own ketch, and then to his service in the navy during World War II. His four years with the war effort further strengthened his respect for the military, and Ford would continue to honor those who served and paid the ultimate price in his films. (Between the end of the war in 1945 until 1964, Ford directed twelve military-themed films.[6]) Even though he was, as John Wayne once noted, "a through and through Navy man," he had a great respect for the US Army and General Douglas MacArthur.

For the cavalry trilogy, Ford's inspiration came from the short stories by James Warner Bellah, the son of an army officer who grew up on military bases. Bellah based his cavalry stories in the Great Plains or the Southwest, providing enough of a plot for Ford to construct a film according to his desire. The three cavalry films saluted the duty and honor of a soldier, as well as offering a touch of romance, humor, reunion of family ties, and the remembrance of lost comrades or lost loves. In *Fort Apache*, Ford was not afraid to show the folly of an officer's ego and ignorance; yet, in the film's conclusion, the officer is a public hero, ignoring his command shortcomings for the good of the regiment.

In all three films, the true heroes are the soldiers. While Colonel Thursday receives posthumous glory and hero worship, it is the men who serve that are the heart of the military. At the end of *Fort Apache*, John Wayne's character reminds the audience that those men who died will keep on living as long as the regiment lives. "The pay is thirteen dollars a month, the diet beans and hay," he states. "They'll fight over cards or rotgut whiskey but share the last drop in their canteens. The faces may change, the names, but they're there. The regiment. The regular army. Now and fifty years from now."

Those words indubitably echoed John Ford's sentiments. The military was everything, and without it, the liberties enjoyed by so many would cease to exist. To celebrate the military's courage and honor the memory of those who served, John Ford turned to the US Cavalry.

* * *

My introduction to a John Ford film was a 1964 Saturday-afternoon roadshow matinee of *Cheyenne Autumn* at the Pantages Theatre in Hollywood. As a cowboy-crazy seven-year-old, the cavalry and the action kept my interest, but it was the land that truly mesmerized me. I had never seen Monument Valley before, and looking at the massive landscape on a big screen ignited my imagination. Subsequently, every tree and bush in my neighborhood stood in for those iconic buttes as my friends and I played cowboys on Saturday afternoons.

My father, character actor Larry J. Blake—who had worked twice for John Ford—introduced me to the director's work. During my childhood, two local television stations showed several of Ford's films, and by 1968 I had managed to watch ten of them. My father would point out "Ford's touches," as he called them, ranging from camera placement, to humor, to performances. For a budding, self-taught film historian, John Ford and his films were my master class. The Masquers Club in Hollywood was a gathering place for actors, and Ford was one of the few directors given an honorary membership. For many years during Easter vacation or in the summer, I often accompanied my dad (who was a member) for lunch. I was fortunate enough to meet several people who worked with Ford, and informed them that I had seen their work in one of his films. This always elicited the reply, "You're too young to know that!" I was not deterred, and realizing my serious interest, they would share stories.

Working as a makeup artist in the film and television industry, I came to appreciate John Ford's talent more and more. For me, working a twelve- to eighteen-hour day on a movie that would take upwards of three months to complete, I was always amazed at how fast Ford shot a film, not to mention only working a ten-hour day. Many directors I worked around spent so much time doing endless takes for a single scene; it reminded me of Ford's comment that additional takes ruined the freshness of a scene.

As a film historian, the background of how a movie was made has always been a great fascination of mine. Perhaps this comes from spending sixty years of my life on soundstages, as well as growing up with my dad's stories about the business. How a production is shot, how locations are chosen, and moving a cast and crew to such a place required immense planning. This process, which began in the silent era, continues to this day. It takes a lot of effort to make a movie, with tremendous help from a lot of unsung heroes.

Ford's cavalry trilogy has never been given the proper attention the films deserve. Unfortunately, when an author is writing a biography of any director or actor, space and word count of a manuscript become the enemy. All too often writers have to make hard decisions on the matter of trimming material. So, much like the cavalry, I have come to the rescue of these three classic films, providing the following account of how John Ford directed his beloved cavalry trilogy.

Author's Note

Film historians rely on many different types of records when researching the history of cinema, including interviews, directors' notes, script drafts, studio memos, and budgets. All of these materials are important in order to separate fact from fiction.

Often these items will divulge previously unknown information, which can bring clarity and greater understanding to the subject matter. However, there are also those occasions when a historian must deal with a major disappointment; for instance, when files and other documentation contain little to no information, and all other avenues of research appear to be just as barren. These annoying stages of research can be quite frustrating, because the author then must work even harder to fill in the gaps.

In my case, I was fortunate to have found an abundance of information regarding both *Fort Apache* and *She Wore a Yellow Ribbon* located in the John Ford Collection at Lilly Library, Indiana University, and the Argosy Productions collection at Brigham Young University. Unfortunately, the files for *Rio Grande* were not as extensive, and equally—if not more—frustrating was the discovery that the files for this film in the Argosy Pictures collection at Brigham Young University held only minimal information. However, the local Moab newspaper, *The Times-Independent*, came to my aid in offering new and previously unknown material.

It is always disappointing when files prove to be as empty as Al Capone's vault. However, when one unearths new material, as I have in this book, you can understand how Indiana Jones felt.

The Director and the Adventurer

John Ford and Merian C. Cooper

That Jack Ford, he yells real loud. He'd make a good director.

—Carl Laemmle

When Peter Bogdanovich asked John Ford how he filmed the land rush sequence of *Three Bad Men* (1926), the director curtly replied, "With a camera."[1]

Concerned Ford was three pages behind schedule, a producer walked on the soundstage to inform him of his tardiness. The director asked for a script and began to thumb through it until he found what he wanted. He ripped out the three pages, letting them fall to the floor. Handing the script back to the producer, Ford commented, "Now we're on schedule!"[2]

During the filming of *Mogambo* (1953), Ford concluded a scene with stars Clark Gable and Ava Gardner, and ordered it printed. (The term means the scene was satisfactory and would be developed to be used in the film.) When Gable asked if he could do the scene again, Ford assured him the last take was fine, but the actor persisted. Relenting to the request, Ford allowed Gable to do it again. He called "Action" and Gable started the scene but soon realized the camera was not filming. Ford had a grin on his face. He had told the actor that he could play the scene again, but didn't say he would shoot it.[3]

Many actors would leap at the chance to work on a John Ford film, while a few regretted working with him and vowed never to do so again. He could be kind, humorous, indifferent, or downright mean. A sentiment held by many who worked with him was "He was a son of a bitch, but he was *our* son of a bitch!"[4] Ben Johnson recalled that "[Ford] had the ability to bring out whatever's inside you. A lot of people can't do that, but he had the ability and he knew what people liked to see and hear. That's why he was so great."[5]

John Ford holds the record of winning four Oscars for Best Director, as well as two additional Oscars for Best Documentary.[6] He's been called one of the greatest directors of cinema. Blessed with a biting Irish wit, which he used to keep producers, actors, and interviewers at bay, Ford carefully crafted a reputation as a hard-nosed director who stinted on praising anyone's work. No one dared to challenge his authority, and if they did, they soon regretted it. In his later years, Ford often gave interviewers minimal answers or a gruff reply, applying a thick layer of Irish blarney that had nothing to do with facts. His lying was never malicious, but augmented the legend. It was good theatrics. He told one interviewer he had been a cowboy early in his life (not true), and told another that the gunfight in *My Darling Clementine* was exactly the way it had happened, as told to him by Wyatt Earp (another tall tale). If he found questions silly or boring, Ford pretended not to hear them, resulting in painful, deadly silence for the interviewer. When a British interviewer pressed him on his treatment of Indians in his movies, it got Ford's Irish up. He shot back, "What about the Black and Tans?"[7]

Despite Ford's brusque demeanor, there was another side to him that he carefully kept hidden, like a gambler hiding an extra ace. When he was about to start a film, he'd find out which older actors, usually from his days at Universal and Fox, needed work. Ford would put these performers on his film, either in a small part or as a background player, often carrying them for days or weeks on the payroll. One day at Fox Studios, an older actor he knew from Universal stopped Ford, informing him that his wife needed an operation, and asking for a loan of $200. Ford yelled at the man, storming away into his office. Moments later, Ford's business manager came out with a $1,000 check, and Ford's driver took the man home, where an ambulance shuttled his ailing wife to the hospital for the surgery.[8]

"One time, just before *Rio Grande*, we were really busted. I owed my mom so much money and I didn't want to ask her for any more," Harry Carey Jr. recounted. "So, I went to Uncle Jack's office over there at Republic, and I sat down and I'm hemming and hawing. He says, 'You want some money?' I didn't give him *any* indication because I never said it before. I said, 'Yes sir.' So, he said, 'What do you want? One week? Two-week salary?' In those days $500 would last you six months. I said, 'Just a week's salary.' Ford called Lowell Farrell (his production manager) in and said, 'Give Dobe $500.' "[9]

Shortly after finishing *She Wore a Yellow Ribbon*, Monument Valley was hit with a hard blizzard, burying it in twelve feet of snow. Learning that many Navajo were in dire straits, Ford used his military connections to arrange for army planes to airdrop needed food and supplies. "Thanks to that, an' the two hundred thousand dollars or so he'd left behind, is why another tragedy was prevented," Harry Goulding stated.[10] To show their gratitude and admiration, the Navajo tribe gifted Ford a sacred deer hide, bestowing the Navajo name *Natani Nez* (Tall Soldier) during the filming of *The Searchers*.

Ford never let on that deep inside was a caring, extremely sentimental Irishman who loved great literature and history, while longing to be just "one of the boys." He fashioned his gruff facade into a myth, much like that of Ransom Stoddard's heroics in *The Man Who Shot Liberty Valance* (1962). He brushed off any praise of being an artist and refused to accept plaudits, claiming it was "just a job." Despite his ornery veneer and biting comments, many people developed a tremendous loyalty to the "Old Man."

"He had more respect from the crew, probably more than any director I've been with," declared stuntman Chuck Hayward. Fellow stuntman Terry Wilson said everyone had so much respect for him they would only address him as "Mr. Ford." There was just one actor (Ken Tobey) who dared to call him Jack, and that only happened once. John Wayne always addressed him as "Coach," or occasionally as "Pappy." "He was a joy to work with, too. He was something," Wilson remembered.[11] These people, who made up what became known as the "John Ford Stock Company," were a group of actors, stuntmen, and crew members Ford used on many of his films. They knew his quirks, understood what he wanted, and catered to his every demand.

When asked why Ford had created such an uncompromising exterior, Harry Carey Jr. simply stated, "On a Ford picture there was one person in charge of the film. *Him.* He didn't want—or need—any input or interference from a producer or an actor. That's why he came off as such a gruff guy. He actually scared a lot of studio executives, and they'd basically leave him alone. That's what he wanted."[12]

John Martin Feeney Jr. was born in Portland, Maine, on February 1, 1894, the ninth of eleven children to Irish immigrant parents.[13] In another example of spreading his Irish blarney, Ford always claimed his name at birth was Sean Aloysius O'Fearna. ("Feeney" is the equivalent of *O'Fearna* in the Gaelic language.) As a child and teenager, often going by the nickname of Jack, Ford engaged in baseball and football, despite his poor eyesight. He also learned to fight against others who besmirched his Irish heritage.

It was during this time that Ford began to craft a rough exterior to hide and protect his sentimentality and love of reading. He was a voracious reader his entire life. John Wayne recalled that on one sailing trip on Ford's boat, the *Araner*, the director had a stack of books and would read three of them while Wayne was still reading his first.

As a teen and young adult, Ford was known for being a gifted storyteller, which likely came, at least in part, from his time working as an usher at Portland's Jefferson Theatre. Standing at the back, Ford would watch the performances, committing the actors' dialogue to memory. It was during this period that he was given a bit part in a play. His role required him to deliver a telegram to actor Sidney Toler. The actor, knowing Ford was an amateur, chose to have some fun. He asked him what was in the telegram, which flustered Ford, who could only offer a stuttered reply. (In later years when both men were working in Hollywood, Toler never appeared in a Ford film.)

Ford's brother, Francis, was thirteen years older than John, and the rascal of the Feeney family. He ran off to fight in the Spanish-American War, only to be sent home when the army learned he was fifteen. A quick romance resulted in a forced marriage, requiring Francis to work in his father's saloon while awaiting the birth of his son, Philip. With the marriage ending as quickly as it had started, Francis packed a bag and left Portland. Drifting into New York City, he soon found a job in a local theater as a stagehand before eventually graduating to acting roles. Like other performers before him, he adopted a new name—Francis Ford. By 1900, he began taking roles in the embryo that became motion pictures, appearing in films for Thomas Edison before hooking up with Star Films, produced by Gaston Méliès (brother of the famous Georges Méliès). Méliès moved his company from New Jersey to San Antonio, Texas, and Francis followed, appearing in many Westerns. Leaving Méliès in 1911, Francis headed to Los Angeles where he joined producer-director Thomas Ince. During this period Francis began directing (mostly Westerns) for Ince and gained a reputation of being brusque and sarcastic to his cast and crew.[14] By 1913, Francis was running his own company at Universal, working as a writer, director, and actor. He teamed up with actress Grace Cunard in these productions, and they became one of cinema's early star duos.

Ever since Francis had left Portland, the Feeney family had not heard a word from him. One day at the cinema, Ford's mother, an ardent fan of the flickers, spotted a young man in a movie produced by Universal Studios. It was Francis! The family sent him a letter in care of Universal, and, in the spring of 1914, there was a grand reunion in Portland, with Francis arriving in style, driving a Stutz Bearcat. John was in awe of the stories Francis told of this new place called Hollywood where they made movies.

Graduating from high school a few months later, John Ford followed in his brother's footsteps and traveled to Hollywood, hoping to find a place in the infant film industry. Not only did he follow his brother to Hollywood, he also adopted his last name, calling himself Jack Ford. At Universal, he worked on his brother's productions as a prop man and stuntman (occasionally doubling for his brother)—even acting.[15] Despite his claims that he never did much acting in his early days at Universal, Ford appeared in at least seventeen films produced by his brother's company. Nearly four decades later, Francis recalled that John's efforts as a prop man "stunk," he was worse as an assistant director, and "as an actor—such a ham!" He admitted his younger brother was "no good" until he was allowed "something to do on his own where he could let himself go—and he proved himself then."

Notwithstanding a familial connection, the relationship between John and Francis was hardly filled with brotherly love. Francis was known to be hard on John, bordering on abusive. In one film, John was doubling his brother in a Civil War battle sequence. An explosion from a hand grenade went off, sending John into the air and breaking his arm. Francis later told his brother that he was relieved the camera didn't catch that it was John, not Francis, taking the hit. John never forgot the incident, or the comment.

Years later, Francis, whose popularity had faded by the mid-1920s, was often cast in small roles in many of John's productions, usually as a drunk. One day on *Judge Priest* (1934), John, who cast his brother as a village loafer, had him sit in a wheelbarrow with a rope tied from the wheelbarrow to the rear of a carriage. As the carriage rides out of the scene, an unsuspecting Francis was yanked out of the wheelbarrow, landing smack on his posterior. With the scene completed, Ford went over to his brother and said, "That was for the hand grenade!"[16]

Exactly how John Ford moved into the director's chair is hard to pin down. According to Ford, he was hurriedly assigned to act like a director (he was a prop man at the time) to impress Universal's founder Carl Laemmle and a group of his friends. Ford gathered a band of cowboys, giving direction for them to race up and down the street, shooting their guns and yelling. When he gave the order by firing a gun, five cowboys he had chosen would fall off their horses. Unfortunately, when Ford shot his gun, *all* the cowboys fell off their horses. Ford also set fire to the town set as a climax. When the studio had an opportunity for someone to direct a two-reel Western, Laemmle reportedly said, "Jack Ford, he yells real loud. He'd make a good director."[17] Another version, possibly closer to the truth, had Francis asking Harry Carey, Universal's leading Western star, to give John a chance at directing. Years later, Olive Carey, the actor's widow, claimed Harry stopped by Francis Ford's set one day and began talking to young Ford, and the two "just clicked." It's entirely possible Francis may have introduced his younger brother to Carey and suggested John as a director, as Carey was unhappy with his current director.

Either way, in 1917, Ford began a forty-seven-year career as a movie director, signing a contract with Universal in September for a weekly salary of $75. Between 1917 and 1920, he directed twenty-two Westerns starring Harry Carey before the two men parted ways. While neither man ever spoke of what caused the relationship to fracture, John's grandson, Dan Ford, believes it was over Carey making more than what Ford was earning. By 1919, Carey was earning $2,250 a week, while Ford's salary was just $300 a week, despite his creative contributions. (Their last collaboration, *Desperate Trails*, was released in June 1921.) It would be sixteen years before Carey would work with Ford one last time in *The Prisoner of Shark Island* (1936).

In December 1920, Ford signed a contract with Fox Pictures for $600 a week. Ford's twenty-one years at Fox allowed his artistic talent to grow and flourish, notably with his epic *The Iron Horse* (1924) and his German cinema–influenced *Four Sons* (1928), both of which were critical and financial successes. (*Cameo Kirby*, released in 1923, was the first film crediting him as John Ford.)

Fox's new studio executive, Darryl F. Zanuck, agreed to a new contract with Ford that granted him the ability to occasionally direct a project at another studio. Ford was invited by RKO studio executive Merian C. Cooper to make *The Lost Patrol* (1934) and *The Informer* (1935), the latter winning Ford his first Oscar for Best Director. Over the next five years, John Ford would make some of his finest films, picking up two more Best Director Oscars for *The Grapes of Wrath* and *How Green Was My Valley*. (Some of Ford's other notable films in this period were *Judge Priest*, *Steamboat 'Round the Bend* [both starring Will Rogers], *Wee Willie Winkie*, *Stagecoach*, *Young Mr. Lincoln*, *Drums Along the Mohawk*, and *The Long Voyage Home*.)

In 1941, America was thrown into the boiling cauldron that became World War II. Ford joined the US Navy, heading up the Field Photographic Unit, populated with several cameramen and editors who had worked in Hollywood prior to the war. His unit was assigned to the Office of Coordinator of Information (COI) at the request of William "Wild Bill" Donovan. Ford answered solely to Donovan, producing various documentaries to support the war effort, as well as training films.

(Ford appeared in one training film, *Undercover* [1944], as an agent discussing a fictitious background for an agent.) In June 1942, President Roosevelt split the COI into two divisions: Office of Strategic Services (OSS) and Office of War Information (OWI). Donovan ran the OSS, forerunner of today's CIA, and brought Ford's unit along with him.

Ford called it the "luck of the Irish" that he happened to land at Midway Island prior to the Japanese naval attack. Armed with his own Bell and Howell 16mm Filmo camera, Ford filmed the June 4, 1942, attack as Japanese fighter planes dropped bombs and strafed the ground. The Japanese navy suffered a crushing defeat, and Ford's subsequent documentary, *The Battle of Midway*, earned his first of two Oscars for Best Documentary.[18]

With the end of the war, John Ford returned to Hollywood. Under his 20th Century-Fox contract he owed one more picture, choosing *My Darling Clementine* (1946), a Western about the exploits of Wyatt Earp and Doc Holliday in Tombstone. Fox studio head Darryl F. Zanuck was eager to keep Ford at his studio, offering him a yearly salary of $600,000, and the ability to work at another studio on selected projects. Ford flatly refused.

Looking to the horizon, Ford, like other directors, longed for autonomy in choosing projects without studio executives looking over his shoulder or questioning his material. It was just a matter of time before John Ford would strike out and form his own company. He just needed the right partner.

* * *

If there ever was a true adventurer in the mold of Indiana Jones, it was Merian C. Cooper.

Born in Jacksonville, Florida, on October 24, 1893, Cooper became fascinated with the life of an explorer after reading Paul du Chaillu's *Explorations and Adventures in Equatorial Africa*, and made up his mind to become an explorer.[19] Du Chaillu's book included his hunt for wild gorillas, a subject that would influence Cooper's cinematic career.

Cooper attended the Naval Academy at Annapolis, but in his senior year was kicked out due to problems caused by his "high-spirited demeanor." He worked as a newspaperman in Des Moines, Minneapolis, and St. Louis, before joining the Georgia National Guard. His unit was detailed to the Texas border to stop Pancho Villa's raids into the United States, but the only action Cooper saw was guard duty. Refusing a lieutenant's commission with the National Guard, he won an appointment to the flight training school in Atlanta, and upon graduation, Cooper was assigned to the 20th Aero Squadron, flying bombing missions over German lines during World War I.

In one mission, his flying group was attacked by German aircraft, and Cooper's plane was hit in the tail before its engine burst into flames. With fire spreading into the cockpit (Cooper's hands were horribly burned), he managed to pull his plane out of a tail-first plunge and land the aircraft. Both he and his tail-gunner partner, Edmund Leonard, managed to get out of the burning wreckage, only to be taken prisoner by German troops. Doctors at the German hospital managed to save Cooper's hands, and he remained there until the end of the war.[20]

After the war's end in 1918, Cooper remained in Europe. Learning from Polish soldiers their homeland was being threatened by the Bolsheviks, Cooper joined a group of fellow Americans who flew humanitarian missions to deliver food and medicine to the Polish people under siege. Captivated by their determination to fight for their freedom against the Russians on the front line, Cooper and other Americans formed a unit as part of the Polish Kościuszko Squadron. Cooper's luck as a pilot ran out in July 1920 when a bullet hit his gas tank, and he was thrown from his plane as it hit the ground. Taken prisoner by Russian Cossacks, Cooper was held in several labor camps near Moscow. Finally, he and two other Polish soldiers escaped a work detail, spending their nights walking to Latvia, a distance of 550 miles. It was there they learned the battle between Poland and Russia had ended. Cooper eventually returned to a hero's welcome in Warsaw, Poland, being decorated for exceptional bravery.[21]

Returning to the United States with nothing in his pockets, Cooper managed to nail down a job as a night reporter for the *New York Times*. This allowed him to spend his days visiting the American Geographical Society, which ignited his flame for adventure. Declining the managing editor job at the *Minneapolis Daily News*, he left New York City behind, signing on as a second officer on a ship that was making travel pictures around the world. Knowing nothing about cameras or filmmaking, Cooper's youthful bluster and drive allowed him to quickly learn how a camera worked, and from his days at newspaper desks, how to tell a story. (Cooper felt most travel pictures were exceedingly dull.)

In India, the company's cameraman quit and Cooper sent a telegram to an acquaintance, Ernest B. Schoedsack, to join them. The two men had met in Vienna after the war, becoming fast friends. Schoedsack had worked as a cameraman at Mack Sennett's studio prior to joining the US Signal Corps during the war. He left Paris and caught up to Cooper's ship in French Somaliland (now known as Djibouti, located on the Horn of East Africa) in February 1923. The ship limped its way to Italy after its keel was damaged in the Red Sea, and while in port a fire destroyed the ship, including some of the film footage. Returning to America, Cooper haunted the American Geographic Society, and earned money by writing magazine articles based on his recent trip. Once again, he didn't stay in New York for long.

Cooper and Schoedsack raised $10,000 to finance a documentary about the annual summer migration of a feudal tribe that moves their livestock across the Zardeh Kuh mountain range in Persia (now Iran). Returning to America to edit their footage, Cooper began showing the completed film, *Grass* (1925), around the East Coast as part of a lecture presentation when Paramount Pictures agreed to release the film theatrically. *Grass* proved to be popular at the box office, making enough of a tidy profit for Paramount executives to offer Cooper and Schoedsack a $75,000 budget for their next project. The two men spent eighteen months in Thailand making *Chang* (1927), a fictionalized documentary focusing on a tribal family's survival in the jungle. (The film included a rousing elephant stampede that would influence other future jungle films.[22]) Like its predecessor, *Chang* did well at the box office, despite running $10,000 over budget.

The Four Feathers (1929), based on A. E. W. Mason's novel, was their next production for Paramount, with David O. Selznick serving as associate producer. Traveling to the Sudan, Cooper and Schoedsack filmed numerous action sequences, with Cooper stepping in as a photo double for actor Richard Arlen. They returned to Hollywood to complete the picture, filming in the desert near Palm Springs. With the release of *The Four Feathers*, Cooper took a break from the film industry and returned to his love of aviation. He invested his money to form the Federal Aviation Corporation, which would soon purchase Pan American Airways (commonly known as Pan Am) and Western Airlines.[23] It was during this period in his life that Cooper, living in New York City, began working on an idea about a giant ape that wreaks havoc in a major city. With the death of John Hambleton, his friend and president of the newly founded aviation company, Cooper left the executive boardroom and returned to Hollywood.

David O. Selznick took over the production reins in the fall of 1931 at RKO Studios, and offered Cooper the position of supervisory producer. Once situated, Cooper sent his new boss an outline for his giant gorilla story, originally titled *The Beast*. Cooper began to work out the details for making this film, with the most complex problem being how to create a giant ape. His answer arrived when he met Willis O'Brien during the making of *The Most Dangerous Game* (1932). O'Brien was the wizard who developed a three-dimensional stop-animation process to create dinosaurs for the 1925 classic *The Lost World.* Marshaling their creative minds, Cooper and O'Brien shot a screen test showing how a giant ape would appear on a movie screen. (While the giant ape appears to be twenty feet tall in the movie, it was really an eighteen-inch-tall miniature with a rabbit pelt covering a machined, ball-and-socket armature.) After showing the test footage to Selznick and the RKO board, Cooper was given the green light to move ahead with production on a budget just over $500,000, a serious monetary gamble for RKO in the midst of the Great Depression.

King Kong premiered at Radio City Music Hall and the RKO Roxy Theatre in New York City on March 2, 1933. Despite the hard times caused by the Depression, people flocked to the two movie houses in the first week, earning the studio over $100,000 in ticket sales.[24] (In the film's climax, Cooper and Schoedsack play pilots who shoot Kong off the Empire State building.)

With Selznick's departure from RKO in early 1933, Cooper took over as production executive. He quickly increased production, utilizing the studio's two lots—one on Gower Street and the other in Culver City.[25] Having seen a screening of a Universal film called *Air Mail* (1932), a film that offered nothing special, Cooper asked the film's director, John Ford, to come see him. Within an hour of their meeting, the two men had reached a deal for Ford to direct two films for RKO, *The Lost Patrol* (1934) and *The Informer* (1935). It marked the beginning of a long and mostly successful collaboration.

Cooper had been an early advocate of the Technicolor process, desiring to produce films in this new medium.[26] While still working for RKO, Cooper and John Hay Whitney formed Pioneer Pictures with the intention to produce full-color films. RKO wasn't keen on making Technicolor films, mainly due to the high costs involved; however, the studio agreed to release Pioneer Pictures' first film, *Becky Sharpe* (1935). When Cooper's RKO contract expired in 1935, he produced, via Pioneer Pictures, a Technicolor short, *La Cucaracha* (1934), winning the Oscar for Best Short Subject. *Dancing Pirate* (1936), the last of the three-picture deal between Pioneer Pictures and RKO, was a box office flop. Looking for another place to do business, Pioneer Pictures merged with the newly formed Selznick International Pictures in 1936.

Western films in the mid-1930s were generally produced by minor studios like Republic Pictures or Poverty Row producers like Producers Releasing Corp. (PRC).[27] The major studios (Paramount, MGM, Fox, Warner Bros.) felt Westerns were only popular to a limited audience (mostly rural and children), and not the general moviegoing public. While Paramount might produce an occasional Western, such as Cecil B. DeMille's 1936 *The Plainsman*, it was rare for a major studio to back an "A"-picture Western. Cooper and Ford agreed to a two-picture deal with Selznick, one based on a short story, "Stage to Lordsburg." Selznick was not impressed with the story, or Ford's choice of a leading man—an actor who had spent the past six years toiling away in low-budget "B" Westerns—John Wayne.

Cooper and Ford managed to convince Selznick to their way of thinking, and he finally agreed to make the picture in Technicolor.

However, the following day he changed his mind and backed out of the deal. Furious that Selznick went back on his word, Cooper resigned from Pioneer Pictures. Ford quit as well, telling Selznick his deal was with Cooper, not him.[28] Ironically, Ford's movie—*Stagecoach*—was released in 1939, the same year as Selznick's *Gone with the Wind.* (Both films were nominated for Best Picture, but Selznick took home the Oscar.) Cooper wasn't unemployed for long, moving over to Metro-Goldwyn-Mayer in 1937, where he began preproduction on *War Eagle*, a film he believed would rival *King Kong*. While some stop-animation test footage was shot, the project was ultimately shelved.

Storm clouds were intensifying over Europe and Asia, signaling another major war was on the horizon. Cooper walked away from Hollywood, returning to active duty with the US Army Air Corps (forerunner to the US Air Force) as a lieutenant-colonel in June 1941. After the Japanese attack on Pearl Harbor on December 7, 1941, Cooper traveled to China where he helped with logistics for the 1942 Doolittle Raid against Japan, and later as chief of staff to General Claire Chennault and his China Air Task Force. Cooper, who was promoted to brigadier-general by the end of the war, was on board the USS *Missouri* to witness Japan's formal surrender in 1945.

Returning to Hollywood, Cooper and John Ford renewed their efforts to become independent producers.

Changing Winds and Independence

Argosy Productions

Freedom is a much-cherished thing. You've got to fight for freedom.
—John Ford

During the war years, box office receipts for Hollywood studios remained high. In 1940, the year before America's involvement in World War II, box office receipts totaled $740 million, while in 1945 that amount had jumped to $1,450,000,000.[1] An estimated 85 million people went to the movies in 1941, increasing to 95 million four years later. The following year, 1946, proved to be the best year yet at the American box office, with grosses earning nearly $1.7 billion. (Even drive-in theaters, which had been discontinued during the war, were making a comeback.)

However, the heady days of 1946 quickly vanished in 1947 when the country hit an economic downturn. Like other industries, Hollywood was forced to tighten its belt in many areas. The normal shooting schedule for an "A" film in 1946 was between fifty to fifty-five days, but the following year studios slashed those schedules down to forty to forty-five days. Shooting a "B" film was generally slated for twenty days, but most were cut to twelve or fifteen days.[2] Production budgets were trimmed, and most films were shot with the less expensive black-and-white film stock versus Technicolor. Some productions filmed on actual locations rather than relying on a studio soundstage and backlot, echoing Italian neorealism productions.[3] Studios took another cost-saving move by not renewing long-term contracts for their producers, directors, and stars, finding it more economical to strike a limited-picture deal.[4]

A tighter economy was also reflected in the overseas market, especially in Europe, as many foreign countries returned to producing films to compete for the audience's attention. Several European countries placed restrictions on how many American-made films were allowed to be exhibited on a yearly basis, as well as freezing Hollywood revenues from previous foreign box office earnings. (It was estimated that in 1946, foreign country earnings of Hollywood films totaled nearly $90 million.) England held $20 million of frozen earnings, which would be available should any American producer choose to produce a film in their country.[5] Walt Disney did just that when he made his first live-action film, *Treasure Island* (1950), and other studios soon followed suit.

Darker storm clouds were beginning to form over Hollywood.

As labor tried to organize in Hollywood during the Depression-wracked 1930s, studio executives strongly hinted that all studio unions were rife with Communist infiltration, even insinuating that several major stars were likely "Red sympathizers." With the outbreak of World War II, the anti-Communist delirium faded as Russia became an ally, but that fever returned with a vengeance in 1946. The House Un-American Activities Committee (HUAC), aided by the conservative Motion Picture Alliance for the Preservation of American Ideals (MPA), was ready and willing to clean out Hollywood's Communists.

Informal interviews began with MPA members who singled out people in the industry they suspected were Communists. With that information, HUAC launched a formal investigation into Communist infiltration and influence in the film industry. While the hearings focused on various people in the industry, several members of the Screen Writers Guild became prime targets because they were either members of the American Communist Party or they attended meetings. Ten witnesses, nine writers and one director, were labeled "unfriendly" and cited for contempt of Congress for refusing to testify. (They were quickly nicknamed "The Hollywood Ten.") Studio executives stated that those witnesses would no longer be employed until they were completely cleared of being a Communist. The ten men were fined and sentenced to prison in 1948, as hearings continued into the 1950s, resulting in more writers, directors, and performers being blacklisted.[6]

Hollywood's major blow came with the Supreme Court's Paramount Decree on May 3, 1948.

In 1938, a government antitrust lawsuit was filed on behalf of independent exhibitors, charging the five major studios with restraint of trade and practicing "block booking" and "blind bidding," which guaranteed studios a positive financial return, even with their less popular films. ("Block booking" forced theater exhibitors to book several films at once, while "blind bidding" compelled an exhibitor to rent a film, sight unseen.) The five major studios—Fox, Warner Bros., MGM, Paramount, and RKO—owned various theaters across the country, with Paramount holding the largest amount, 1,250 theaters in forty-three states. In November 1940, the studios agreed to a consent decree that outlawed blind bidding and would limit block booking to a group of no more than five pictures. This consent decree was to last for three years while the government and studios worked to reach a more equitable agreement.

With the expiration of the consent decree, it was business as usual, as the studios continued to employ blind bidding and block booking, until the Justice Department revived their antitrust actions in 1945. The Justice Department was now determined to completely separate the studios from their theater chains and put an end to blind bidding and block booking. The Supreme Court ruled that the studios had violated antitrust laws, and forced them to relinquish their movie theater ownership.

It was the beginning of the end of the fabled studio system.[7]

* * *

The war had not just changed the world, but also the people in Hollywood. Many stars had long resented the constraints of a studio contract. Actors wanted the freedom to pick and choose projects, not be assigned a film that was just another warmed-over plot from a previous film. Refusing to appear in a movie resulted in suspension for the rebellious performer, such as Bette Davis, Olivia de Havilland, and James Cagney. They were all suspended by Warner Bros. for refusing to accept certain roles. (Jack Warner called Cagney "the professional againster.")[8]

The quest for independence was not limited to actors, as several directors also yearned for greater artistic autonomy. The directors who served in World War II had seen the horrors of war and the ugliness of mankind. Returning to work for a studio executive who acted like a dictator simply held no appeal.[9] Autonomy would allow a director the freedom to make the kind of film story he wanted to tell.

In January 1946, Frank Capra, William Wyler, and George Stevens formed Liberty Films. The three filmmakers agreed they would act as independent producer-directors, with RKO Pictures handling distribution of their films. Each partner was to make a total of three films, each investing $150,000 to handle preproduction costs. Only Capra had a film ready to go into production, *It's a Wonderful Life* (1946), which proved to be the first—and only—film produced by Liberty Films. Stevens had no project that interested him, while Wyler was completing *The Best Years of Our Lives* (1946) for Samuel Goldwyn.

Awaiting the release of Capra's film, the company had no infusion of cash, causing the partners to chip in to meet expenses. (Although now considered a classic, *It's a Wonderful Life* was not a box office hit when released.) As financial demands drained the partners' wallets, they agreed to sell Liberty Films to Paramount in January 1947. As part of the deal, George Stevens and William Wyler agreed to direct five films for Paramount.

* * *

John Ford and Merian C. Cooper discussed plans to form their own company back in 1937, although nothing came of it until three years later when they created Argosy Pictures. (*Argosy* in Italian means a large ship or a prosperous supply, and the company's logo was a three-masted ship.[10]) *Stagecoach*, produced by Walter Wanger for United Artists, was unofficially an Argosy production, with Cooper serving as uncredited producer. The Western that Selznick walked away from proved to be a great success, both at the box office and with critics. Wanger quickly agreed to sign up Argosy Pictures for two more films. *The Long Voyage Home* (1940), based on several Eugene O'Neill one-act plays, focused on the lives of merchant seamen who fight to battle loneliness as well as an upcoming world war. While critics praised Ford's film, it was nothing short of a washout at the box office. The second film, *Eagle Squadron*, centered on American pilots who join a British RAF squadron in 1940 to fight Germany's aggression. With the box office disappointment of *The Long Voyage Home*, Wanger was hardly in a rush to jump into another production, and they parted ways.[11]

World War II put a halt to any future Argosy projects, but the company was restructured on January 2, 1946, with Ford serving as chairman of the board and Cooper as company president. Argosy was funded with half a million dollars, half of the amount coming from Ford and Cooper, while twelve other investors (made up of OSS colleagues) contributed the remaining share.[12] Ford's Argosy contract stated he would direct at least one film per year over a three-year period, with a yearly salary of $150,000, while Cooper would be paid $50,000 a year.

The ultimate goal of Argosy wasn't just to make their own films, but to own them outright. Ford and Cooper realized that owning their own movies would allow Argosy to rerelease them to theaters, pocketing a larger percentage of the profits. While television was just beginning to make its debut as a form of entertainment, studios and independent producers realized that in the not-too-distant future, previously released films would provide a gold mine of ready-made product for television.[13] Cooper attempted to purchase *Stagecoach* and *The Long Voyage Home* from United Artists, but was met with silence. Summing up his feelings about being an independent filmmaker, Ford once told his grandson, Dan, that "Freedom is a much-cherished thing. You've got to fight for freedom." Cooper and Ford were soon to learn that forming a company was easier than securing a deal beneficial to Argosy.

Cooper approached United Artists about producing Argosy's first production, *The Last Outlaw*, a remake of the 1919 version Ford directed at Universal. A deal was struck with United Artists, who purchased the story rights and would handle all distribution, with Argosy receiving 70 percent of the profits.[14] When the deal collapsed, Cooper turned to Monogram Pictures to produce the film. Monogram was notorious for producing extremely low-budget productions featuring B- or C-grade stars in a week—or less. As Ford biographer Scott Eyman noted, attempting to strike a deal with Monogram, Ford and Cooper showed how "committed they were to independence."[15] (While Monogram would have loved to be associated with Ford and Cooper, the deal fell apart over financing.) Both men came to the realization that the company's best bet was securing a multipicture deal instead of an individual project. On September 27, 1946, Argosy signed a four-picture deal with RKO. A clause in the contract noted that if Argosy's first film was successful, Ford's passion project, *The Quiet Man*, would be put into production.[16]

Argosy chose *The Fugitive*, an adaptation of Graham Greene's novel *The Power and the Glory*, as their first release. It is about a priest who doubts his faith and calling, and is caught in an unnamed Mexican state that denounces any form of Christianity and enforces the murder of every priest. Attempting to escape by ship, the priest (Henry Fonda) stays when a villager's religious needs force him to make a choice. Eventually captured by the state police, the priest walks to his execution with a rebirth in his faith. In the end, as parishioners privately pray for the dead priest, another arrives to carry on.

The film is visually stunning, due to Gabriel Figueroa's wonderful camera work, but suffers from a heavy dose of symbolism. In Greene's novel, the priest is an alcoholic and womanizer, subjects that never would have received approval from the Production Code Administration. Instead, writer Dudley Nichols crafted the script to show the priest's failings were limited to his self-doubt as a man of the cloth until the need to fulfill his religious calling takes over. Fonda was chosen because of his popularity as a box office attraction, while Ward Bond was cast as "El Gringo," a wanted criminal, echoing the priest's attempt to escape the country. Dolores del Rio, stunningly photographed, is a Mary Magdalene–type character who aids the priest, while Pedro Armendáriz (in his first of three films with Ford) is the brutal police lieutenant. John Qualen, Robert Armstrong, J. Carrol Naish (giving an excellent performance as the police informer), Chris-Pin Martin, Miguel Inclán, and Leo Carrillo rounded out the cast.

Ford and Cooper decided to film entirely in Mexico, as it not only fit the story's locale, but production costs would be considerably lower. The film's budget was $1.13 million, with Argosy putting up $782,000 (as well as $100,000 in cash), and RKO providing $250,000. Released in New York City on Christmas Day, 1947, critics generally approved of *The Fugitive*, but the box office held a disparate opinion, taking in a slim $818,000. After subtracting RKO's distribution fee, Argosy was left with just a little over $500,000, with a debt load of over a million dollars.[17]

The Fugitive begs the unanswered question: Why did Ford and Cooper choose this story as the basis for their first film? It's hardly box office material, as the narrative echoes the totalitarian actions by the Soviet Union at the time. Along with the heavy visual symbolism, *The Fugitive* simply is not the type of movie to attract huge audiences. The studio newspaper ads did not help create much interest by proclaiming it a "peril-laden adventure of a man's desperate plight!" Another ad relied on Ford's stature as a filmmaker, stating it was directed by "John Ford, who gave you *The Informer*, *The Hurricane*, *Stagecoach*, [and] *The Grapes of Wrath*."

After the war, several smaller theaters, mostly in large metropolitan cities, became known as "art houses," screening various foreign or American-made independent films, as well as documentaries. *The Fugitive* was the type of film that would have easily appealed to that circuit, albeit smaller than major theater chains. Prior to production, Ford admitted in a letter to Darryl F. Zanuck that he knew the film wasn't "a sound commercial gamble," but his heart and his faith compelled him to make the picture. Whatever his attraction, *The Fugitive* not only put Argosy Pictures into a financial hole right out of the starting gate, but firmly torpedoed any chances for Ford to make *The Quiet Man* at RKO.

Ford and Cooper realized they needed to turn things around quickly in order for Argosy to survive, let alone be successful. Ford's next project for Argosy would see him return to a genre he knew well—the Western.[18]

Fort Apache

Colonel Thursday, I gave my word to Cochise. No man is gonna make a liar out of me.

—Captain York (John Wayne)

The Indian Wars period (1865–1890) in the American West was a brutal time—for both sides. Some historians say nowhere was it harsher than in the Southwest territory of Arizona. It wasn't just the climate and terrain, but the guerrilla-style fighting by Apache tribes that often disheartened the shrewdest military officer.[1] To the military, their foe was a ghost that swiftly attacked without warning, and evaporated without a trace. Cavalry units were worn ragged across the Arizona desert chasing this phantom enemy. The actions by the US Cavalry became a popular scenario that was played out numerous times, in various forms, dating back to dime novels, Buffalo Bill's Wild West show, and various backyards where children re-created such heroics. Little wonder writers and filmmakers were drawn to the dramatic aspects.

To relax from the stress of making movies, John Ford loved devouring books on history (Civil War, American West, and Irish), biographies, and magazine short stories. The latter also was an avenue to discover a story that could serve as a future production.[2] One night, traveling to San Francisco to board a ship for Hawaii, Ford read the short story "Massacre" by James Warner Bellah in the latest issue of the *Saturday Evening Post.*

> I told Barbara [Ford's daughter], the next [train] stop send a telegram—a night letter—to Cooper saying "Buy 'Massacre.' It's a good

> story." Cooper called me up on the boat's radio and said there was no such race horse as Massacre. Barbara had garbled the message. Barbara, my pride and joy, is a lousy secretary.[3]

James Warner Bellah and John Ford were an unlikely pair—totally different types who only socialized when working, and even that was minimal. However, Bellah's stories struck a chord in Ford's imagination. Bellah's stories about the US Cavalry celebrated the valor and glory of the military, something Ford understood and embraced—men in the harshest environment doing a thankless but necessary job, willing to make the ultimate sacrifice.[4]

The author's short stories paint a picture with crisp, descriptive words, giving the reader a true, gritty feeling for the location, the men, and the Indians. ("The sun in August is a molten saber blade. It will burn the neckline and the back of the head to blistered uselessness as you watch it.") Bellah's material gave Ford the liberty to enhance and expand a narrative into his distinct style, something a novel did not always easily provide. Ford once stated that short stories allowed one to develop a better storyline, versus a long novel which often had to be trimmed due to length.

* * *

In "Massacre," Bellah describes the Indian as having a smell that is "resinous and salty and rancid. It is the wood smoke of his teepee and the fetidity of his breath that comes from eating body-hot animal entrails. It is the uncured tobacco and the sweat of his unwashed body. It is the animal grease in his hair and old leather and fur, tanned with bird lime and handed down unclean from ancestral bodies long since gathered to the Happy Lands."[5] In seventy-five words he has painted a vivid, albeit harsh and insensitive, portrait for the reader. Reading his work today in a more politically correct world, one cringes at the way he portrays the Indian, yet his words offer a coarse reality of the period. Characters such as Flintridge Cohill, Clay Sitterding, D'Arcy Topliff, Toucy Rynders, Pennell, Tyree, Allshard, and Brome Chadbourne populate his stories. Although to the modern ear these names sound implausible or absurd, historically, they are not far from reality. During the 1800s, many people had individualistic names such as Law Olmsted, Green Manning, Osum Latrobe, Orange Judd, Dorsey Pender, Leander Alley, and Fletcher Stockdale.

James Warner Bellah Jr. recalled his father as an "absolute military snob" whose political beliefs were "just a bit right of Attila the Hun," and described him as "a fascist, a racist, and a world-class bigot." He believed his father had great contempt for Ford, not so much as an artist, but from a social outlook, often referring to him as a "shanty Irishman." (Bellah described Ford as either a loner or a "most effusive mad Irish gentleman.") While Bellah disdained Hollywood, his son stated that he liked the money they offered a writer.[6]

Born in New York City in 1899, Bellah, a seventh-generation American, was born into a military family and grew up around various military outposts. During World War I, he served as a pilot for the Canadian Royal Flying Corps. Returning home in 1918, Bellah attended college, earning a master's degree in history, before finding employment at various New York City advertising agencies as well as teaching English courses at Columbia University. During this period, he began writing short stories and submitting them to various magazines such as *The Saturday Evening Post*. Bellah and Ford crossed paths during World War II in New Delhi; although Ford maintained they had met previously, neither man could recall when or where.[7]

* * *

"Massacre," which Argosy bought for $3,000, tells the story of Major Owen Thursday, who is sent to take command of fictional Fort Starke.[8] Bellah describes Thursday as "a tall man, dried out to leather and bone and sinew." The former Civil War major-general is now "back in the slow Army runway again, with the flame of glory burning low on his horizon." (The character of Philadelphia, Thursday's daughter, does not appear in Bellah's story.) Lieutenant Flint Cohill greets Thursday as he arrives at the fort in the early morning hours, while Curtis Meacham, the Indian agent, has requested Thursday make a show of military strength to deter Stone Buffalo and Running Calf from causing further trouble.

(In the story, the Indians are part of the Cheyenne tribe.) Thursday announces he will escort two companies to the White River Agency, insisting the troopers bring their polishing kits and boot blacks, items reserved for formal dress, not field campaigns. "A little more military dignity and decorum out here, and a little less cowboy manners and dress, will engender a lot more respect for the Army," Thursday states.

In the field, Lieutenant Sitterding notifies Thursday that he has seen Stone Buffalo's camp, and the dispute between Stone Buffalo and Running Calf, which threatened to spill into warfare, has calmed down. Thursday believes it is because the Indians knew the troopers were on the way. Stone Buffalo has requested to come into the army's camp to talk, but Sitterding advises the major against that, as it would reveal how many men are present. Thursday quickly rejects the suggestion, adding, "When I want advice from my officers, Mr. Sitterding, I ask for it. Will you remember that, please?" At their meeting, while Stone Buffalo talks about how his tribe is made up of great hunters, Cohill whispers to Thursday that the chief is stalling for time, adding that his speech is "an insolent attempt at reconnaissance." Thursday interrupts Stone Buffalo, ordering him to return to the reservation or face the consequences, before walking away.

The following morning, Thursday and his two columns charge down the canyon where the Indians ambush them. Cohill, on the ridgetop with the supply wagons, spots Thursday moving near the group of dead soldiers. He runs down to his commanding officer, urging him to come up to the ridge. Instead, Thursday asks for Cohill's pistol and goes to rejoin the dead troopers. ("I've had all that I can have," he says softly. "This is where the road stops at last.")

When the relief column arrives several days later, they inspect the dead command and notice that Thursday has a bullet wound on the side of his head, but the pistol is missing. Prior to the column's arrival, Cohill had removed it, honoring his final words to Thursday that, for the good of the service, he would never reveal the officer's suicide.

* * *

To turn the short story into a screenplay, Ford made a unique choice for a screenwriter.

Frank Nugent, a native of New York City, worked as a reporter for the *New York Times* after graduating from Columbia University. He covered the Lindbergh kidnapping case and subsequent trial before landing a job as the paper's film critic in 1936. Nugent's reviews were tough and demanding, championing quality over typical studio meat-grinder stories. His review of 20th Century-Fox's *The Story of Alexander Graham Bell* (1939) so infuriated the studio and the Roxy Theatre (where the film was playing in New York City) that they pulled their advertising for over six months, reportedly costing the paper about $50,000.[9] In 1940, Darryl F. Zanuck offered him a position at Fox as a script critic, paying him close to $1,000 a week, three times the salary he'd gotten at the newspaper. (Industry rumor claimed Zanuck hired him so he would stop writing negative reviews of the studio's popular films.)

Nugent also wrote various magazine articles, including a *Saturday Evening Post* feature about Ford on the set of *The Fugitive*. A few months later Nugent visited Ford at his office, and during the conversation Ford mentioned he had a cavalry film in mind, commenting that in most Westerns the cavalry comes to the rescue and then rides off, such as in *Stagecoach*. "I've been thinking about it—what was it like at a cavalry post, remote, people with their own personal problems, over everything the threat of Indians, of death," Ford mused.

Nugent thought the idea was great. The director asked if he'd like to write the script, and the stunned writer immediately accepted. Ford gave him a list of fifty books to read (novels, memoirs, etc.) and told him to go explore the Apache country. Nugent hired an anthropology major from the University of Arizona as a guide, and the two visited the ruins of Fort Bowie and walked Apache Pass, among other places. After several weeks, he met with the director, who asked him if he had done enough research. Nugent replied affirmatively. "Good," Ford said. "Now just forget everything you've read and we'll start writing a movie."[10] (In the film's budget file, under the heading of Story-Title, Frank Wead was paid $25,000, but there are no memos or notes to explain why he was paid that amount.

It is possible Ford either had Wead write a script draft before Nugent's hiring, or that Wead possibly polished the script.[11])

Ford had Nugent write a complete biography of every character before ever working on the script. In later years, Nugent recalled this process.

> Never occurred to me before, but something I've practiced ever since . . . where [they were] born, educated, politics, drinking habits (if any), quirks. You take your character from childhood and write out all the salient events in his life leading up to the moment the picture finds him—or her. In some cases, a full page or more, single spaced, was required to describe the character. The advantages are tremendous, because having thought a character out this way, his actions, his speech are thereafter compulsory; you know how he'll react to any given situation. This is in marked contrast, as you must know, to the usual thinking where a character is described as an "Alan Ladd type" or a "sort of Humphrey Bogart guy," or a "Gilda character." None of this for Ford. Anyway, that was how *Fort Apache* was born.[12]

Nugent said Bellah's short story "touched on the character and provided the ending." Now it was his turn to contribute 80 percent of the story that leads up to the ending. The key for the writer was character development. Ford worked very closely with him, although Nugent didn't think that Ford "[saw] his story in its entirety when he [began]." Ford would have an idea for a scene and discuss it with the writer, who would chime in. If Ford approved the basic idea, the writer would go off and write the scene. Then the two would sit down and read the scene, discuss it, make suggestions, and then do another rewrite. If Ford felt the scene worked, it was approved and they'd move on to the next piece. "With Jack, once the scene is okayed, you can put it behind you—certainly until the first draft is completed," Nugent stated. The pace of writing was not slave-driving, but more leisurely, with a few hours in the morning and a few more hours in the afternoon. Nugent said the script was done in eight weeks, with an additional seven for his research.[13]

The biography created for Owen Thursday is very interesting, given that Bellah only provided a minor hint of his background and personality in the short story. It was Nugent who fleshed out Owen Thursday to become the character we see in the film.

> Graduated West Point in '55 . . . second or third in his class. First assignment Third Cavalry detached for Staff Duty in Washington with General Hallock [Halleck], outbreak of Civil War. Made Lieut. Colonel of newly formed Tenth Ohio Cavalry . . . close of war was brevet Major General of U.S. Cavalry. Assigned as Provost Marshal. Remained in Washington until '69 and was sent as Military Observer to Europe . . . was Military attaché and observer for Prussian Army throughout Prussian-Franco War. Whereupon he was recalled to Washington. Great student of military affairs. A reputation as a brilliant Cavalry Tactician and very strict soldier. Thursday had been detailed to Europe with the Prussians both at Sadows and in the Prussian-Franco War. He had been forcibly impressed not only by their stern discipline . . . going into minor details of their dress, but also their thesis of the power of frontal attack . . . Having served exclusively with Prussian Officers who despised cunning and believed only in crushing the opposition at the point of impact by the weight and power of attack, regardless of loss, he can little appreciate what swift moving Indian warriors can do maneuvering over vast distances in the West . . . is the son and grandson and great-grandson of Regular Army soldiers and in politics is a Republican . . . At the start of our story, Thursday is a bitter, disillusioned soldier. He thinks he should have a bigger job; rails against political machinations on the part of his enemies; has written numerous letters to Congress. He goes to Arizona to fight against the Apache whom he despises in his ignorance, not knowing he is up against the best light Cavalry that ever lived.[14]

When it came to the backstory of the character of Captain Kirby Calvin York, Nugent stated that York did not attend West Point, but volunteered in 1861 when Lincoln called for additional soldiers. He became a first lieutenant of a volunteer cavalry regiment and held an "honorable war record." At the end of the war, York, a brevet colonel, applied for a commission in the army and was given a first lieutenant rank, serving mainly along the border. "He is Washington to Thursday's Braddock. He knows the country. He knows the Indians . . . Kirby is a great admirer of the

Plains Indians as a soldier and as a man. He believes they have been badly treated by dishonest Indian agents, carpetbaggers, and politicians. He has a great and particular respect for the Apache. Like most men constantly at warfare, with one enemy, he unconsciously has taken on some of the fighting attributes and characteristics of the Indian warrior."[15]

Nugent's biography of Cochise describes him as "a highly intelligent Indian, great strategist, philosopher . . . His name will strike terror and dread in the hearts of men, but when we meet him, he will prove to be an impressive and dignified man, no more vengeful fighter, but a man who has suffered much at the hands of the whites and has, in fact, right on his side . . . Cochise would not give his word readily unless he meant to keep it . . . In our story, he is presumed to have known Kirby York, and, when they meet, will make some special gesture toward him acknowledging this fact."[16]

* * *

It is very rare that any film follows the final draft of a script. Depending on time, budget, or the director's choice, many scenes might be discarded before filming, or photographed only to be excluded in the editing room. While a scene may appear solid in the script, John Ford was well known for cutting out loquacious dialogue in any script on the set, saving only the words that made the scene stand out. The following examples highlight the differences between Nugent's script and Ford's final cut of the released film.

Nugent's script opens the same way as the film—a stagecoach making its way through a desolate Arizona desert. The stage stop at Hassayampa (northwest of present-day Phoenix) is described as a "huddle of adobe huts in the middle of nowhere. The chief building would be the stage stop, with its corral and Ma Breen's hostelry." (Below this description Nugent has added, "Note: possibly Goulding's, in Monument Valley, will serve for this scene."[17]) Inside the stagecoach, Thursday, accompanied by his daughter, Philadelphia, shows an immediate repulsion toward the country. Examining his small notebook, Thursday comments on the various stops they have passed. "What a country! Forty miles from mud hole to mud hole," he says disdainfully. "Mule Creek, Dead Man's

Squaw, Schmidt's Wells, Hangman's Flats, Hassayampa. The end of the rainbow, Fort Apache." From this dialogue the audience quickly becomes aware that Thursday is a bitter, angry, and pompous man. (Nugent's script placed the story at Fort Bowie in southwest Arizona territory.[18])

At the stage stop, Thursday's daughter, Philadelphia, meets young Lieutenant Michael O'Rourke. It's obvious she finds him very attractive, and Michael tries his best to hide a similar feeling, especially since her father is Michael's commanding officer. Three sergeants, Schattuck, Mulcahy, and Kramer, arrive with a military stagecoach to transport Michael to Fort Apache. (Two of the four sergeants' names were changed before filming commenced. Kramer becomes Quincannon, and the fourth sergeant, Pierre St. Pierre ["Pete"], becomes Beaufort.[19]) The sergeants are unaware of Thursday's arrival due to the telegraph wires being cut by the Apaches. The script does not mention that Mulcahy is Michael's godfather, although Michael later relates to Philadelphia that the three sergeants helped raise him. (In the film, Mulcahy introduces Michael to Philadelphia as his godson during this sequence.) Schattuck gets a grip on Michael's skin-tight trouser seat and comments, "There ain't too much slack in these pants." Philadelphia, who has now exited the washroom, comments that she thinks the trousers fit perfectly. (Both lines were cut, as the Production Code Administration would deem them too suggestive.)

The script mentions Thursday winding his watch after checking the time, and Nugent has noted: "We will see the timepiece frequently during the picture." Aside from this notation, there are perhaps three more instances of Thursday checking his watch, as a hint to the character's rigidity.

As Thursday and Philadelphia ride in the ambulance to Fort Apache, she quickly glances at Michael riding along. Thursday, who observes her looking at Michael, reminds Philadelphia that there will be a lot of men at the post, and how lonely it can be for women on the frontier. He admits, cautiously, that he knows little about women, stating that he and her mother had "a very short time together before the war." He urges her to be careful around men and any thoughts of marriage. Ford dumped all of this dialogue, instead choosing to have Philadelphia act covertly to watch Michael riding. She looks quickly at him but, afraid of being caught by her father, opens her hatbox and adjusts the mirror. Pretending to wipe her eyes, she watches Michael in the mirror.

At the fort dance, Captain York and Mrs. Collingwood are finishing a dance as she scans the room to find her husband, Sam. York goes into the smoking room, where Sam is drinking, and guides him out to the dance floor as the band plays a waltz for the Collingwoods. When Thursday enters, Collingwood greets him and starts to extend his hand. "Something in Thursday's air makes him let it fall at his side," the script notes. Thursday's greeting of Collingwood is described as "almost grudgingly."[20] (Ford discarded the sequence of York getting Sam and the Collingwoods dancing, but kept the meeting of Thursday and Collingwood.) As the band plays another number, York asks Philadelphia for a dance and other couples join in, leaving Thursday to stand alone to watch. (With Thursday standing by himself, Ford suggests at this early moment in the film the colonel's isolation from his men.)

The script included a sequence showing the early morning at the fort, starting with Mulcahy rousting the troopers out of their bunks, horses led out to graze, and troopers hurrying to various duty posts before the cannon goes off, which awakens Philadelphia, who walks out on the balcony to watch the activity. Ford condensed all of this by opening with the cannon booming, and the camera following Philadelphia out onto the balcony. (He omitted the barracks piece entirely.) With the camera on the balcony, Ford uses a panning shot of the fort grounds to capture the morning activity. The director also added Michael riding up to Thursday's quarters to deliver a calling card. He meets Philadelphia before York arrives, who informs Michael he's assigned to Thursday's troop.

Entering headquarters, Thursday meets Sergeant Major O'Rourke, Michael's father. (Hearing the last name, Thursday comments, "Place seems to be full of O'Rourkes.") Learning Michael is his son, and has received a presidential appointment to West Point, Thursday states that such acts were reserved for sons of Medal of Honor recipients. "That is my impression, too, sir," O'Rourke flatly replies. Nugent inserted several shots of officers looking surprised when officers' call is sounded, but Ford did not shoot any of these reaction shots.

In the officers' meeting, we quickly become aware of Thursday's low opinion of the Apache and their fighting skills. He derogatorily refers to them as "gnat stings and the flea bites of a few cowardly digger Indians." York, who holds a higher opinion based on his field experiences, cautions him not to take the Apache for granted.[21] Thursday quickly dismisses York's comments, further illustrating his arrogance, and a harbinger of what is to befall him.

The script then features Michael attempting to drill new recruits, with little success. The men march more like a muddled mob than soldiers. (In reality, the recruits would already know how to march, having gone through a minimum training of four weeks at Jefferson Barracks in St. Louis.) O'Rourke talks to the three sergeants and they conspire to create a plan. Michael is told to go to the stables to pick out a horse, while the sergeants take over drilling practice. (In the film, the sergeants handle the drilling exercise as O'Rourke takes Michael to the stable and gives him the horse.) Nugent's draft included a quick montage of shots featuring Sergeant Schattuck yelling, men sweating, carbine rifles being shifted raggedly onto shoulders, feet marching in the dust, and ending with the group coming to a sloppy halt. Michael is given a beautiful saddled horse as his father watches from afar and smiles proudly. Another montage followed with Mulcahy yelling at the recruits, who are now marching in good rhythm and formation, and concluded with them coming to a halt in smart fashion.

Ford eliminated the entire montage, instead creating a sequence displaying his boisterous physical humor as the sergeants berate and rough up the men into shape. He included a humorous touch when Sergeant Mulcahy asks if any man is from a certain county in Ireland. The first three names are met with silence, but on the fourth, County Sligo, a man speaks up. Smiling broadly, Mulcahy says he doesn't want to show any favoritism, but he now has promoted the man to acting corporal.[22] As Mulcahy walks down the line, the man puts down his rifle and picks up a large wooden slat like the other sergeants hold in their hands, and mimics the sergeants by looking at the men. Seeing this, Mulcahy physically throws the man back into line, where he knocks over another recruit.

Living in the barest of quarters with no furniture, Philadelphia goes to Mrs. Collingwood, who enlists Mrs. O'Rourke's help. The following scene in the script has Mrs. O'Rourke overseeing the cleaning of Thursday's living quarters, placement of furniture, and ordering soldiers around like a sergeant major. Dr. Wilkens brings his favorite chair, and as he sits in it, it collapses under him. When Thursday arrives home that evening, he is surprised at the redecorated quarters. The script has Philadelphia at the piano playing "Regular Army, O!" as he walks in. She has him sit in the chair donated by Dr. Wilkens, and as Thursday sits down, he falls into the chair "like a jack-knife, his knees against his chin." Attempting to get up, Thursday has no luck, commenting, "This is no chair—it's a bear trap!" Philadelphia tries to pull him out with no success, and then calls for the two Mexican female cooks to help. They free Thursday from the chair, with him landing on his hands and knees on the floor. The script notes that there is a hint of anger on his face as he stands up, which causes Philadelphia to step back, but his anger quickly fades.

Ford kept the scene of the two military wives offering to help Philadelphia, but once in the editing room, he deleted the part with Mrs. O'Rourke overseeing the cleaning and placement of furniture in Thursday's quarters. Instead, Thursday returns home, greeted by Guadalupe (the house cook) and Philadelphia. His daughter shows him the various items given to them, before leaving the room to help prepare dinner. Thursday lights a cigar, looks at Michael O'Rourke's calling card before sitting in the chair. As he sits down, the back legs collapse, leaving Thursday in an awkward position where he cannot get up. Philadelphia and Guadalupe watch, trying not to laugh, before attempting to help him up. Their second attempt is successful, and Thursday straightens his coat, trying to maintain dignity. Philadelphia sheepishly says, "I'm sorry, I forgot to tell you. It does that sometimes." (Ford deleted the scene of Dr. Wilkens collapsing in the chair, as it would diminish the humor of Thursday's predicament.)

When it came to editing the film, Ford did not always follow the order of scenes in the script. For example, he placed the scene of Philadelphia asking Mrs. O'Rourke and Mrs. Collingwood for help after the officers' meeting with Thursday. He also moved Thursday's arrival to his newly furnished home after the sequence of the new recruits being drilled by the three sergeants.

The script's version of Michael and Philadelphia's horseback ride begins with the couple riding around the parade grounds. Mrs. Collingwood watches and smiles, while Mrs. O'Rourke has "an anxious look" on her face. Another sergeant's wife comments that Michael is "aiming a bit high, isn't he now?" Mrs. O'Rourke says nothing and walks away. The script then covers the riding lesson of the new recruits, describing them as "riding like sacks of grain or swaying beanpoles" on saddled horses walking around in a circle. One recruit, Kelsey, has his arms wrapped around a horse's neck, causing Schattuck to shout, "I know you're fond of that horse, but this is no parlor!" The recruit releases his grip and falls off. Mulcahy tells Kelsey not to worry, as they will have him riding "as if you're part of the horse." Quickly turning to others before a reply can be made, Mulcahy shouts, "AND DON'T SAY IT!" (Another example of Ford switching the script's order of scenes happens when the recruits' riding lesson is placed after the scene of Philadelphia visiting the Collingwoods, York, and Michael at dinner.)

When it came to filming the horse-riding lesson, Ford tossed the script's version in favor of a more raucous free-for-all. (Actual cavalry recruits would already have had a basic knowledge of riding a horse from their training at Jefferson Barracks.) Sergeant Beaufort addresses the assembled recruits, asking if any man served with the Southern Army during the war. One recruit comes forward, noting that he served with Nathan Bedford Forrest. Beaufort shakes his hand and makes him an acting corporal, before announcing "this gallant soldier, a member of the greatest cavalry force that ever lived, will show you Yankees how to ride." The man hops on the horse and gallops off, shouting out a rebel yell. Beaufort asks for another volunteer and the beginning of the rambunctious riding lesson takes off. One man tries to mount a horse and goes flying over the animal, while another horse rears up and dumps the rider into the dust. The area becomes a circus of chaos: men falling, horses neighing loudly, and dust flying. Sergeant Quincannon yells out orders as a rider goes by, landing in the sergeant's arms before he dumps him on the ground. The former Southern rebel returns on his horse, dismounts, and salutes Sergeant Beaufort, explaining he "lost his Yankee cap." Beaufort, smiling, shakes his hand. He does it again, takes a few steps, and returns to repeat the gesture.

After the riding lesson sequence, the script returns to Michael and Philadelphia riding out of the fort and across the open land. Nugent suggested that "the nature of this and successive shots of the riders will be determined by the terrain. The effect of them, however, will be to suggest that Philadelphia, all curiosity, is constantly suggesting a turn in a new direction—wherever a ridge or a knoll promises a wider view." In the course of this sequence, the two rest their horses and Philadelphia comments how much she loves this area, never wanting to leave. She mentions wanting to settle down and marry, stating the man she wants to marry is "just like you." (Michael is completely oblivious to Philadelphia's not-so-subtle hint.) The scene continues with them riding on and discovering the two dead troopers and the burned-out wagon, before concluding with Michael and Philadelphia returning to the fort.

Ford did film Michael and Philadelphia riding around the parade grounds, but dropped it in the editing room. Instead, he chose to open the couple's riding sequence with a wide shot of the couple cantering across the desert, making a brief stop to enjoy the view. Addressing her as "Miss Thursday," Michael points out a distant mesa, which causes her to ask if he doesn't like the name "Phil," her nickname. Michael, smiling, replies, "Of course I do, Phil." Philadelphia smiles and they continue to ride, stopping at another overlook where Michael points out where the telegraph line wires keep getting cut by the Apaches. Philadelphia, noticing smoke in the distance, asks if it is an Indian signal, but Michael knows it is something more serious. He discreetly unsnaps the flap covering his pistol.

Ford then cuts to the telegraph operator delivering a message to Thursday that Diablo's band left the reservation. Thursday orders Michael to go with a squad, only to learn his daughter and Michael are out riding. Ford cuts back to Michael and Philadelphia riding up to the burned-out wagon and the two dead soldiers. Quickly examining the area, Michael finds a bloody Apache headband and stuffs it into his pocket before leading Philadelphia away. Galloping away in a wide shot, Philadelphia loses her hat. Michael turns around, retrieves it, and they continue on.

Without breaking up the composition of this scene into closer angles, Ford lets the viewer take in the vastness of the Arizona desert, building tension as Michael and Philadelphia are in the open where Apaches could attack them at any moment. Ford condenses Nugent's dialogue to a minimal amount, yet maintains the couple's growing romance. As Michael and Philadelphia return to the fort, Thursday sees to her comfort before returning to his office. Passing O'Rourke on the porch, Thursday looks at him before walking away. This brief exchange, which was not in the script, enhances the division between officers and noncommissioned officers, as well as concerned fathers.

As Thursday leads a platoon in hopes of catching Diablo's band, the script describes Philadelphia watching them from the balcony. She "brings her hand up as though to wave, but lets it drop. We know Thursday has not looked back." According to the script, the next time we see Thursday and the soldiers, it is obvious they have traveled a good distance. The script notes that "Thursday, without protection, is a mess. His lips are caked and his immaculate uniform is a wreck." York, the veteran of many campaigns in this region, has a bandana over his mouth, while Thursday tries to wipe the dust from his face with a white linen handkerchief. York offers him a red bandana, which he takes. (Ford used none of this.)

The sequence of Michael and the repair wagon returning to the burned-out wagon was split up into two scenes in the script, the first featuring the men riding toward the area with one sergeant needling Beaufort that he knew nothing about repairing telegraph wires, to which Beaufort states, "I wish I had a drink for every Yankee wire I cut in the war!" The other sergeant replies he just wishes he had a drink. (Ford dropped this whole scene.) In the second scene, as they arrive at the burned-out wagon, Michael orders the men to recover the bodies and repair the telegraph line as he climbs up a small ridge to survey the area. When a shot is fired at him by an Apache, Michael orders the men to take off. The wagon and Michael's horse race across open terrain as Diablo's band chases them. The canvas that covers the wagon "catches the wind . . . and balloons like a sail, then flies out behind the wagon—dragging and throwing an immense dust cloud—but also destroying the wagon's balance." Michael, saber in hand, rides up and slices the rope holding the canvas. The tarp goes sailing, "engulfing an Indian and pony who have been blinded by the dust and ride into it . . . They go down." (Ford filmed all this action, discarding the Indian and horse being caught in the canvas cover.)

York's platoon arrives, surrounding the Apache, forcing Diablo to throw down his rifle and, in the Apache language, utters, "Curses." As Thursday arrives on scene, his comment to York is disdainful. "So that's Diablo and your crafty Apache! No Sioux or Cheyenne, Captain, would have let himself been caught like this! Crafty Apaches! Hah!" Thursday orders Michael to go back and repair the telegraph wires, adding, "My compliments on your handling of the detail. Smartly done." York, disgusted by Thursday's comment, tells Michael that Philadelphia is a nice girl, but "you can't take him as a father-in-law." Ford eliminated Thursday and all of his dialogue in this sequence. In the film, we only see York and his troop riding in and circling Diablo's band.

The script then follows Thursday, York, and the four sergeants riding up to Meacham's trading post. Nugent paints the area as populated with a few wikiups and a decent amount of empty whiskey bottles. A male Apache runs from one of the wikiups with a Winchester in his hands, but Mulcahy rides him down. He yanks the rifle from the Apache, handing it to York as the men dismount. In front of the entrance to Meacham's post, an Apache woman and her child "sit stoically" beside a male, likely her husband, lying prone with an empty whiskey bottle near his hand.

Ford ignored all of this detail; instead, York is already carrying a Winchester rifle (presumably taken from the captive Diablo), and as the bugler raises the flag to full staff, he kicks aside an empty whiskey bottle. Ford cut the script's action to one small moment, yet gives an indication the trading post is a blighted area. Describing the inside of the trading post, Nugent describes it to reflect the man: "vile, degraded, false." Much of the dialogue in this sequence comes directly from Bellah's short story, including Meacham stating he pays no attention to titles, after addressing Thursday as "Mister," much to the officer's displeasure. Going into the storeroom, Thursday asks Mulcahy his opinion of the newly discovered whiskey. The script has him reply, "I wouldn't disgrace the good name of whiskey by calling this that, sir." Thursday, before walking out, orders the whiskey and Winchester repeaters destroyed.[23]

Ford changed Mulcahy's comment about the whiskey, having him state, "It's better than no whiskey at all." He concludes the scene with the four sergeants dipping cups into the whiskey barrel, as Mulcahy comments they "have a man's job ahead of us." Schattuck takes a sip and suddenly stands at attention and hiccups.[24] The film dissolves to the guardhouse sign, panning down to see Mulcahy and the other sergeants (now reduced to privates) behind bars. O'Rourke orders them out, stressing they are now privates, and sends them to work the manure pile. Meeting with Thursday, York requests that Beaufort accompany him to speak with Cochise, since he speaks Spanish. As they ride out, Ford has Beaufort yell, "Private Mulcahy, my compliments, sir!" Working the manure pile, the three watch their comrade (his sergeant's stripes restored) gallop off, with Mulcahy commenting, "Officer's pet. Officer's pet, that's what he is." (To avoid any issues with the PCA, Ford has the manure pile appear more like dirt and hay.)

Prior to York and Beaufort crossing the Rio Grande River, Nugent inserted a scene where they stop, taking a drink from York's silver flask before throwing it into the gorge below. Coming up on the riverbank side of Mexico, Beaufort dismounts and scoops up a bunch of dirt. "He kneels, kisses the handful of soil, presses it to his heart . . . rises slowly, and lets the soil drift down. In Spanish he says, 'My mother's land.'" Riding into the entrance of Cochise's stronghold (described as a "natural gateway of stones"), the ground slopes gently upward on an empty path until coming around a slight bend where it ends in a cul-de-sac filled with armed Apaches. The two men dismount, as York, speaking in Apache, says he wants to see Cochise. The Indian leader appears, standing in front of them. He takes something from another Apache and hands it to York, asking in Spanish if it belongs to him. It is York's discarded silver flask.

Eliminating the scene on the Mexican soil, Ford has York and Beaufort stop at an overlook of a winding, erosion-carved canyon and river (the location was Gooseneck Valley). The captain hands Beaufort a small whiskey bottle, and before taking a drink, Beaufort raises the bottle and says in Spanish that it is the land of his mother. Finishing the contents, Beaufort hands it back to York, who then pitches it into the canyon. (This made more sense than York throwing away a silver flask.) They cross the river, going into Mexico, eventually stopping to look ahead and then at each other. Taking a drink from a canteen, they see a flash of a mirror off to the left. Scanning the area, York sees another mirror flash in the distance to his right, before they ride on.[25]

As the camera looks down on the two cavalrymen riding into the canyon, we see three Apache warriors watching. The camera pans to the right, following the riders, as a larger gathering of warriors watches from both sides of the canyon. Dismounting, York and Beaufort (carrying a makeshift pole with a bandana on it as a sign of peace), walk up a small incline. Beaufort greets Cochise in Spanish, and introduces York, who salutes. Cochise gives York a quick glance from head to toe, sizing him up. York looks at Cochise for a moment, then at the stoic face of another Apache who we later learn is Geronimo. Walking closer, York extends his two arms with palms down (sign for conference), in front of Cochise. "*Buenas tardes*, *jefe*," he says.[26] Cochise places his right hand on top of York's hands and replies *Buenas tardes*, before dropping his right hand. York slightly smiles as he drops his hands and the scene fades out.

Prior to the noncommissioned officers' dance, Nugent had written two scenes, the first involving Collingwood and his wife at their living quarters. He notices his dress coat has the shoulder bars displaying his former Civil War lieutenant-colonel insignias. Mrs. Collingwood takes the jacket and begins to sew on his captain bars as he comments, "Just shows how long it's been since I've worn my full dress." Sitting next to her, he admits he is sorry for failing—even failing her. "It's *our* opinion that counts—not your Owen Thursday and others like him!" she reminds him. As she helps him into his dress jacket, they kiss.

The second scene took place in Philadelphia's room, where Guadalupe is helping her dress. Hearing the strumming of guitars and the beginning of a Spanish love song, she opens the French doors of her small balcony. Michael, accompanied by a small group of mariachis, informs her he will not be able to attend the dance because he's been assigned to be officer of the day.[27] Philadelphia realizes this is her father's doing and refuses to attend the dance, but Michael urges her to go. "I'll pretend you're in my arms, not theirs," he says. Just then Thursday calls for her, with Philadelphia replying she'll be ready in a minute. Two men from the mariachi band lift Michael up to Philadelphia, where they kiss briefly before she leaves her room.

While Ford did film both scenes, he dropped them in the editing room. Ford once commented that Nugent was repeatedly "putting in cute pieces of business" in the script, which he would always cut out. He also said Nugent "became an expert on the West—and he's always wrong." At one point while working on the *Fort Apache* script, Nugent had a line where one of the sergeants tells the men to get their Sharps rifles ready. Ford insisted it be changed to Winchesters, but Nugent insisted cavalrymen did not carry them. "I don't give a damn. Winchesters sound better," Ford stated.[28]

At the noncommissioned officers' dance, Ford shows Dr. Wilkens being helped up on the stage by the bandmaster, as it is obvious the good doctor has sampled a sizable portion of the spiked punch. Greeting the bandmaster, Wilkens compliments the food and the punch ("The food is exquisite, and the punch-wow!") before turning once again to greet the band leader.[29] (There is no indication in Nugent's script that Wilkens is drunk.) In many of his films, Ford attempted to include a dance, feeling they were part of the story and provided a good interlude. Ford noted, "The 'Grand March' in *Fort Apache* is typical of the period—it's a ritual, part of their tradition. I try to make it true to life."[30] Ford enjoyed filming Henry Fonda in a dance sequence, dating back to the high-stepping dance the actor did in *Young Mr. Lincoln* (1939), later taking advantage of Fonda's unique stride in *My Darling Clementine* (1946).

When O'Rourke steps up to ask Philadelphia to dance, Nugent has her say "Of course," before whispering "Father." O'Rourke "goes brick-red as she takes his arm." (None of this is in the film.) York arrives at the dance with word that Cochise has returned to American soil to talk peace. Thursday orders the dance to end, and the regiment to form ranks to move out at dawn. York reminds Thursday he gave his word to Cochise, adding "no man's going to make a liar out of me!" Thursday's anger begins to rise, calling Cochise "a breach-clouted savage . . . an illiterate, uncivilized murderer and treaty-breaker!" He reminds York that he "will obey, not challenge my orders." York, with a clenched fist, steps toward Thursday, who is unyielding. Collingwood's hand catches York's arm, stopping him. After a moment, York storms out of the building.

The script then has Dr. Wilkens dancing with Philadelphia to the strains of "Goodnight, Ladies" as he guides her through the main door and out onto the veranda, where Michael is waiting. He wheels her to face Michael and they finish the dance. They hold each other for a moment until the bugler blows "Officers' Call." Michael kisses Philadelphia before returning to headquarters. Nugent's direction added: "Mrs. Collingwood comes up and stands beside her—and other women move into matching positions—with their husbands running past them down the steps and down the company street." (It was Ford's idea to include in the script the band playing its final song, "Goodnight, Ladies."[31])

Ford follows the script, with York informing the colonel about Cochise's return, although he does not step toward Thursday with a clenched fist, nor does Collingwood attempt to stop him. Instead, after Thursday dresses York down, he turns on his heel and walks out, followed by other officers. York stands alone for a minute, slapping his hat against his leg before exiting.

As the final dance begins, Beaufort walks to the punch bowl, followed by Mulcahy, Schattuck, and Quincannon. Throwing his hat aside and letting out a rebel yell, Beaufort dunks the ladle into the bowl and takes a big drink as the others watch for his reaction. "Is it to your taste, Johnny, darlin'?" asks Mulcahy. Schattuck and Quincannon dunk crystal cups into the bowl, after which Mulcahy picks up the bowl and drinks from it. Ford then cuts to the outside of the building where Michael and Philadelphia find a secluded spot on the veranda to dance a few steps before kissing as the scene fades out.

As the troop leaves the fort to meet with Cochise, the women are standing on the headquarters' balcony when the telegraph operator rushes in to notify Mrs. Collingwood that her husband's transfer to West Point was approved. Mrs. Collingwood hands the telegram back to the man, telling him to wait until her husband returns. As the regiment has gone out the fort gates, Mrs. Collingwood, "peering off at the dust of the receding column," says almost to herself, "I can't see him . . . nothing but the dust . . . the red dust." Mrs. Collingwood's line was changed by Ford to "I can't see him. All I can see is the flags." Peter Bogdanovich asked Ford if the line was symbolic. "More as a slight touch of premonition about her husband's death," Ford replied.[32]

Ford's relationship with Frank Nugent was never close, unlike the one he shared with Dudley Nichols.[33] Ford said years later that he and Nugent "never fit." While Ford and Nugent were friendly, Ford rarely engaged in the give-and-take of crafting a scene as he did with Nichols. A perfect example was when Nugent and Ford held a discussion about the meeting between Thursday and Cochise. Ford said he saw the Indian leader standing against the sky, holding a pipe in one hand. Nugent interrupted him, stating that Apaches did not smoke from a pipe, but used cigarettes rolled in corn husks. Ford paused—one of his deathly silent moments—before continuing that Cochise would be holding something. "That hand may have a flute, it may have an ax, I don't give a damn what he has . . . but he isn't smoking any cigarette."[34] (In later years, Ford was often dismissive of Nugent's contributions.)

"Jack was very patient with writers," John Wayne once observed. "[He'd] take a scene and make the writer write and write and then reach in and pull three lines out of it that could tell everything." However, Wayne noted, in later years Ford "lost his patience with writers and it ultimately hurt his work."[35]

From this point on, the film followed the script, although Ford did change certain things, either dropping scenes or condensing dialogue or script direction. At the meeting between the officers and Cochise, Nugent has Cochise offering cigarettes, while Thursday prefers his cigar. (Ford discarded this piece.) Thursday is introduced to Alchesay, head of the White Mountain Apache tribe; Santana, leader of the Mescaleros; and "the Chiricahua medicine man, named Jerome in our language, but in Spanish, Geronimo." (Ford featured each man in a close-up as they are introduced.)[36] As Cochise begins to speak, the script noted that "his voice is faded," as Beaufort's voice translating "comes over—sentence by sentence."

When Cochise speaks about Meacham, the Apache leader's voice "comes through loudly in his denunciation of Meacham," calling the Indian agent (in Spanish) "an evil man, a cursed man, who speaks no truth and spreads illness and vice through my nation." When Thursday asks what he said, Beaufort, "relishing the opportunity," says that a "free translation" was Cochise called him "a yellow-bellied polecat of dubious antecedents and conjectural progeny." Cochise continues to speak, and, again, Beaufort's voice becomes louder as he translates. When Cochise states for every Apache killed, they will kill ten white men, Thursday's patience explodes. He orders Beaufort to tell the leader he finds him without honor and demands they return to the reservation or he will attack. Beaufort translates in "rapid-fire Spanish, but in a monotone of a man reading a death warrant—possibly his own."

As both Thursday and Cochise leave the talks, Nugent describes the other men as "stunned and stricken—all but Meacham, who—with a gloating smile—is the first to turn and follow his man Thursday." When it came to filming this scene, Ford ignored Nugent's version and instead had Cochise (a blanket draped over his left arm) speak in Spanish, then letting Beaufort translate.

Before ordering an attack, Thursday surveys the narrow defile but cannot see anything. York, thinking like Cochise, tells him the Apache are hidden in the rocks above the passageway. Ignoring York's observations, Thursday announces the regiment will charge in a column of fours. York is shocked, explaining that such a move is suicidal. Thursday will not listen to reason and relieves him of his command. York flings his gauntlet to the ground in front of Thursday, stating, "At your service, sir!" Thursday draws "his saber and, with its tip, neatly pins the gauntlet which he extends on the point to York." Thursday states he will decide later whether he will answer York with pistols or a general court-martial, ordering York to take the supply wagons up to the ridge, with Michael O'Rourke to go with him. York gallops off. (Ford's only change in this sequence was having Thursday order the bugler to return the captain's gauntlet to him.)

As the charge begins, Nugent describes Collingwood's expression as "one of sardonic amusement tinged with bitterness. It is the expression of a man whose destiny—to die in a stupid charge—finally has caught up with him."[37] Mulcahy leads his troop with "a fierce grin of a fighter" and yells to Beaufort, "Come on, Reb!" Beaufort, his saber pointed forward, releases a rebel yell that is taken up by the troop. Nugent describes a camera angle that looks down into the defile, featuring Thursday and his men galloping in, as five or six carbines slide into the camera's foreground. "Shooting past their sights we see Thursday, Collingwood, the bugler, and others lined up as they still race on with the sights holding them. Then we hear a savage Apache yell and the carbines blast fire—the smoke filling the screen." The script included a closer shot that dimly revealed through the dust "men and horses falling." The passageway is a dead end, causing the cavalrymen to turn around and run through the gauntlet again. Thursday's horse is stricken, and he cannot control it, the animal wheeling around on its own and galloping "back through the stricken troop," passing Collingwood and others. Collingwood, grabbing the guidon from a stricken soldier, leads the remaining men to follow Thursday.

During one discussion about the climactic fight, Ford came up with an idea for a shot involving the bugler. "A bugler will be sounding the charge. Then the bugler's arm will weaken, the bugle will start dropping down in the limp hand. The bugler will slowly slide, not fall, from his horse. The camera will continue on the riderless horse for twelve feet."[38]

Nugent created moments showing the sergeants meeting their fate. Schattuck, on his horse, is rallying the men when he is suddenly shot. Swaying in the saddle, saber in his hand, he pitches forward from the saddle. His saber is "driven, point first, into the ground and remains there quivering.[39] Then horses ride by, obscuring it, and dust again fills the screen." As Thursday's horse falls, just beyond the entrenched troopers, O'Rourke runs out and pulls him to safety. Thursday apologizes to the sergeant major, who replies, "Save *yer* regrets for the grandchildren we'll never know or see." O'Rourke is then shot and goes down, as Mulcahy stands over his body, cursing the Apache as he fires at shadows in the rocks. He is hit three times, "toppling like a giant tree, across O'Rourke's body." Suddenly, it becomes completely silent. Beaufort holds the flag at an angle as it "flutters across his face." Beaufort smiles at "the symbolism of a Confederate fighting under the Union banner—and holds it erect again."

Ford never shot the deaths of Schattuck, O'Rourke, and Mulcahy as detailed in the script. Instead, he has the cavalry charge in, many being picked off, while the surviving troopers turn around and race back to take cover in a small circular dirt mound. Ford uses a wide shot, showing the men taking position and returning fire, while one corporal tends to a wounded colleague. Ford keeps three characters (Thursday, Collingwood, and O'Rourke) in a medium shot as O'Rourke hands the colonel his pistol. As Thursday moves toward the front of the circle of men, the director features all of the men in a medium-wide shot. As the silence enfolds the area, Ford returns to a wide shot as we see the Apaches descend on the soldiers.

The final scene in both the script and film takes place in the fort's headquarters, a few years after Thursday's death. York is addressing four newspaper reporters who will accompany the regiment as they go after Geronimo. On the wall above the fireplace is a painting of Thursday and his broken saber mounted in front of the painting. The newspapermen are hailing Thursday's charge as a heroic action, which York does not dispute. The real truth remains with the men who were there and will not sully the regiment's honor. As the troopers move out through the gates, the women watch as the military band plays "The Girl I Left Behind Me."[40]

* * *

In 1922, Will Hays, former postmaster general, was chosen to head up the Motion Picture Producers and Distributors of America (MPPDA). This association was formed by studio executives in an effort to head off threats of government censorship of motion pictures after three scandals brought unwanted attention.[41] The MPPDA, also known as the "Hays Office," created guidelines labeled "Don'ts and Be Careful" for producers to follow to avoid any censorship problems. For instance, a kiss between a couple could not be any longer than ten seconds, and married couples had to sleep in separate beds.

In 1933, the Production Code Administration (PCA) replaced the MPPDA after the Catholic Legion of Decency and other religious groups demanded stricter censorship rules on movies. (Between 1930 and 1933, many films had suggestive dialogue and/or scenes, gaining the moniker "Pre-Code" movies.) With the formation of the Production Code Administration, rules of what was and was not acceptable were heavily tightened and enforced. Just like with the Hays Office, studios had to submit the script prior to production for approval, including song lyrics or poems. (Anything the PCA found objectionable had to be either rewritten or eliminated.) Once the film was completed, PCA officials screened it so they could demand changes before granting its seal of approval. PCA was also vigilant for things deemed offensive in a foreign country that would forbid the film's release there, which would mean lost revenue for a studio.

With the script completed, Ford sent it to Joseph L. Breen, president of the PCA, for his approval. In a letter, dated July 17, 1947, Ford commented to Breen:

> We contemplate calling it *War Party* or *Fort Apache* or preferably *Boots and Saddles* if the title can be cleared. I hope you enjoy reading it, Joe, for I'm quite enthused about it as a bit of Americana. The subject of the Garrison Post in the Arizona Apache country has never been quite fully exploited. I repeat, I think it is a good Americanism and good Americana.
>
> I hope you observe with the same sympathy I do the introduction of Irish characters into American History. As you no doubt already know, a lot of the Irish went West after the Civil War. Some stayed in the Regular Army . . . some went to California, and others went to the mines in Butte, Montana. Many of their descendants became famous. The best literature of the period came from some of the old Irish Regular Soldiers.
>
> The bit about the "manure pile" naturally is in your hands entirely. I don't know whether it offends the Code or not. I hope it doesn't. I also hope we may be able to use the expression "rump spring," as it is a period piece and was accepted in those days.[42]
>
> We already heard through our research department in the East, headed by Miss Katherine Spaatz, daughter of General Carl Spaatz,[43] that the idea of the story was received most favorably—in fact,

> enthusiastically—by those apprehensive lads in Washington who are trying to hold some semblance of a fighting force together.

Signing the letter "Jack," it is interesting how he lays on his Irish charm to Breen.[44]

It is notable that this letter was written during the HUAC hearings about Communist influence in Hollywood. Ford emphasizes that this film would reflect positive aspects of the country's history and patriotism, using the term "Americana" twice. When it came to the manure pile sequence, he places the decision in Breen's hands, careful not to come off as adversarial. Ford was also not afraid to drop names, noting that the daughter of General Spaatz was his head researcher, and that the Washington military people were very supportive of the project. This letter illustrates Ford taking every advantage to get the project into production. In the past, he generally refrained from writing anything to Breen when it came to script approval, letting a studio executive like Zanuck handle such issues. For future productions, either he or Cooper would serve as point man dealing with Breen, but the letters were usually brief.

Breen gave approval to the script—"except as noted." He stressed that the script contained "little, if anything, that is even questionable from the standpoint of political censorship." He also requested that Mel Morse at the American Humane Association (AHA) be contacted regarding any scenes involving horses or other animals.[45] Breen cautioned that they "make certain that there will be no toilet shown" in the scene between Mickey and Philadelphia in the washroom at the stage stop. (In reality, there would have been an outhouse at the stop.) He was adamant that throughout the film they "keep to an *absolute minimum* all scenes of drinking. This is important." Breen also expressed his concern when it came to showing the two dead troopers burned and spread-eagle on two wagon wheels. He stated that such scenes be "shot in such a way as to make certain that the scene not be unduly gruesome."[46]

Breen also commented that the various battle scenes between the cavalry and the Indians "not come through too realistically gruesome." He also requested the list of songs they planned on using in the film, which Katherine Cliffton, Argosy's story editor, forwarded. The list comprised songs from the period, including "Captain Jinks," "Cuckoo Waltz,"

"Fiddler's Green," "Garryowen," "For Seven Long Years," "For Her Lover Who Was Far Away," "The Girl I Left Behind Me," and "Regular Army, O!" On July 30, 1947, Breen replied that all songs were approved except for "Fiddler's Green" and "For Her Lover Who Was Far Away." Noting that "Fiddler's Green" contained the word "hell" (one of the "forbidden words," per the Code), Breen commented that if they used the song, the word would have to be deleted. Breen warned that lyrics from "For Her Lover Who Was Far Away" would either have to be changed or excluded due to including the word "lover."[47]

* * *

As Nugent began his research for the script, Ford hired Katharine Spaatz for historical research and D. R. O. Hatswell as military wardrobe advisor. No detail was too small or insignificant when it came to military life, drills, and uniforms. Ford was not a stickler when it came to army uniform regulations, most notably his version of trooper's campaign hats. In his films, they bore little resemblance to military issue of that era. Ford didn't care, as he wanted what looked good cinematically.[48] While his research team went to work, Ford read numerous books and journals from the period. Katherine Cliffton, who also assisted in the military research work, said, "He wanted to know what was right, even if he chose to overlook it."[49]

In Ford's *Fort Apache* papers, he made a notation: "Col. Tim McCoy, Technical Advisor." Growing up in Saginaw, Michigan, McCoy had dreams of being a cowboy. While attending college in Chicago, he caught a performance of the Miller Brothers 101 Ranch Wild West show and quickly ditched his education. McCoy went to Wyoming to follow his childhood dream, becoming friendly with the Arapaho, Shoshone, and Sioux tribes. He quickly adapted to conversing with the tribes in sign language, learning their customs and history. After serving as a lieutenant-colonel in World War I, McCoy worked as an Indian agent in Wyoming, and this is where he had his first brush with Hollywood, serving as a technical advisor and coordinating the Indian extras for Paramount's 1923 epic, *The Covered Wagon*.[50]

McCoy would not work for Ford, but he found another former military man who served as technical advisor on all three cavalry pictures. Philip Kieffer was born into a military family, as his father was a Union captain in the Civil War. Kieffer graduated from West Point in 1911 as a second-lieutenant with the 4th Cavalry. Between 1916 and 1917, he was part of the Punitive Expedition on the border against Pancho Villa, and after World War I, left the army. Kieffer found work in Hollywood as a military technical advisor and played small parts, often in Westerns.[51]

* * *

The *Hollywood Reporter* reported on March 31, 1947, that *Fort Apache* had been planned as a United Artists release for later that year. Since their RKO deal wasn't exclusive, it's possible Cooper and Ford may have shopped this production to another studio, hoping for a more favorable contract. The article went on to state that Argosy decided to make *Fort Apache* at RKO due to the "unsettled status" at United Artists, as it was heavily in debt. At this period in Hollywood, major studios viewed independent producers as a threat to their well-oiled machine, fearing that if an independent producer was successful, other producers would demand a similar deal. Even with the Paramount Decree, the major studios still held the upper hand, and they were not about to let an independent producer get the better accord.

To finance *Fort Apache*, Argosy acquired another large bank note for $1.64 million. They asked director Leo McCarey for a $360,000 loan through his Rainbow Productions company, plus an additional $220,000 for a completion bond.[52] Both Cooper and Ford agreed to defer a portion of their salaries ($37,500 and $112,500 respectively), as well as getting Henry Fonda and John Wayne to equally defer $25,000 of their salaries in exchange for 5 percent of the profits. With all of this done, Argosy then arranged a $610,000 loan (at 5 percent interest) from RKO that allowed them to pay off Leo McCarey's loan, as well as repay Cooper, Ford, Fonda, and Wayne their deferments.[53] (The studio loan would be "payable only from gross receipts.") The contract stated that "amounts received from box offices of theatres either owned or controlled by RKO" would *not* be considered gross receipts. When it came to RKO's distribution fee, things did not get better for Argosy. The studio would recoup their distribution fee from gross receipts: 25 percent from domestic release where they distribute, 30 percent deducted from other territories where RKO distributes directly, while 15 percent from receipts received to RKO from sub-distributors.[54]

All of this meant that once RKO, the bank, Fonda, and Wayne received their fees, Argosy would collect 60 percent of any residual amount. No matter how they looked at it, the deal was stacked in favor of RKO, not Argosy. It should be noted that this deal was signed before *The Fugitive* was even released. That film's box office failure guaranteed any profit Argosy earned from *Fort Apache* would go against the debt caused by the company's feature debut.

* * *

Turning to casting the roles, Ford brought in Henry Fonda for the role of Colonel Thursday and John Wayne as Captain York.[55] Many of the supporting and smaller roles were filled by performers of the director's well-established stock company. "I used my friends in pictures because I like an atmosphere in which people can work well together," Ford said years later. "Besides, I knew what they could do, and I don't coach acting."[56]

Danny Borzage held the record of being the longest member of the director's stock company, starting with *The Iron Horse* in 1924. He was the younger brother of director Frank Borzage, and found a niche in silent movies by playing his accordion to provide mood music for the performers. Ford took a liking to the man and took him on every film thereafter, as well as giving him an occasional small bit part in many of his films. (Borzage plays one of the new recruits in *Fort Apache*.) No matter if it was on a soundstage or location, everyone knew when Ford arrived. Someone would holler out, "He's comin,' Danny!" and Borzage would begin playing "Bringing in the Sheaves" on his accordion, which was Ford's "theme song." Over the years, Borzage adopted other songs for certain actors, such as "Red River" for Fonda, "Lorena" for Wayne, and "Streets of Laredo" for Harry Carey Jr. (When asked if he'd play "Bringing in the

Sheaves" at Ford's funeral, Borzage shook his head, saying he'd never get through it.[57])

Jack Pennick, who played Sergeant Schattuck in *Fort Apache*, was the second-longest member of the stock company, first working for Ford in *The Blue Eagle* in 1926. He would go on to appear in forty films, as well as serving as his adjutant during World War II.[58] Wayne said Pennick was a "valuable asset" to Ford, and that the two men had "a loyalty that didn't require a lot of thank-yous." Others in the cast who were part of Ford's stock company included Victor McLaglen (*Sgt. Mulcahy*), Ward Bond (*Sgt. O'Rourke*), Anna Lee (*Mrs. Collingwood*), Mickey Simpson (*Sergeant*), Ray Hyke (*Irish Recruit*), Fred Graham (*Cavalryman*), Frank McGrath (*Cpl. Derice, Bugler*), Mae Marsh (*Officer's Wife*), Harry Tenbrook (*O'Feeney, Telegraph Operator*), Jane Crowley (*Officer's Wife*), and Francis Ford (*Stagecoach Guard*). Ford rounded out the cast with Pedro Armendáriz (*Sgt. Beaufort*), Irene Rich (*Mrs. O'Rourke*), Guy Kibbee (*Dr. Wilkens*), Grant Withers (*Silas Meacham*), Dick Foran (*Sgt. Quincannon*), Miguel Inclán (*Cochise*), Hank Worden (*Southern Recruit*), and Mary Gordon (*Ma*).[59] Chris-Pin Martin, who had appeared in *Stagecoach* and *The Fugitive*, was cast as Francisco, the father of Lupe, who becomes the housemaid for Thursday's quarters. Fernando Fernández, referred to as "Mexico's Sinatra" because of his popularity as a singer in Mexican films of the late 1940s, was hired to play Esteban, who sings a love song when Mickey shows up at Philadelphia's balcony.[60] Both Martin and Fernández (who also appeared in *The Fugitive*) filmed their scenes, but were cut from the final print.

Fort Apache was a reunion for Ford and actor George O' Brien. Ford first hired the actor to play the lead role in his 1924 epic, *The Iron Horse*. The two men quickly became close friends as well as working colleagues in five additional films. After finishing *The Seas Beneath* (1931), they went off on a boys' adventure of the Philippines, Indochina, Hong Kong, and Japan. During their stay in Manila, for reasons unknown, Ford went on an alcoholic bender for nearly two weeks. Nothing O'Brien could do or say would get Ford to stop drinking. Leaving Ford to his own devices, O'Brien went on to visit other places in the Philippines while Ford remained in a drunken haze. Ford, now sober, reunited with O'Brien after his solo jaunt, and the trip continued as if nothing had happened.

O'Brien did not realize he had committed a serious misstep in Ford's eyes by abandoning him during his stewed condition, and Ford banished him from working in his cinematic world for sixteen years. O'Brien would not be the only one to suffer this fate in Ford's universe.

With the birth of talking pictures, O'Brien quickly became a popular star of "B" Westerns at Fox, and later, at RKO. After serving in the navy during World War II, O'Brien found that Hollywood had forgotten him. The lack of work, among other things, put a severe strain on his marriage, which led to his wife reaching out to Ford. She asked him to give O'Brien a part in his film, but Ford flatly refused. O'Brien's wife played her ace, claiming that if Ford didn't cast him, it would shatter a Catholic family. The ploy of playing to Ford's devout Catholic faith worked. The friendship between the two men took up where they left off, as if nothing had ever happened. (O'Brien's wife wound up filing for divorce a year later.)

For the roles of Philadelphia Thursday and Michael O'Rourke, David O. Selznick made a deal to loan out Shirley Temple and her husband, John Agar.[61] Temple was seventeen when she married Agar, who was twenty-four, in 1945. At the time of their marriage, Agar had no aspirations of becoming an actor, but Selznick put him under personal contract at $150 a week, without Temple's knowledge.[62] The teaming of the newlywed couple may have been good publicity, but privately the marriage was in trouble, even before they worked together, and they eventually divorced in 1949.

A new group became part of the Ford stock company, stuntmen who would work with Ford throughout the rest of his career. They included Cliff Lyons, William Steele, Fred Kennedy, Post Park, John Hudkins, Slim Hightower, and Frank McGrath. Three more stuntmen, Chuck Hayward, Chuck Roberson, and Terry Wilson, would join Ford's "Iodine Squad" on *Rio Grande*.[63] (The term was an industry nickname for stuntmen, who often used the medicine to treat cuts and scrapes.)

When it came to casting a Ford film, there was a ritual that played out among the stock company members. Word would get out that Ford was gearing up for a new film, and one by one, stock company members would make the pilgrimage to Ford's office and pay a visit. They would talk about various things that had nothing to do with the film, and Ford *never* brought up the film or a potential job until the end, when he'd tell the actor or actress briefly what the film was about and if they had a role. There was no haggling over pay, no coming in and reading for a role. Ford knew what his actors were capable of, and if they didn't fit a role, he wouldn't cast them. Even the performers who were not part of his stock company never had to read for a role, as Ford was able to judge their ability by just having a conversation, well aware of their previous work.

* * *

The Navajo call it *Tsé Bii' Ndzisgaii.*[64]

No other location is so identified with one director and his films. Between 1939 and 1964, John Ford filmed seven pictures in Monument Valley. It has become so identified with the director that many filmmakers avoided using the location lest they be accused of copying Ford. When it came to choosing locations for *Fort Apache*, there was no question he would return to the valley for numerous exteriors.

Monument Valley waited a long time for its cinematic debut.

It began its creation over twenty-five million years ago. Like a great artist, wind and rain slowly etched the land into unique formations depending on the varying hardiness of the rocks, while red iron oxide stained the floor and the sandstone. Millions of years later, this land continues to evolve on its own schedule. Monument Valley defies any ability to describe it. Only by seeing it in person and walking the land can one truly appreciate its majesty. However, its beauty belies a harsh and unforgiving environment. Living in such a habitat requires resilient people who can adapt and survive. In the Navajo language they refer to themselves as *Diné*—"The People." Like the magnificent buttes, they have endured and survived in Monument Valley and the surrounding country for centuries. Evidence points to the arrival of the Navajo in the Four Corners area between 1100 and 1300 BC.[65] The agricultural influence of the Puebloans led the Navajo to engage in farming (corn, beans, and squash), while contact with Spanish explorers introduced them to raising livestock, mainly sheep and goats. From the sheep, the Navajo women spun and weaved wool into blankets and clothing.

A section of land in northeastern Arizona and southeastern Utah (which includes Monument Valley) was set aside for the Southern Paiute tribe, called the Paiute Strip. In the early 1920s, Utah's state legislature offered the tribe a more fertile territory, which they accepted. By 1922, the Paiute Strip was considered public domain, allowing anyone to homestead the land. A lanky Colorado sheepherder named Harry Goulding visited Monument Valley and quickly fell in love with the region. Goulding scraped together $320 to purchase 640 acres in Monument Valley at the base of Tsay-Kizzi Mesa (Rock Door Mesa) in 1923. Harry and his wife, "Mike,"[66] packed up their belongings and made the difficult trek across unpaved roads and sand hills to their new homestead. Setting up a big tent, Harry planned on raising sheep and trading with the Navajo. The Gouldings pitched their tent on the mesa that backed up to a sheer, eight-hundred-foot rock cliff, which not only offered protection from the wind and the heat, but provided a magnificent view. While the Navajo traded with the Gouldings, they were far from welcoming, but Goulding's good-natured humor and honesty proved he was a man to trust, and tribal members soon treated them as family. In 1928, he built a two-story stone trading post, with the second story serving as their living quarters. In 1963, Harry Goulding sold his trading post, which has since expanded into a motel. (The trading post is now a museum.)

Exactly how John Ford chose Monument Valley as a film location varies depending on who is telling the story. Ford told director Peter Bogdanovich that he came across the area as he was driving through Arizona on his way to Santa Fe, New Mexico, in the early 1930s.[67] This is an example of "Ford's blarney," as there were no paved roads in the area at that time, and well out of the way if you were traveling to Santa Fe. In later years, Ford told his grandson, Dan, that George O'Brien had seen the area and raved about its beauty. John Wayne once said he told Ford about the location after having worked on a film in a nearby area.

The most credible story comes from two separate interviews with Harry Goulding by film historian Todd McCarthy and author Samuel Moon.[68] Learning a Hollywood movie company was planning on making a film around the Flagstaff area, Harry was determined to get Hollywood to come to Monument Valley, as a film company would provide much-needed financial help to the Navajo tribe, hit hard by the Great Depression.[69]

Harry and Mike packed some bags, along with a batch of eight-by-ten photographs, and drove to California, staying with Mike's brother. Locating Walter Wanger's offices in Hollywood, Harry presented himself and his photos. He was eventually introduced to John Ford, who, like Harry did seventeen years earlier, fell in love with the landscape. Once Ford chose Monument Valley, the plan was to house the cast and crew in the town of Kayenta, about twenty-five miles southwest of Monument Valley, at John Wetherill's trading post quarters, and Goulding would handle any overflow.[70] Goulding's location proved more beneficial, since Wetherill's post had limited housing, and was a good half-hour drive (one way) to the valley. Goulding had more than enough space to handle the entire cast and crew (living in tents), including an eating area for their meals, and it was within minutes of where the company would be filming. Goulding also served as the liaison with the Navajo, translating what was required of the tribal members who acted in the film. It was the beginning of a long relationship with Ford. By the late 1940s, Frank and Lee Bradley eventually took over as Navajo liaisons, working on every Ford film shot in the area.

* * *

With the Monument Valley location locked up, Ford and Cooper made a deal with actor Ray Corrigan to build the exterior Fort Apache set on his ranch.[71] Corrigan, an actor in "B" Westerns, purchased 1,500 acres in Simi Valley (about ten miles past Iverson Ranch in Chatsworth) for $11,400 in 1937. The land had plenty of oak and evergreen trees, a man-made lake with a waterfall, rock outcroppings (courtesy of the Santa Susana Mountains), and plenty of open space.[72] As companies began to use his ranch, Corrigan negotiated a deal: Any sets a production company built on the ranch would remain on the property for use in other productions. To make this agreement more appealing, he likely either cut the rental price, or waived it entirely. This was the case for *Fort Apache*, as Argosy agreed to leave the set standing, which was later featured in numerous movies and television shows, including *The Adventures of Rin Tin Tin* (1954–1959).[73]

* * *

Both Cooper and Ford had hoped to film *Fort Apache* in Technicolor, but the cost for film stock and the specific camera proved too expensive. Instead, cinematographer Archie Stout came up with a different idea: All exterior scenes would be photographed with black-and-white infrared film. One of the unique aspects of using this film stock was that it turned objects that normally appeared dark to the human eye as nearly white, such as foliage, clouds, and sand.[74] This stock was sensitive to blue, making the blue sky in Monument Valley photograph slightly darker than normal, which caused the white clouds to stand out on the screen. Using infrared stock required some changes while filming on location; for example, the cavalry guidon—normally a red top and white bottom—saw the red replaced with a light or medium brown. To avoid actors' faces having a chalky appearance, makeup artist Emile LaVigne had to use a light brown makeup base. (Stout reverted to traditional panchromatic black-and-white film stock for all of the studio interiors, which did not require any changes.)

Stout, who had a reputation for being headstrong, clashed with Ford throughout the making of the film, with the cameraman later saying working with Ford was "not a piece of cake." Normally, Ford would have fired such a person, but he felt duty-bound, as Stout's son was killed in World War II while serving in Ford's Field Photographic Unit. When things turned tense because Stout refused to shoot a scene due to the lighting, Ford turned to assistant cameraman William Clothier as an intermediary.[75] While Ford and Stout may have had difficulties, the cinematographer worked again with Ford on *The Quiet Man* (1952) and *The Sun Shines Bright* (1953). As second-unit cinematographer for *The Quiet Man*, Stout shared the Oscar for Best Cinematography with Winton Hoch, marking the only time a cinematographer won an Oscar for his work on a second unit.[76]

* * *

Budgeting and scheduling a film that travels to a remote location requires a tremendous amount of planning. Weather problems or a leading actor getting hurt can cause serious delays, driving the budget even higher. With a $2,520,000 budget, Cooper reminded Ford that this was all they could spend; he was counting on Ford's resourcefulness to complete the film in less than the sixty days allotted on the schedule.

When it came to the salary for the lead actors, Fonda, Wayne, and Shirley Temple each earned a weekly salary of $10,000 for ten weeks. Victor McLaglen was paid $35,000 a week for five weeks, while Ward Bond got $2,500 a week for ten weeks, plus a $15,000 bonus. (Why he was given a bonus is unknown.) John Agar, making his film debut, was paid $500 a week for ten weeks; however, since Selznick loaned him out, $350 of his salary went directly to the producer. George O'Brien's weekly salary was $1,875 for five weeks; Dick Foran signed for $1,000 a week for ten weeks; and Pedro Armendáriz was paid a flat salary of $16,578. Jack Pennick earned $350 a week for his seven weeks of acting duties, while collecting $3,748 as production assistant and an additional $200 for recording military counting cadence. Both Anna Lee and Irene Rich had a four-week contract, with Lee earning $1,750 weekly and Irene Rich making $1,250 a week. Then there were the bit players like Ruth Clifford ($275 a week for nearly three weeks), Mae Marsh ($350 a week for nineteen days), Harry Tenbrook ($55 a day for nine days), and, of course, Ford's brother, Francis ($150 a day for four days).

Stunt Coordinator Cliff Lyons was paid $500 a week, plus an additional $300 for doing stunts. Frank McGrath, who played the bugler Derice, earned $300 a week for seven weeks, plus stunt adjustments that totaled $1,879. (A stunt adjustment, or stunt check, is industry parlance for paying a stuntman an extra fee to perform a specific stunt.) Hiring background players (also known as extras) to play cavalrymen on location was budgeted at $12.50 an hour for an eight-hour day, while Navajo men were paid $6.50 an hour for an eight-hour day.[77] No matter what tribe the Navajo people would portray in Ford's films (Apache, Comanche, or Cheyenne), they always spoke in their own language, usually telling jokes with each other.

Fort Apache also had other expenses, such as livestock, especially horses. Navajo tribal members who owned their own horses were paid $1.50 an hour per head for an eight-hour day, while other horses for the cavalry were rented from local ranchers, an amount that totaled $6,151. The eleven principal horses (for the star or featured performer to ride in the film) cost $550 a week for ten weeks ($5,500). Then came the six-up and four-up teams at $30 a day, for the stagecoach and repair wagon sequences.[78] Renting horses for filming at Corrigan Ranch was budgeted at $5 a day ($2,920), while "falling horses" were paid $5 a day to be on standby, with adjustments for stunt work running an additional $2,085. (A "falling horse" was one that was trained to take a fall with a stuntman aboard.) Hay and feed costs on location ran $3,675, while in California it was $452.

An independent film production had to rent their wardrobe and props, while a studio-produced production mostly relied on their departments. When it came to renting wardrobe, the go-to place was Western Costume, which could supply anything from Roman era to modern day.[79] (Argosy rented wardrobe from Western Costume not just for principal performers, but also the numerous background players.) Shirley Temple had ten wardrobe changes, which cost $3,645 (her photo double's wardrobe cost $850). Wayne's wardrobe rental ran $1,300, while Fonda's was $950. Cavalry uniforms (totaling 140) cost $14,456, for both Monument Valley and Corrigan Ranch locations, and 250 costumes for the Indian extras rented out at $3,825. The company also rented 103 brass spurs ($148), 216 pairs of socks ($72), 60 gauntlet gloves ($206), 60 suspenders ($61), and four pairs of boots for principal performers ($247).[80]

Props were another part of the budget, including 50 sabers with rubber blades ($540), 50 Indian daggers, 30 bows and quivers, and 283 arrows (6 weeks rental, $495). Rifle and gun rentals cost $1,485; renting 115 saddles, blankets, bridles, and other accessories for a six-week period totaled $6,612; sixteen McClellan saddles (including bridles and blankets) ran $920. Six army freight wagons were rented for six weeks ($150 a week), an army ambulance for eleven weeks ($50 a week), and a stagecoach for six and a half weeks ($100 a week). An additional $711 was added to "rebuild stagecoach and wagons."[81] (Saddles and tack were either supplied by various stables that catered to the film industry, or rented from various studio departments.)

Moving a film company to and from a location is the equivalent of a military operation. This was Ford's third film shot in the valley, which meant everyone at Goulding's Trading Post knew what was needed. (Goulding was paid $12,981 for his assistance and use of the facilities.) The biggest task was providing living quarters and meals for the cast and crew, and those duties fell to Anderson Boarding Supply and Company. (Beginning with this production, the company worked on every Ford film in the valley.) The camp was located on the flats below Goulding's Trading Post. Each tent housed four people—hardly luxury accommodations—with the dirt floor covered by a Navajo blanket, and each person given a small dresser for clothing. A large tent served as the mess hall for meals, served at a specific time. For all of this, Anderson was paid $85,842, which also included $15,500 for dismantling and moving out of Monument Valley. Portable toilets ($950) and a water tank ($250) for showers were brought in, and additional portable toilets were provided at shooting locations ($550). Navajo tribal members employed as laborers earned $6.60 an hour (an eight-hour minimum) for unskilled workers, while skilled workers and interpreters earned $9.50 an hour (eight-hour minimum).

* * *

Getting a company to a remote location required the use of railroads, planes, and cars. All cast and crew left from Union Station in downtown Los Angeles and traveled overnight to Flagstaff. (A round-trip ticket was $29.75, amounting to a total of $7,484 for the entire cast and crew.[82]) From Flagstaff, Ford and some cast members took a small plane to the valley where a dirt landing strip was built near the camp. The majority of the cast and crew were driven by car or bus. Getting to Monument Valley today on paved roads is much different from 1947, when the roads were dirt and mostly unpaved. If it rained, one was in for a very long drive to the valley.

A film company heading to a location generally moved in waves. For *Fort Apache*, the first group included the production unit manager, the second assistant director, the auditor, and the head wrangler, who left on July 21, 1947.[83] Their job was to set up shop, making sure the necessary equipment and material was already there, or in the process of being set up. They were followed by the wardrobe foreman, special effects department head, assistant property man, grips, and electricians. Twelve wranglers and two train cars carrying horses also left on July 21, as did Ford, Lowell Farrell (first assistant director), stunt coordinator Cliff Lyons, cinematographer Archie Stout, Ford's ever-present assistant Jack Pennick, wardrobe department head Mickey Meyers, and prop master Jack Golconda. (Ford, with his assistant director, cinematographer, stunt coordinator, and other technicians, began scouting locations upon their arrival in Monument Valley.) Merian Cooper, Ford's longtime secretary and script supervisor Meta Stern, John Wayne, George O'Brien, John Agar, Pedro Armendáriz, Philip Kieffer, stuntmen Frank McGrath, Fred Graham, Bob Rose, Post Park, Bryan "Slim" Hightower, John Hudkins, William Clothier, and crew departments such as camera, electric, makeup/hair, and wardrobe all departed on July 23. Victor McLaglen, Henry Fonda, Dick Foran, and Miguel Inclán left four days later, while Grant Withers (the last cast member needed on location) left on August 2. That same day, four stunt "falling" horses and their owners left for location by truck.[84]

* * *

Location work on any Western movie is challenging. While a location can feature a lot of natural beauty, it is also fraught with hardships ranging from minor problems like insect bites to a major quagmire like unpredictable weather. A film crew, similar to the pioneers heading west, have to learn to live with the elements, and Monument Valley was no different. Daytime temperatures routinely climbed past 110 degrees, and an occasional sandstorm brought filming to a sudden halt.

Ford began filming on Friday, July 25, using photo doubles of Michael and Philadelphia for wide shots of the couple's ride through the valley.[85] The following day was spent filming the stagecoach making its way across the desert, as well as the cavalry ambulance on its way to Fort Apache, using photo doubles for not only Thursday and Philadelphia, but

Michael, Quincannon, Schattuck, Beaufort, and Mulcahy. Sunday, July 27, Ford spent the day shooting scenes of York and Beaufort looking over Gooseneck Valley (the dialogue in this scene was shot on a soundstage in Hollywood) before moving to the San Juan River location near Mexican Hat, Utah, to film the two men riding across the river into Mexico.[86] It was common practice for film companies to work seven days a week on a distant location (i.e., away from Hollywood), but once the company returned to Los Angeles, they returned to the normal six-day work week, with Sundays idle. By the early 1960s, both movies and television series went to a five-day shooting schedule in town (Hollywood), and six days a week on distant location, with Sundays off.

Running shots of the repair wagon escaping the Apaches were done on the open flat land near Square Rock the following day,[87] while on Tuesday, July 29, the company moved to Rock Door Canyon to photograph wide shots of the massacre sequence of the Apaches overrunning the troopers. (Ford relied on stunt and photo doubles for the doomed troopers instead of using the actors.) The company spent Wednesday morning working at Goulding's Trading Post, which served as the exterior Hassayampa stage stop, as well as filming the cavalry ambulance's approach with the four sergeants. Once these shots were completed, Ford moved the company to the other side of Rock Door Mesa to film Michael and the four sergeants making their way to the burned-out wagon prior to the Apache attack. July 31 and August 1 were spent photographing the repair wagon escaping the Apaches, along with York's column coming to the rescue and capturing Diablo's band.

Sharp-eyed viewers might catch a glimpse of a car as the camera pans off the repair wagon moving along to a group of mounted Apaches on a ridge. Behind the Indians in the lower right camera frame, one can spot a car driving down a dirt road. (A similar incident shows up in Ford's *The Searchers* when the cavalry escorts Comanche Indians across a snow-covered stream; one can spot a car coming to a stop on the road in the background.)

In one shot in this sequence, Ford broke the cinematic rule by filming the horses from "the wrong side." The director had the performers moving from right to left on the screen; however, in one cut, the Apaches are now moving *left to right* on the screen. The cardinal rule is if you show a figure going from right to left on the screen, the camera must remain on the figure's left-hand side. Switching the camera angle to now feature the figure's right-hand side gives the appearance they have changed direction. (Ford had previously done this several times during the climactic chase in *Stagecoach*.) Asked why he chose to break this rule, Ford stated that it was getting late in the day and, had he kept the camera on the "correct" side, the Indians and horses would have been backlit. Backlighting the rider and horse minimizes a viewer's perception of the animal's speed. By Ford switching the camera to the other side, he was able to properly capture the speed of the horse with the natural light on them.[88]

York and Beaufort meeting Cochise (with nearly two hundred Navajo extras) was filmed on Saturday in Rock Door Canyon. The following day, Sunday, August 3, Ford covered scenes of York and Beaufort making their way to Cochise's encampment, near the Totem Pole and Yei Bi Chei formations. According to the shooting schedule, Ford set aside two days (August 4 and 5) in the Square Rock vicinity to film the peace talk with Cochise, employing one hundred cavalrymen and two hundred Indian background players. Wednesday, August 6, found the company in front of the East and West Mitten formations (commonly called "the Mittens") to film York, Michael, and the supply wagons taking a defensive position, and Cochise and his warriors riding up with the guidon after the massacre.

Ford returned to Rock Door Canyon on Thursday, August 7, to complete the dialogue scenes of Thursday rejoining the troopers as they await the final charge of the Indians. Friday was spent filming the cavalry charging into the narrow canyon in the same location, while the following day the company returned to the Square Rock location. It was here that Ford shot the scene of Thursday announcing that the cavalry would charge and York speaking against it, throwing down his gauntlet. Once this was finished, Ford then covered scenes of York saying good-bye to O'Rourke and ordering Michael and the wagons to the ridge.

The last day of location work, Sunday, August 10, was spent filming various angles of Thursday leading his troop in a charge. Using the flatland area across from Square Rock, Ford filmed the stunt of Frank

McGrath (Derice, the bugler) falling from his horse at a gallop. The camera is traveling alongside the galloping horses as the bugler blows "Charge." Another cavalryman, riding slightly ahead and to the right, leads the bugler's horse with a short rope attached to the bridle. (This was done to keep the horse running straight ahead instead of slowing down when McGrath takes his fall.) We hear a gunshot and the bugler slumps forward and to the left, the bugle hanging on the side of the saddle. After letting go of the bugle, McGrath, holding on to the pommel and the cantle with his hands, sets himself up for the fall, then slides off and away from the horse. After cutting to the charging troopers, Ford returns to show the bugler's horse still charging ahead with an empty saddle.

All went well for this shot, but then came a serious accident.

As the cavalry is charging, the Apaches begin firing at the oncoming troopers. As the camera races alongside a group of troopers, we see one soldier (carrying a guidon) get shot. He drops the flag and slips forward from his galloping horse, which goes down on top of him. It was an impressive and dramatic stunt, which still makes a viewer cringe today. After dropping the guidon (carried on his right side), stuntman John Hudkins leans forward on the left side of his galloping horse, and his body, coming completely out of the saddle, begins to fall to the ground. Just then, his horse tripped in a hole and landed on top of him. Years later, Hudkins recalled that the horse "drove me into the ground," breaking his back.[89] (Doctors had to fuse his spine, and the following year Hudkins was back doing stunts.)

When it came to planned horse falls, the "Running W" was considered the most dangerous stunt. A leather hobble was attached to each of the horse's front legs (above the hooves), with a thin flexible wire anchored to the back of the hobble on a D-ring. The wire was run up the side of the horse's saddle and measured out from the starting point to where the fall would occur, then anchored to a secured post or log in the ground. As the horse gallops off, the wire runs its length and goes taut. The horse's front legs are pulled under them, causing the horse to tumble or somersault, and launching the rider forward into the air before hitting the ground. In several cases, the stunt reportedly either killed or severely hurt a horse, causing it to be put down. (Some veteran stuntmen said horses that did survive this stunt were never able to be used again, as they were fearful of galloping.) According to film historian Ed Hulse, Yakima Canutt was adamant that in the three hundred Running W stunts he staged in his career, he never crippled a horse with a Running W. The problems came with stunt coordinators who didn't take the proper time or care to rig the stunt.[90] (Yakima Canutt performed this stunt several times in Ford's *Stagecoach*.) In 1941, the American Humane Association (AHA) took over monitoring animals used in films from the Society for the Prevention of Cruelty to Animals. They put pressure on the studios to ban the use of the Running W, and the studios entered into a "gentlemen's agreement" around 1941 that the practice of using a Running W would be phased out. However, the official ban did not take place until 1983.[91]

Cliff Lyons helped develop a different way to train a horse to fall, and the technique is still in use today. The first step was picking the right horse, preferably one that is docile and heavy-boned. (The stuntman who owned a falling horse did all the training, and only he would perform the stunt on the animal.) The training begins with the animal's front left leg tied up, leaving it to stand on three legs. Once the horse has shown that it's comfortable with this, the second step involves slowly pulling the right rein until the horse is unbalanced and falls to the ground, usually on its left shoulder, landing on five inches of sawdust shavings. This teaches the horse to overcome its fear of falling, and that the pull of the right rein is the cue to fall. This step is repeated until the horse has mastered the fall easily.

The trainer then will get on the horse's back and start doing the fall from a standing position, then at a slow walk, before graduating to a trot. When a horse falls, the stirrup on the left side (where the animal lands) is made of a soft rubber so it will not hurt its ribs, while the saddle horn is removed to protect the rider.[92] When it comes to performing the stunt, the chosen area is on flat ground and dug out to a minimum of fifteen inches deep, at least six feet wide and six to ten feet in length. All rocks and other debris are removed, before filling the open space with sand.

In the late 1940s and into the 1950s, a falling horse earned upwards of $400 a week, and the stuntman got a hefty stunt adjustment for performing the fall. Ford commented that falling horses were never used in any chase scenes in his films, and that the animals were very pampered.[93] (From 1946 to the late 1950s, trained falling horses numbered around twenty.[94]) Between 1946 and 1951, horse falls were accomplished with horse and rider coming in at a trot or slow canter, while the camera speed was slowed down. When the exposed film was projected, the action appeared to be going faster; however, the movement looks slightly unnatural to the human eye. (This is noticeable in *Rio Grande* when Tyree gallops by an Apache, knocking him off the horse.)

* * *

"In the barrel."

This was a well-known term for those who worked for John Ford. It meant that someone, generally an actor, became the victim of the director's wrath and would be picked on mercilessly or become the brunt of one of Ford's jokes. Most crew members were exempt from such suffering, except for the wardrobe and prop departments. "When they [wardrobe department] went on location, they took everything," stuntman Chuck Hayward recalled. "First thing he's gonna ask for is a purple neckerchief with red diamonds in it."[95] Harry Carey Jr. echoed that statement, noting that every department had to be "fully prepared" for anything Ford would request at any time. If a department did not have what Ford requested, they rued the day.

Actors were Ford's favorite target. No one was immune, including John Wayne, whose first experience of being in the barrel happened on *Stagecoach*. One day Ford asked him to go view footage of the film, and when he returned the director asked Wayne how he liked it. Wayne said everything looked great, offering no criticism. Ford repeatedly asked the actor if there wasn't anything wrong, until Wayne finally took the bait. He mentioned that the scenes of Andy Devine driving the stagecoach didn't look very real, even after Wayne had suggested to the prop man that the lines should be attached to suspenders, which would give them more of a pull and appear realistic. Ford yelled for everyone's attention and called all the cast and crew together. He told the assembled group that Wayne had seen footage of the film and liked everyone's performance, except Andy Devine's. With that, he dismissed the crowd and went back to work.[96]

This wasn't the only way of being in the barrel. When it came to directing his actors, Ford could be tough on them, usually in scenes where they had little to do. Wayne recalled a scene in *Stagecoach* where all he had to do was wash his face, as the other actors had all the dialogue. Ford continually berated Wayne about the way he washed his face between takes, frustrating the young actor. Finally, the other cast members came to his defense, helping Wayne throughout the film. This was Ford's plan all along. "He has a way of picking on actors when they're not too important in part of a scene, in order to get them on their toes so they'll come in ready when they really have something to do," Wayne recalled. "And then he handles you like a baby."[97] Actor Larry Blake said that Ford would repeatedly pick on an actor for what appeared to be no reason. "You'd get so angry at him, that you'd go into your scene determined to show him how good you were. It was his way of getting a performance out of you," he said.[98]

Every member of Ford's stock company had been in the barrel at least once, and if they tolerated his actions, he rewarded them with steady work. Not every actor would tolerate it, such as Walter Brennan, when he worked with Ford on *My Darling Clementine* (1946). During one scene, Brennan had difficulty mounting a horse, which elicited a biting question from Ford, asking the actor if he could mount a horse. "No, but I have three Oscars," the actor abruptly replied. Things between the two men got so troubled that at one point, Brennan told Ford he never wanted to work with him again—and never did.[99]

On *Fort Apache*, John Agar found himself in the barrel on a daily basis, with Ford picking on his delivery of a line, how he wore his wardrobe, or sat on a horse. He also took to calling him "Mr. Temple" in front of the crew. Agar got so mad one day that he walked off the set, saying he was going to quit the film, pack his bag, and leave the business—even his wife. John Wayne pulled the young man aside, explaining that he had felt the same way on *Stagecoach*, and urged him to tough it out and ignore Ford.

A few days later, Ward Bond arrived by train in Flagstaff and boarded a small prop plane to the Monument Valley location. Bond convinced the pilot to fly over the crew while they were working. As the plane buzzed by, interrupting a scene, Wayne looked at Agar and told him he could relax now, as Ford's favorite whipping boy had just arrived.

Ford took to calling Bond "my favorite shit."[100]

Harry Carey Jr. recalled that Ford was relentless in picking on Bond. The more Ford did it, the more the actor loved it, making him feel part of the group.

> Ward had a hide like a rhinoceros [when it came to being picked on]. He literally asked for it . . . Ward would always talk back to him, unless it was really serious. Uncle Jack had a way with Ward Bond. One was "Now I'm bawling ya out because you're a horse's ass," and then there was another time when he really meant business. When Ward was on a picture it was a great show, because like the Duke said, it's always gonna be somebody's day in the barrel, but when Ward's along you can always depend on him to take the heat off you, because he'll pull some goddamn thing.[101]

Bond's antics provided Ford and Wayne with endless laughs both on and off the set. Their favorite inside joke was to pose with the ass-end of a horse and have a picture taken, signing it, "Thinking of you." They would send it to Bond, who'd roar with laughter. Ford sometimes worked this inside joke into a scene by staging Bond so that his back end was to the camera. (This happens a few times in *Fort Apache*.) No one took more abuse, and enjoyed it, than Ward Bond. When Ford learned of Bond's death while he was filming *Two Rode Together* (1961) in Texas, he suddenly turned to actor Andy Devine, pointing a finger at him. "Now, you're my favorite shit! Ward just died," he said.[102]

* * *

Shirley Temple had worked with Ford in *Wee Willie Winkie* (1937) when she was only nine years old and was 20th Century-Fox's biggest moneymaker. It was said that when studio head Darryl F. Zanuck told Ford he'd be directing the young starlet his face fell to the floor. Ford thought working with a child star was a "most horrible thing." No matter what Shirley did to gain Ford's approval, she was greeted with a miffed look and a disgruntled noise. Temple felt Ford regarded her as "someone to be endured, not embraced as a colleague."[103] It was her performance in Victor McLaglen's death scene that won Ford over. Afterwards, he put his arm around her and complimented her performance.

On *Fort Apache*, Ford treated her warmly from her first day, even allowing her to sit in his director's chair, something no one—not even Wayne—dared to do. However, there was one moment when Shirley spoke up that caused everyone to hold their breath. Shirley, Irene Rich, and Anna Lee were standing on the balcony watching the cavalry column disappear into the distance, when Lee says, "I can't see him. All I can see is the flags." After the scene was shot, Shirley stated that the line was not very good grammar. A deathly silence hung over the set, everyone bracing for Ford's Irish wrath to be unleashed. He calmly asked her why. "It should be, 'All I can see *are* the flags,'" she replied. Ford looked at her and then asked, "Where did you go to school, Shirley?" Quickly realizing she had stepped into a potential minefield, Temple offered an apology and all was forgiven.[104] Unlike others, Shirley Temple never once was in the barrel with the old man.

* * *

Like a circus, the company packed up its equipment and performers and traveled back to Los Angeles. (Ford spent seventeen days filming in Monument Valley.) Production resumed on Wednesday, August 13, at RKO-Pathé Studios in Culver City. Interior scenes in the stagecoach stop were first up on the list, followed by three days (August 14 to 16) covering various scenes in Thursday's headquarters, including his greeting other officers, talking to O'Rourke about his son, and learning of Mickey and Philadelphia out riding.

Whether a John Ford production was on location or on a soundstage, every day at 4:00 p.m. there was a twenty-minute break for tea. This was a tradition on Ford's pictures for over thirty years, where Ford, his script supervisor, Meta Stern, and cast members would sit down at a table and relax. There was only one rule that was strictly enforced: no shop talk. John Wayne said the tea break was a way of keeping the actors from complaining about sitting around all day if they weren't in a scene. "At that tea thing, he [Ford] made more of a point to [speak to] those people who were not working in a scene."[105] On every film, Ford always had all the actors on the set, whether scheduled to work or not, as he might suddenly get an idea to place one actor into a scene.

The company moved to the Corrigan Ranch on Monday, August 18, filming exterior scenes of Thursday, York, and the four sergeants arriving at Meacham's trading post. Returning to the studio, Tuesday and Wednesday were spent filming the interior scenes of Meacham's trading post and storeroom. The following three days (August 21 to 23) were devoted to completing scenes all in Thursday's home quarters, which included the sergeants' wives cleaning up the quarters and Thursday's arrival at the newly furnished home, with the chair collapsing under him.

Over the next seven days, August 25 to September 2, the company remained on the RKO-Pathé lot filming scenes of Thursday's arrival at the fort during a dance, and the entire noncommissioned officers' dance. (The company was idle on September 1, in observance of Labor Day.) The next four days, Wednesday to Saturday, involved shooting scenes in the O'Rourkes' quarters (Michael's return home, Philadelphia visiting them, and her father's arrival), as well as Philadelphia getting ready for the NCO dance in her room when Michael arrives with the mariachi band and they kiss.[106]

The company returned to the Corrigan Ranch on Monday, September 8. That day was spent filming scenes of the cavalry leaving to speak with Cochise, which involved 125 background players (100 troopers, 25 wives), an 8-man band, over 100 horses, and 6 wagons. Like Monument Valley, Corrigan's Ranch was miserably hot in the summer, with temperatures easily pushing beyond 100 degrees. Ford had the actresses standing in place on the upper porch of Thursday's quarters where they waited and waited in the sun, while Ford got the men, horses, and wagons properly aligned for the shot. Finally, Anna Lee fainted. John Wayne ran up and carried her down from the upper deck. ("I woke up in John Wayne's arms, which was lovely," she recalled.) When she came to, Ford was looking over her and asked, "Anna, are you pregnant?"[107] During the filming of *How Green Was My Valley* (1941), Lee was pregnant but never mentioned it to Ford. One day she filmed the scene where her character had to fight through a crowd and collapses when she sees her dead husband. That evening, Lee suffered a miscarriage, losing one of the twins she was carrying. Ford was crushed, blaming himself, and visited her every day in the hospital. From that point on, before filming any scene involving Lee, Ford would always ask her if she was pregnant.

The rest of the week, September 9 to 13, was spent at the ranch shooting scenes of the new recruits drilling, the brouhaha riding lesson, and Philadelphia asking Mrs. Collingwood for help in furnishing the quarters. Four days of the following week, September 15 to 18, Ford shot various scenes around the fort set that included Michael and Philadelphia riding around the parade grounds (which he deleted), Philadelphia going to the Collingwoods' quarters at dinner, the four sergeants taken from the guardhouse to the manure pile, York and Beaufort riding off to see Cochise and their return, and the ambulance arrival with Thursday and Philadelphia at the fort.

On Friday, September 19, Ford completed the sequence of Michael and Philadelphia riding up to the burned wagon and bodies. He also shot the dialogue scene between York coming to Thursday's aid during the final ambush, and watching him ride off to rejoin the remaining soldiers. Ford then finished the day with starting the sequence with Michael and the four sergeants returning to the destroyed wagon and dead bodies.

The following day Ford completed the scene, then filming the repair wagon and men galloping off after Michael is shot at by the Apaches. The wagon, driven with a six-up team by stuntman Post Park, leads off as stunt doubles for Michael and Beaufort (Cliff Lyons and Frank McGrath) come up alongside the wagon, leading it up a small rise at a full gallop. The next shot features riders and wagon galloping down a narrow path toward the camera (going left to right) before making a hard right turn on the road. The camera pans to the right as the doubles for Michael and Beaufort race past, followed by the wagon. As the wagon makes its turn, it starts to swerve in the dirt, giving the impression it would capsize before Ford cuts to a low angle shot (filmed in Monument Valley) of the two riders and wagon racing by.

What viewers did not see was a potential deadly accident that might have happened if it hadn't been for the quick thinking of a young stuntman named Ben Johnson.

As the wagon made its turn, it did flip over on its side with the three stuntmen aboard. The galloping horses were running wild, dragging the wagon to a sheer rock wall. If the wagon hit the wall, the three stuntmen would be killed. Johnson, astride a horse next to the camera, saw what had happened and galloped in, grabbing the bridle of the lead horse on the left, bringing the team to a halt. In doing so, the horses "stacked up" (ran into each other) but were not hurt, while the three stuntmen lived to tell another war story.

Ford, who had been on a high platform watching the entire thing, climbed down and told Johnson he'd be well rewarded for his action. The young stuntman took the comment to mean he'd probably get additional stunt work on the film. About two weeks later, Ford asked him to come to his office, where he handed Johnson a large envelope, saying he should have his lawyer look at it. The envelope was not sealed, so Johnson opened it. It was a seven-year contract with Argosy Productions, and the fifth line stated he'd get five thousand dollars a week. Without hesitation, Johnson took a pen from Ford's desk and signed the contract.[108]

Monday and Tuesday (September 22 and 23) marked the company's last days at Corrigan Ranch, completing scenes of Philadelphia and Michael riding in after seeing the burned wagon, and Michael leading out the repair wagon with the four sergeants (this scene was deleted). Ford returned to RKO-Pathé Studios where he spent two days (Wednesday and Thursday) completing all the scenes inside the Collingwoods' quarters, such as Collingwood and his wife before the NCO dance (cut from the film), Philadelphia arriving for dinner, Michael asking if she'll go riding with him, and Quincannon arriving at the door to sing a song.

The director then spent two days (Friday and Saturday) in Thursday's headquarters set finishing the scenes where Michael explains about the burned-out wagon, and Thursday forbidding him to see Philadelphia.

Ford then moved on to the scene of Thursday granting York permission to talk to Cochise. (Completing the coverage shots of this scene lapped over to the following Monday.) Tuesday, September 30, was devoted to the final scene that takes place several years later, where York speaks to the newspapermen and introduces his adjutant, Michael; Michael's wife, Philadelphia; and their son before walking out of headquarters. (This completed Wayne's work on the picture.)

On Wednesday, October 1, Ford began filming the rear-screen process scenes involving Thursday and Philadelphia on the stagecoach, as well as scenes with the stage driver and shotgun guard. Once completed, the next rear-screen sequence covered Thursday and Philadelphia in the army ambulance making its way to Fort Apache, which included Philadelphia using her hatbox mirror to watch Mickey ride alongside. In order to achieve this shot, it was not done on location with an actual moving stagecoach, but rather a carefully angled rear-screen projection shot that featured Michael riding as reflected in the mirror. Rear-screen projection was achieved by placing the actors in front of a screen with the appropriate background film projected and running in sync with the camera. (This process was common throughout the late 1920s and into the mid-1960s.) One of the advantages of shooting scenes with rear-screen projection was that a director did not have to be concerned about outside noise or inclement weather.

The last day of production, October 2, was spent completing the rear-screen projection scenes between Mickey and Philadelphia during their horseback ride.[109]

Ford completed *Fort Apache* fifteen days ahead of the sixty-day schedule, and $363,229.10 under budget. (Total picture cost was $2,156,770.95.)[110]

* * *

Since the start of production, the film's title was *War Party*; however, neither Ford nor Cooper was terribly happy with it. An RKO memo, dated January 19, 1948, reveals the studio conducted a survey of six titles: *Fort Apache*, *None But the Brave*, *The Girl I Left Behind Me*, *War Party*, *War Paint*, and *Boots and Saddles*. The memo noted that "Although certain of the titles test higher, it would mean clearing them with one or more studios. In view of the time element involved, RKO strongly urges *Fort Apache*, [of] which Argosy has clear [ownership] and tests quite high, to be used."[111]

* * *

With the project completed, Ford turned everything over to the editor, Jack Murray, to assemble the film. Unlike some directors, Ford disliked doing numerous takes of a scene. His longtime assistant director, and brother-in-law, Wingate Smith, said Ford rarely printed more than one take, while Henry Fonda noted Ford didn't shoot "a hundred feet of film," leaving an editor struggling to put it into shape for months. "He just shot what he wanted and he cut it in the camera, so there wasn't any film to play with and there wasn't the problem of what scene do we use, any of that shit, not with Ford," he said.[112] While Ford was known to discard scenes from the script prior to filming, in *Fort Apache* he did shoot several scenes, eventually choosing to eliminate them in the editing process.

"Cutting in the camera" meant Ford (or any director) shot a scene in a certain way, such as a medium shot of two actors talking on horseback. Satisfied with the performance, he'd either say "Right!" or "That's well," which meant the shot was to be printed and to move on to the next scene, eschewing any coverage shots, such as a master shot or a close-up. Traditionally, a director first shoots the scene as a master shot (a long or wide shot), then covers it with a two-shot (medium shot of two actors), possibly an "over the shoulder" angle, and finally, individual close-ups. To Ford, all that was unnecessary and a waste of film stock. He'd shoot the scene the way he wanted it to look, and move on. In some cases, he *might* shoot another angle, or even a close-up, but only if it added something to the scene. Nor did he often move his camera much, if at all. Ford maintained that a camera should not move in a scene except for a valid reason. He preferred to have his camera on "sticks" (industry term for a tripod), a throwback to his days making silent films. Ford felt too much camera movement made the audience aware of the camera, taking them out of the scene. By Ford cutting the film in the camera, he was able to keep the film close to his vision, thus denying a producer the chance to try to "improve a scene."

When it came to making a film, *all of it* was in Ford's head. Harry Carey Jr. observed that Ford often gave the impression he did things "off the top of his head," but when he finished the day's work, he'd begin his homework for the next day's scenes. "That's when he thought up the stuff he'd do the next day," the actor recalled. "I've never seen anybody as creative."[113] Unlike other directors, Ford never looked at the script during a day's filming, as he already knew what scenes were to be shot and how he'd cover them. There were no notes in his pockets to remind him. It was all in his head.

Wingate Smith, who served as Ford's assistant director on thirty-four films (his first being 1929's *The Black Watch*), stated that when Ford walked on the set in the morning, he knew what he was going to do. "There was no guessing about it, no getting the producer down [on the set]. He had worked it out in his mind," he said. "The overall picture, I'm convinced, he had in his head, and as he went along, he'd improve [things]." Smith also knew not to approach Ford with a question if he was sitting in his director's chair by himself, as it meant he was working out a scene in his head.[114] On set, Ford appeared to have an underlying sense of inner stress, his mind constantly working. His most outward example of this was constantly chewing on the ends of a handkerchief.

* * *

Ford left for Mazatlán on his boat, the *Araner*, a 110-foot ketch he bought in 1934, with Wayne, Fonda, and Bond joining him for some deep-sea fishing. The *Araner*—named after the Aran Islands off the coast of Ireland, where his mother's family came from—was Ford's only luxury. It was his place to relax and ignore the hypocrisy of the industry. Here, with his close friends like Wayne, Bond, and others, Ford would play cards, swap tall tales, and fish. Drinking was very common, as all the participants enjoyed themselves. For Ford, alcohol was a problem that plagued him all his life. He was an alcoholic, yet would never admit he had a problem. "The sad thing was he just couldn't handle it," John Wayne recalled.[115] Work is what drove Ford. He thrived on it. When he was working, he never drank, and it was forbidden for others to imbibe.[116] The creative process fed a need in him, and without that he was lost. Having no work often meant he'd start drinking, many times into an alcoholic oblivion that required hospitalization. Once Ford recovered, he'd usually stay sober and begin work on another production.

Other than making movies, his boat, and reading, Ford had no hobbies to occupy him during downtime. He didn't play golf or tennis, didn't paint, nor was he a car or plane fanatic. Reading had always been a major part of his life going back to childhood, and on the *Araner* he could go through a large stash of books. The *Araner* also served as a secondary office, allowing Ford to work on scripts with writers like Dudley Nichols or Frank Nugent, in what he called his "lucky spot."

* * *

To score *Fort Apache*, Ford turned to Richard Hageman, who worked with him on seven films, beginning with *Stagecoach*. Unlike other composers in Hollywood, Hageman was a latecomer to film scoring, starting in 1938.[117] Hageman's musical scores for Ford films tended to be oversaturated, often overplaying scenes that would have been better with either a minimal melody or nothing at all. In *Fort Apache*, Hageman avoids his normal routine by leaving some scenes without a score, such as York and Beaufort riding to Cochise's encampment. (How much of this was Hageman's choice or Ford's is unknown.) Throughout the film, Hageman has populated the musical score with traditional songs from the period, including, "Beautiful Dreamer," "Oh, Dem Golden Slippers," "Home Sweet Home," "Sweet Genevieve," "The Girl I Left Behind Me," and "Regular Army O!" (Hageman also uses "You're in the Army Now," which was composed in 1917 during World War I.)

Hageman's score opens with a mounted bugler blowing the "Guard Mounting" call before switching to his "Indian theme," filled with strings and deep drumbeats. (Hageman repeats this theme in *She Wore a Yellow Ribbon*.) It then reverts to military themes accompanying footage of the cavalry moving through the desert, before once again returning to the Indian theme as a band of Indians rides past the camera. As the credits end, Hageman's score takes on a vigorous modified version of "Bury Me Not on the Lone Prairie," echoing the stagecoach's movement across the desert. Hageman makes good use of violins and horns to create the feeling of the coach's rolling motion, and it continues, albeit softly, under the scene between Thursday and Philadelphia inside the stagecoach. He returns to the score's original intensity as the coach approaches the stage stop.

For the scene of the army wagon making its way to Fort Apache, Hageman creates a theme which later becomes identified as the riding theme for Philadelphia and Michael. This melody is accompanied by a strong use of violins and muted horns, eventually dissolving into the music for the fort dance. As the dance resumes after Thursday's exit, it breaks into "Home Sweet Home," which Hageman carries over to Michael's return to his family, creating the proper sentiment.

With the four hungover sergeants in the guardhouse, Hageman uses a refrain of "You're in the Army Now" for comedic effect. The tune is played in a light fashion, with low, soft notes as we see the unhappy face of Mulcahy before he and the others are removed from the guardhouse. As they are marched off to the manure pile, Hageman makes good use of the horn section, playing harsh, sour notes to emphasize the men's misery.

The use of "The Girl I Left Behind Me," a traditional song played as military units left for field duty, creates a somber moment as the women watch their men riding out of the fort, accompanied with a chorus singing the lyrics. It is the song's melody, along with the reaction of the men's wives, which gives this scene its poignancy.

When one reporter comments in the final scene that the other soldiers are forgotten, York replies that they are not forgotten, as Hageman softly incorporates "Battle Hymn of the Republic" under York's speech. As the cavalry heads out of the fort, the score returns to "The Girl I Left Behind Me," along with another brief choral reprise of the lyrics. This time the melody has more of a heroic tone, with strong use of horns and strings, as the film fades out.

* * *

"A rootin' tootin' Wild West show, full of Indians and United States Cavalry, dust and desert scenery, and a nice masculine trace of romance, has been honestly put together under the masterful direction of John Ford," wrote *New York Times* critic Bosley Crowther.

> Folks who are for action in the oldest tradition of the screen, observed through a genuine artist's camera, will find plenty of it here. But also apparent in this picture, for those who care to look, is a new and maturing viewpoint upon one aspect of the American Indian wars. For here it is not the "heathen Indian" who is the "heavy" of the piece but a hard-bitten Army colonel, blind through ignorance and a passion for revenge. And ranged alongside this willful white man is a venal government agent who exploits the innocence of the Indians while supposedly acting as their friend . . . Mr. Ford never disappoints us. Every episode, every detail of drama and personality is crisply and tautly realized. Whether it be a highly humorous incident of raw recruits being taught to ride or a hell-for-leather chase across the desert, he makes it sharp and intensely visible . . . Performing this dandy panorama of frontier cavalry life is a cast, which, in every aspect, is nigh impeccable. Henry Fonda is withering as the colonel . . . John Wayne is powerful as his captain . . . Victor McLaglen, Jack Pennick, and Dick Foran honor the virtues of whiskey and low-humor as three Irish noncoms. Even Shirley Temple is ingratiating as the colonel's lass who falls in love with a noble young lieutenant, played patly by her husband, John Agar . . . In his rich blend of personality, of the gorgeously picturesque outdoor western scenery, of folk music and intrinsic sounds, plus his new comprehension of frontier history, Mr. Ford here again fires keen hope that he will soon turn his unsurpassed talents to a great and sweeping drama of the old west.[118]

The industry trade paper *Hollywood Reporter* found *Fort Apache* "a vigorous, sweeping Western adventure drama done with effect and spectacular action sequences that is the invariable characteristic of John Ford . . . [the production] reflects a fine degree of showmanship that will pay off handsomely at the box office."[119] Hollywood's rival trade paper, *Daily Variety*, felt "*Fort Apache* undoubtedly will cause considerable critical pro and con because of the openly commercial approach John Ford has used on the subject. He has aimed the picture directly at the average theatregoer, bypassing non-profitable art effects. As a consequence, the film has a mass appeal, great excitement, and a potent box office outlook . . . For sheer seat-edge attention, *Apache* is socko. Mass action, humorous byplay in the western cavalry outpost, deadly suspense, and romance are masterfully combined in the Ford–Merian C. Cooper production to stir the greatest number of filmgoers."[120]

Motion Picture Exhibitor, a trade paper for theater owners, was not terribly effusive in its review, noting that movie patrons "looking for a different treatment of a familiar story by John Ford won't find it [in *Fort Apache*]." Observing that the film was the "usual story" of soldiers versus Indians, with "the windup slightly different in that the Indians come off best in the only conflict . . . All in all, this is made for the box office, even though it charts no new trails."[121] The other exhibitor journal, *Motion Picture Herald*, noted that Ford's film is "One of his best. His basic ingredients have been presented in many other attractions down through the years, but *Fort Apache* finds its answer in the superior and careful craftsmanship which extends to its making."[122]

The box office response was a strong one, with *Fort Apache* earning $2,986,934.61 in domestic rentals, eventually tallying nearly $4.9 million worldwide.[123] The film held two premieres: in Phoenix, Arizona, and Chicago, Illinois. The Phoenix premiere, held on March 26 and 27 at the Orpheum Theatre, saw George O'Brien, Victor McLaglen, Irene Rich, Mae Marsh, Grant Withers, Dick Foran, and Anna Lee in attendance. (An article in the *Arizona Republic* listed the actors as "all Hollywood stars.") In front of the theater was an Apache village, and over fifty tribal members were on hand, presenting traditional dances as part of the event. Shirley Temple and John Agar (with a newspaper ad claiming "Direct from Hollywood!") attended the Chicago premiere at the RKO Palace on March 30, which served as a fund-raiser for the Wounded Veterans Fund.

* * *

On May 8, 1949, John Ford introduced a condensed version of the film on the *Screen Director's Playhouse*, an NBC radio program sponsored by Pabst Beer. Wayne reprises his role as Captain York, while Ward Bond (with a slight touch of an Irish brogue) took on the Colonel Thursday role. The half-hour performance, complete with orchestra and sound effects, mainly focused on York and Thursday dealing with Cochise. The Michael O'Rourke character, as well as Sergeants Schattuck and Quincannon, are only mentioned in passing. Beaufort's character makes a brief appearance when he and York meet with Cochise.

At the end of the show, Wayne says, "Let's have a word from the director, if Ward Bond will bring over Pappy."

Ford replies, "What do you mean, bring Pappy over here? That's the trouble with you actors—just because I'm a director, you think I'm afraid of a microphone."

"Well, Pappy?" Bond asks.

"Well, I am! That's why I'm gonna say good night and get out!"

As he leaves, you can hear Ford yell, "Good night, folks!"[124]

* * *

Arrogance and wounded pride. Corruption from Washington, DC, to the Indian reservation post. A societal caste system that jeopardizes a true love. People struggling to survive the elements while others see their way of life disappearing. All of these elements make up John Ford's *Fort Apache.*

The film opens with the Western desert in all its vastness and beauty. Yet there is an underlying harshness to the land, unforgiving to those who do not respect it. Passing through this region is a stagecoach, easily making its way past mesquite and chaparral. The driver, like others who live in this region, has adapted, knowing what places to avoid. These people have learned—possibly the hard way—that no human can conquer these Western lands, and the surest way to survive is to acclimate themselves to the elements. Failure comes at a high cost. Despite warnings and examples, there are some people who believe the terrain can submit to their will.

Inside the stagecoach is just such a person, Colonel Owen Thursday. Arrogant, with a sense of superiority, Thursday will not tolerate any change, especially in the army. His dogmatism is obvious as he complains to the driver about being an hour late to the next stage stop. Thursday is so rigid a man, he cannot accept tardiness due to traveling over a rough landscape. In this brief moment, Ford quickly paints for the audience an outline of Thursday's character. His disgust is further amplified when he states, "Forty miles from mud hole to mud hole." Thursday is so indignant over the "ungrateful War Department" sending a man with his pedigree to this barren land, that he is myopic when it comes to recognizing his daughter's happiness at their reunion. When Philadelphia acknowledges his position will at least give her more time with him, unlike his years in Europe, Thursday bitterly replies, "Better there than here." Her reaction to his verbal slap leads him to offer a weak explanation by blaming it on being shunted aside. Thursday is determined not to allow Fort Apache to be his Waterloo.

In military life, there is a definite caste system between officers, noncommissioned officers, and enlisted soldiers.[125] Thursday treats Sergeant Major O'Rourke with indifference, not attempting to build a working relationship, a direct contrast to the rapport shared by York and O'Rourke in *Fort Apache*, or Brittles and Tyree in *She Wore a Yellow Ribbon*. His attitude is discernible when he inquires if Michael is related to O'Rourke. "Not by chance, sir. By blood. He's my son," O'Rourke acknowledges. Dubious about Michael's appointment to West Point as a son of a noncommissioned officer, Thursday comments that a presidential appointment is reserved for sons of Medal of Honor recipients. "That is my impression, too, sir," the sergeant major calmly replies.

Despite O'Rourke being awarded the prestigious medal, Thursday is not impressed, very likely due to a personal dislike for the Irish, which many officers held during the Civil War. His belief in the caste system and disdain for Michael's heritage is apparent when he addresses Michael several times using other Irish surnames, not his own. Nor does Thursday hesitate to drive a wedge between Philadelphia and Michael, feeling he is unworthy of his daughter's hand. He further illustrates his need for control when he orders Michael to "bow to my wishes" and never see his daughter again.

Thursday also will not forgive a previous misstep. Arriving at the fort, Thursday interrupts a dance and is greeted by Collingwood with an open hand. Thursday indifferently replies, refusing to shake his hand. In taking over the fort's command, Thursday removes Collingwood from his position as regimental adjutant, later telling him it wasn't a personal decision. Collingwood says no explanation is needed, although he tries once to ask for one. Thursday curtly cuts him off, stating there is nothing to explain. (All of this goes back to Collingwood's performance during the Civil War.) Collingwood wryly notes that he did what he did, while Thursday went on to glory, yet here they both are at Fort Apache, a dead-end position. Dismissing the comment, Thursday says he will find something to distinguish himself.

Despite a weak attempt to assure his officers he is not a martinet, Thursday is the walking embodiment of one. His bullheadedness, strict following of the US Army guidebook, and West Point education have blinded him so much that he cannot adapt to his surroundings. This demeanor is demonstrated in many ways, notably when he criticizes York and his troopers for not being properly dressed for field duty in the Arizona desert. Stating that their uniforms remind him of "scratch farmers on market day," Thursday castigates York and the men for wearing exposed galluses (suspenders) over their shirts and hats not properly creased per army regulations.[126] This line likely was suggested by Ford, after he and D. R. O. Hatswell, the costume advisor, locked horns over soldiers and some officers wearing exposed suspenders. Hatswell, British by birth, insisted they would not be wearing them, but Ford's Irish nature overruled him.[127]

Thursday lacks any knowledge of the Apache or their fighting skills, and is only too quick to deride the tribe. He concedes that their brother officers are involved in campaigns against the more impressive Sioux and Cheyenne, while they are left to deal with "gnat stings and flea bites." Captain York counsels him that the Apache made quick work of a Sioux tribe that raided in Arizona, but Thursday refuses to listen. A more subtle way of displaying Thursday's contempt for the Apache happens when Michael is giving his report about the burned-out wagon and dead men. He removes from his pocket the bloody headband of a dead Apache. Collingwood and York do not hesitate to pick it up to examine it, while the colonel refuses to touch it, instead using a pencil to study the bandana.

Unlike York and other officers at the fort, Thursday displays no sympathy toward the Apache or their conditions at the hands of Meacham, the reservation agent. Thursday despises Meacham, but is forced to respect his position as a government agent. However, he is not blind to the fact that the man is corrupt, and verbally castigates him as "a blackguard, a liar, a hypocrite and a stench in the nostrils of honest men." Unlike York, who does not hesitate to hit the man, Thursday's obduracy forces him to follow the law.

When York proposes to speak with Cochise, Thursday seizes it as an opportunity for advancement. "The man who brought Cochise in," he says quietly to himself. His thinking is void of what is best for the Apache or the United States; instead, he is consumed by the fact that this would mark him for greater glory. Days later, when York returns from meeting Cochise, Thursday nullifies the captain's plan of taking a small, unarmed group to meet the Apache leader. Thursday intends to punish the leader and his tribe, making them bend to *his* will. York protests against Thursday's plan to bring the full regiment, stating that he gave his word to Cochise. Thursday crassly replies that there is no question of honor between an army officer and Cochise.

When they meet, Thursday is dismissive of Cochise and refuses to stand, unlike Collingwood and York. Removing his kepi hat and dusting the dirt from his clothes, Thursday sits on a camping stool, only half listening to Cochise's words. When the Apache leader warns that for every Apache the soldiers kill, he will kill ten whites, Thursday jumps to his feet. Angry that a man of his standing is being threatened by a "savage," Thursday's blind rage erupts. As York and Beaufort try to explain that Cochise is speaking the truth, Thursday demands that Beaufort tell Cochise his exact words. He orders him and his people to return at once to the reservation; failing to do so, the cavalry would attack at dawn before walking away. Knowing Cochise will not return to the reservation, Thursday seizes this moment to advance, to break loose from the confines of a dead-end post. He recklessly believes this charge and forcing Cochise and his people to submit to his demands will pave the way for greater glory.

Captain Kirby York is the antithesis of Thursday. He is very much secure in his position, as years of experience with various Indian tribes have given him a greater understanding. While his duties as a military officer may force him to face off against the Apache, York recognizes they are victims of the corrupt Bureau of Indian Affairs and Washington politics. Seeing what Meacham has done, he greatly respects Cochise taking his people off the reservation. York tolerates Thursday's martinet persona, brooking his verbal abuse solely due to his rank, even though Thursday has nary a clue of how to deal with the Apache. It isn't until Thursday has destroyed any hope of peace that York finally loses his temper, flinging his gauntlet to the ground in front of Thursday. Despite his anger over Thursday's foolishness, he comes to his aid, only to see it refused for a final time.

In the final scene, York, now the commanding officer, speaks with four newspaper reporters. As one reporter reverently looks at the painting of Thursday, he suggests the colonel must have been a great man and a great soldier. York takes a moment before replying, then flatly states, with no emotion in his voice, "No man died more gallantly, nor won more honor for his regiment." Another reporter, brimming with excitement, comments on the now-famous painting in Washington, DC, of Thursday's charge. "There were these massed columns of Apaches in their war paint and feathered bonnets and here was Thursday leading his men in that heroic charge!" he gushes. York looks into space, avoiding any eye contact, before saying the painting was "correct in every detail."

Peter Bogdanovich suggested to Ford that this scene anticipates the end of *The Man Who Shot Liberty Valance* (1962) with the famous line, "When the legend becomes fact, print the legend." Ford agreed, adding that he thought it was good for the country. "We've had a lot of people who were supposed to be great heroes, and you know damn well they weren't. But it's good for the country to have heroes to look up to," he noted. "Like Custer—a great hero. Well, he wasn't. Not that he was a stupid man—but he did a stupid job that day . . . On the other hand, of course, the legend had always had some foundation."[128]

One may wonder why York goes along with perpetuating the myth of Thursday's heroic charge. Why doesn't he reveal the truth to the reporters? Like Ford's response, York understands Thursday's image is a positive one for the country and the army. He personally believes Thursday's decision was a serious blunder, but the myth of the charge has given the regiment glory and honor. As one reporter comments that people remember the Thursdays, while the others are forgotten, York, looking out a window onto the parade grounds, says none of the men are forgotten because none of them died. (As he reminds the reporters they are still living, Ford creates a ghostly double exposure of York looking out the window while the regiment, with Thursday in the lead, marches on.) "They'll keep on living as long as the regiment lives . . . faces may change, the names, but they're there. The regiment. The regular army. Now and fifty years from now."

* * *

Ford's love of the military, its sense of honor, duty, self-sacrifice, and courage, only grew during his service in World War II. He was present in the heat of combat, even receiving a wound during the Battle of Midway Island.[129] After the war, Ford bought eight acres in the San Fernando Valley where he built a large clubhouse, two swimming pools (one for paraplegics), a baseball field, and tennis courts, all ringed by huge eucalyptus trees. It was named the Field Photo Farm, in honor of the men who had served in his unit, where they could gather, relax, and share an unspoken camaraderie that only military veterans understand.[130] Every Memorial Day, Ford held services at the farm to honor those no longer present. The United States military was built on traditions, and John Ford would not let America forget them.

In later years, Ford said that *Fort Apache* and the character of Thursday were based on Custer, "laid against an Apache background," but the film was not a "true character study of Custer."[131] Ford's reason for setting the story in the Arizona territory was twofold: It allowed him to return to Monument Valley and the Navajo tribe, both near and dear to him; and, setting it in Arizona helped to distance Thursday's character from Custer's image and his defeat at Little Bighorn. (Bellah's short story takes place against the Cheyenne tribe.)

No actor could have played Owen Thursday better than Henry Fonda. His stiff-legged gait, used to advantage by Ford in other films, paints a different character here. Thursday's rigid stride is a reflection of the man's authoritarian persona. With the use of three gray hairpieces (temples and forehead), a mustache, and a small soul patch under his lower lip, combined with a lack of much facial expression, Fonda transforms himself into a different character. We despise Thursday, yet we come to understand his actions. He is not a villain, but more of a tragic figure who cannot accept that his placement at Fort Apache is likely his own doing. Ford carefully avoids letting Fonda's Thursday become the stock villain of the piece. Noting that some critics said Fonda was miscast as Thursday, Ford praised the actor's performance as "very good," although in later years Fonda reportedly stated he was unhappy with the role. "All these stories are legendary. Most of them aren't true," Ford replied when asked if the actor was disappointed with the part.[132]

John Wayne's Captain York is the opposite of Thursday. Ford lets Wayne's natural warmth imbue York, making him the type of leader one would follow. York is a true soldier, having come up through the ranks, and understands when the rule book is to be ignored in favor of common sense. He has a deep hatred for the injustice Meacham has brought to the Apache, wanting to see the tribe treated fairly. The audience easily identifies with York's frustration when dealing with his commanding officer, which Wayne communicates with simple body language and vocal or facial expressions.

Shirley Temple's character, Philadelphia, is the opposite of her father. She is a cheerful, outgoing young woman one cannot help but like. Philadelphia's personal warmth easily wins the audience over in the first few minutes of the film, gaining sympathy when reacting to her father's callous words. Temple does not have much material to work with, as Philadelphia basically serves as part of the romantic duo creating conflict for her father. However, Temple's Philadelphia is very likable, due to the natural charisma the actress was known for since childhood. John Agar's role as Michael O'Rourke isn't a very demanding one, but offers him a decent debut performance. (He received separate billing in the opening credits as "Introducing John Agar.")

Miguel Inclán as Cochise, who speaks all his lines in Spanish, gives a standout performance in one of the few Indian roles that is not a stereotypical renegade Indian. His scene when attempting to talk peace with Thursday comes across as strong and meaningful. There is a beautiful moment when Ford shows Cochise's frustration and disappointment after the meeting. Flanked by Geronimo, Alchesay, and Santana, Cochise comes up to a bluff, watching Thursday form his troops to attack. Cochise picks up a handful of dirt, holding it for a moment before casting it down. His whole body slightly slumps before he walks away. Ford's shot expresses the Apache leader's frustration and futility, his throwing of the dirt to signify his acceptance of what is to come. It is a brilliant, moving moment.

The three sergeants, played by Victor McLaglen, Jack Pennick, and Dick Foran, are the film's court jesters, providing comic relief in various spots. While Pedro Armendáriz is part of this group, Ford uses him sparingly in the humorous situations, relying primarily on Victor McLaglen to deliver the bulk of the laughs in various moments, from drilling the new recruits to drinking from the spiked punch bowl at the dance. McLaglen's Mulcahy is a sample of what he will bring in the next two cavalry films.

George O'Brien plays Collingwood as a man with past failures weighing heavily on his shoulders. With Thursday's arrival, the old wound is reopened. He tries, once more, to explain himself, but that door is verbally shut in his face. O'Brien's Collingwood is a man at the end of the line. He is stationed at a forlorn post, hopefully waiting for a transfer to teach at West Point. When Thursday offers Collingwood a drink, he pauses before speaking. "No, thank you, Owen. It's a little early in the day—even for me." O'Brien delivers his last line with a bite in his voice, giving an indication that his character's drinking may have been a problem in the past.

Ward Bond could easily have played O'Rourke in a more broad and boisterous way, echoing the three sergeants. Instead, Ford has Bond underplay his part. He is the straight man to the three sergeants' comedic actions, especially in the scene before the dance when they, Dr. Wilkens, and another officer bring separate whiskey bottles for the punch bowl.[133] With Michael's arrival from West Point, Bond displays the slow realization that his boy is now an officer, hugging him tightly. Then, with his back to the camera (again, Ford playing his practical joke on the actor by showing his rear end), he reaches into his vest pocket for a handkerchief and blows his nose and wipes his eyes before turning around and announcing to his wife that their son is home.

The rest of the cast, including Irene Rich, Anna Lee, Guy Kibbee, Grant Withers (as a very slippery Meacham), Hank Worden, and the remaining actors, down to the smallest role, provide substance in their work.

As he does in so many of his films, Ford lets the landscape become an integral part of the story. The land offers a stark beauty (as in the opening segment) or increases the tension of certain scenes, such as when Michael and Philadelphia race away from the burned-out wagon over sand dunes. The large buttes stand silently in the background as the dramatic music swells; Philadelphia's hat flies off as she continues to ride up to a rise, while Michael turns around and retrieves her hat. (The script does not mention Philadelphia losing her hat; it was an accident, and Ford kept the cameras rolling, adding to the scene's tension, as they are alone in the desert.)

Another sequence of Ford's integration of the land as a character is displayed when York and Beaufort make their way to Cochise's camp. Riding across wide-open terrain, overlooking a vast winding canyon, and crossing the Rio Grande is enhanced by the musical score, which takes on an energetic theme that carries on through the river crossing. The next time we see York and Beaufort, the musical score is more subdued in its energy as the two men stop to drink from a canteen out in the open, with no cover. At this point, the music takes on a more cautionary theme before suddenly halting when York and Beaufort see a flash of a mirror from a distant mountain. The openness of the area and the silence has created its own tension. As they ride on, the audience hears only the rhythmic clip-clop of their horses' hooves and several dogs barking as they enter the Apache camp, conveying a feeling of isolation and tension.

In most of Ford's films, women are presented as strong-willed, determined characters. Like their men, they have faced hardships; it can be doubly so for the wife of an army officer. In one sequence, Ford shows their strength—and private fears—as they watch the regiment leave the fort to meet Cochise. Philadelphia, Mrs. Collingwood, and Mrs. O'Rourke stand on the upper porch, watching stoically.[134] There are no tears, no waving of hands. The women just stand and watch, knowing this could be the last time they see their husbands. Ford further emphasizes their fears and concern with a shot of two other women (Mae Marsh and Ruth Clifford) watching, before Marsh briefly looks at Clifford and then walks away.

As the women watch the troop disappear, the telegraph operator rushes up with news of Collingwood's transfer. She is torn between wanting her husband back, but not wanting him to be labeled a coward for letting the rest of the troop go without him. Despite the urgings of Mrs. O'Rourke and Philadelphia to call him back, she hands the telegraph operator the telegram, asking him to hold it for her husband's return. (Anna Lee makes the most of this scene, displaying the perfect amount of anxiety and courage.)

In *Fort Apache*, the Apache is not a stock villain, but is presented with a great honesty and dignity, earning the audience's sympathy. Cochise is portrayed as the great leader he was, and a fearsome adversary when provoked. The Apache is forced to fight despite the pleas for peace from Cochise. This storyline defied cinema's stereotypical theme of the cavalry being heroic and the Indians as villainous. Some believe the credit for this trope came from screenwriter Frank Nugent's liberal feelings, but Ford was equally sympathetic to the problems faced by Native Americans. No doubt Ford saw the struggle of Native Americans as similar to the treatment of the Irish under British rule.

In many of John Ford's films, the death of a character is either shown in a medium to wide shot, or not at all. In the latter case, Ford leaves it to other characters to communicate the loss of life, such as he does in the scene where Michael and the four sergeants return to the burned-out wagon. Ford frames a two-shot featuring Michael and Beaufort in front of the wagon. He lets Beaufort's facial reaction tell everything, glancing at the bodies of his comrades before looking straight ahead, holding his feelings in check.

The same is true in the final attack. Thursday stands at the head of the small group of men waiting for the inevitable. There is a silence before a deafening roar of horses galloping and yelps from the Apache. As they swarm over the men like locusts, the area is swathed in dust, and once they have ridden on, we see Thursday and his men have fallen. Throughout this scene, Ford keeps the camera in a wide shot in order to capture the action, but also because viewing death from a distance (or not at all) is not as emotionally poignant to the audience.

After the death of Thursday, Cochise and his men ride up to York and the supply wagons. The roar of the horses is thunderous as York orders his men to hold their fire. Cochise's warriors halt, Ford staging them in a single line behind their leader as the dust envelops them. York walks out to Cochise, who approaches on horseback with Thursday's guidon, planting it into the ground. Turning his horse around, the Apaches gallop off, creating a cloud of dust which further obscures them. York is left standing alone as the dust cloud covers him. It is one of the most compelling shots in the film.

* * *

When historians asked Ford questions about the theme of *Fort Apache*, or attempted to dig for a deeper meaning, he brushed them aside. His only comment was, "It was a good moneymaking picture."

But *Fort Apache* is more than that.

It is a story about devotion to duty, courage in the face of death, attempting to right wrongs for victims of corruption, a man's arrogance leading to a last stand, and doing the right thing for the honor of the regiment. As York tells the reporters, the names and faces may change, but the military remains. It does not change. It will always be there in time of need.

FORT APACHE

Argosy Pictures–RKO Radio Pictures. *Released:* March 27, 1948. *In production:* July 25, 1947, to October 2, 1947, forty-five days. *Producer:* Merian C. Cooper. *Director:* John Ford. *Screenplay:* Frank S. Nugent, based on the short story "Massacre" by James Warner Bellah. *Cinematographer:* Archie Stout. *Second Unit Cinematographer:* William Clothier. *Editor:* Jack Murray. *Art Director:* James Basevi. *Set Decorator:* Joe Kish.

Musical Score: Richard Hageman. *Musical Director:* Lucien Cailliet. *Sound:* Joseph Kane, Frank Webster. *Assistant Director:* Lowell Farrell. *Second Assistant Directors:* Frank Parmenter, Jack Pennick. *Second Unit Director:* Cliff Lyons. *Production Manager:* Bernard McEveety, William Forsyth. *Wardrobe:* Michael Meyer (men's), Ann Peck (women's). *Makeup Artists:* Emile LaVigne, Webster Phillips, Steve Clensos. *Props:* Jack Golconda. *Set Dressing:* Joseph Kish. *Camera Operator:* Eddie Fitzgerald. *Dolly Grip:* Carl Gibson. *Still Photographer:* Al St. Hilaire. *Art Department Foreman:* Robert Clark. *Special Effects:* Dave Koehler, Daniel Hays. *Wardrobe Researcher:* D. R. O. Hatswell. *Script Supervisor:* Meta Stern. *Military Technical Advisor:* Major Philip Kieffer, US Army (Ret'd). *Dance Choreographer:* Kenny Williams. *Set Accordionist:* Danny Borzage. *Historical Researchers/Advisors:* Katharine Spaatz, Katherine Cliffton. *Set Medics:* James Green, Robert Neilson. *Running Time:* 127 minutes. *Budget:* $2,156,770.95. *Domestic Rental Gross:* $2,986,934.61. *Working Title: War Party*. Rereleased in 1953.

Filmed at RKO-Pathé Studios, Culver City, California. Corrigan Ranch, Simi Valley, California. Goulding's Trading Post, Monument Valley. Mexican Hat, Utah. Gooseneck State Park, Utah.

Cast

John Wayne (*Captain Kirby York*), Henry Fonda (*Lt. Colonel Owen Thursday*), Shirley Temple (*Philadelphia Thursday*), John Agar (*Lt. Michael "Mickey" O'Rourke*), Ward Bond (*Sgt. Major O'Rourke*), George O'Brien (*Capt. Sam Collingwood*), Victor McLaglen (*Sgt. Festus Mulcahy*), Pedro Armendáriz (*Sgt. Beaufort*), Dick Foran (*Sgt. Quincannon*), Guy Kibbee (*Dr. Wilkens*), Grant Withers (*Silas Meacham*), Miguel Inclán (*Cochise*), Jack Pennick (*Sgt. Schattuck*), Anna Lee (*Mrs. Emily Collingwood*), Irene Rich (*Mrs. Mary O'Rourke*), Mae Marsh (*Mrs. Martha Gates*), Movita (*Guadalupe*), Francis Ford (*Stagecoach Guard*), Mary Gordon (*Ma, Stage Stop*), Cliff Clark (*Stage Driver*), Hank Worden (*Southern Recruit*), Danny Borzage (*Recruit with Mustache*), Frank Ferguson, William Forrest, Archie Twitchell (*Newspaper Reporters*), Frank McGrath (*Cpl. Derice, Bugler*), Harry Tenbrook (*O'Feeney*), Mickey Simpson (*NCO at Dance*), Frank Baker (*Officer*), Brick Sullivan (*Officer at Dance*), Fred

Graham, Phil Schumacher (*Cavalrymen*), Ruth Clifford, Jane Crowley, Eleanor Vogel (*Officers' Wives*).

Stunts

Richard Farnsworth, Fred Graham, Ben Johnson, Frank McGrath, Gil Perkins, Henry Wills, Fred Carson, John Epper, John Hudkins, Walt LaRue, Cliff Lyons, Ted Mapes, Bob Rose, Barlow Simpson, Don Summers.

She Wore a Yellow Ribbon

Tyree, it's about time I did retire.

—Captain Brittles (John Wayne)

The financial success of *Fort Apache* did not ease or erase Argosy's debt relating to *The Fugitive*. Still carrying a heavy liability, Ford and Cooper once again sought financial assistance by making another Western. This time Ford turned to a familiar source: Peter B. Kyne's novel, *The Three Godfathers*. (Ford directed Harry Carey in 1919's *Marked Men*, based on Kyne's book.)[1]

Ford and Cooper approached Metro-Goldwyn-Mayer about making another version, this time in Technicolor. (MGM produced a version in 1936 and still maintained the film rights to the novel.) Originally, Ford and Cooper planned to finance the film through Argosy, with MGM handling worldwide distribution for a 30 percent cut, and an additional 25 percent for use of the story and box office profits. Unfortunately, Argosy was too overextended to apply for another bank loan. Instead, Cooper proposed that MGM finance the film, with Argosy producing.

MGM's contract with Argosy stated that if Ford remained within the $1.25 million budget, the studio would pay Argosy an additional $100,000. Should the film go over budget, MGM would deduct 50 cents for every dollar the company went over from Argosy's $100,000 bonus. The contract stipulated that if the film reached domestic box office earnings of 170 percent of the negative cost, the company would receive an additional $100,000, ending Argosy sharing any further profits. The negative cost of *3 Godfathers* (1948) was estimated at $1,243,000, and domestic box office earnings were $2,078,000, while foreign box office was about $763,000. According to MGM's account books, as of December 20, 1950, the film had earned $1.98 million in domestic revenue. The studio sent the promised $100,000 not to Argosy, but to Bankers Trust, who held one of the several notes Argosy had taken out. (Negative costs did not include marketing or publicity for a film upon release, such as posters, newspaper ads, or radio spots.)

* * *

With the completion of *3 Godfathers* in early June of 1948, Ford started looking for his next project under Argosy's RKO contract. Once again, he returned to the cavalry and two short stories by James Warner Bellah, "The Big Hunt" and "War Party." (Argosy bought the film rights for both stories for $12,000.)[2]

"The Big Hunt" follows Major Allshard's plan to capture the gunrunners supplying Henry repeating rifles to Comanches. When US senator Brome Chadbourne arrives to inspect the conditions on the Indian reservations, Allshard informs the senator about the gunrunners and his suspicions that Indian agent Toucey Rynders is involved. Sergeant Tyree and his patrol have gathered a large herd of buffalo in the area, knowing the Comanches want to launch a big hunt. In order to do that, they need rifles, and the gunrunners are only too happy to take the money the tribe stole from the murdered US Army paymaster.

Following the buffalo herd, Allshard and his troop discover the Comanches are heading toward Jackknife Canyon. Lieutenant Pennell, who scouted ahead, notifies Allshard that Rynders is in the canyon with the gunrunners and handing out rifles to the Comanches. Catching Rynders in the act, Allshard fires his gun and yells down to Rynders that he is under arrest. The buffalo, located on the rim of the canyon (just under Rynders and the gunrunners), are spooked by the gunfire and stampede toward the edge. Hundreds of buffalo fall into the canyon, landing on Rynders and others, killing them.[3]

"War Party" details the final day of duty for Captain Nathan Brittles at Fort Starke. Broken Wrist of the Comanches has led his tribe, as well as those from the Kiowa and Arapaho tribes, off the reservations.

Threatening the area around the fort, the army has issued orders not to engage in any hostilities, forcing Lieutenant Cohill's troop to only track the tribes' movements.

After morning inspection of Company B, Sergeant Tyree presents Brittles with a silver watch and chain from Kansas City. (There is no inscription on the back of the watch.) Brittles, touched by the gift, calls Company B the "best I've seen in all my time. Tough in the rump, but good." Stopping at Major Allshard's office, Brittles learns that his application for civilian scout was turned down. Brittles requests permission to go help Cohill, but the major refuses, as it is the captain's last day of service.

Walking past the post cemetery, he sees the graves of his wife and two sons, both victims of smallpox a few years before. (In the film, the two children were changed to daughters.) Their deaths had sent him into an alcoholic downward spiral, until he eventually pulled himself out of it. As he leaves the fort for the last time, Brittles bids good-bye to Allshard and other officers. Finding Cohill's company, Brittles hands a written order which turns the company command over to the captain immediately. Leading Company C in a night charge of the Indian camp, they stampede the pony herd, firing their pistols and killing the animals. The tribes are now forced to walk back to their reservations, with Company C following them. With his mission accomplished, Brittles rides off into the West.

Two days later Lieutenant Pennell arrives with a telegram appointing Brittles as chief of scouts with a rank of major, signed by General Sherman, General Sheridan, and President Grant. Returning to the fort with Brittles, Cohill reminds the captain that he has been absent without leave for forty-eight hours. "Don't ever apologize," Cohill says, quoting the former captain. "It's a mark of weakness."

* * *

Preparing this film, Ford wrote a detailed letter to Bellah expressing his ideas for the story and the look. The director asked Bellah to write the script and worked with him on the story layout and dialogue. Focusing the story on Captain Nathan Brittles, Ford envisioned the film would look like "a Remington canvas." Men with "broad shoulders . . . wide hats," Indians with "war bonnets and eagle feathers trailing in the dust . . . the brassy sounds of bugles in the morning . . . the long reaches of the prairie . . . the buttes and mesas in the distance, and the buffalo." Ford wanted to "work Custer into it some way" without his actual presence, indicating that their story would take place months after the Battle of the Little Bighorn.

Ford proposed they should "lay out our important scenes" and between them "build some action." One scene he wanted to include featured Brittles and Oldroyd, the scout, riding into the Indian camp to "argue with the Chief." The young warriors have finished their Buffalo Dance and are "now in mass hysteria . . . almost into the Ghost or War Dance." He mentioned the Chief of the Cheyenne Dog Soldiers would shoot an arrow between Brittles' feet, with the captain breaking it in two, spitting on it, and tossing it over his shoulder. (Such an action is considered an insult, causing the warrior to lose face among his fellow braves.) "A sharp argument with the Chief and his headman, who are tired of war . . . but the young bucks who have never been blooded are frantic in their desire to join the Cheyenne." Ford suggested after this sequence would come the stampeding of the pony herd, "which I think is a wonderful sequence." He also commented that the scene when the watch is given to Brittles was "truly swell."[4]

Ford admitted they were "suffering from the greatest of all boons . . . an overabundance of great material. If we can tie this together simply and in a straightforward line, we've got something." He noted that Monument Valley had never been shot in Technicolor, adding it "should be breathtaking."[5] Ford stated that he had his own group of Navajo Indians "who are great riders, swell actors," and the Navajo men were "tall, sinewy, and as the poor bastards never get enough to eat unless I make a picture there, they have no excess fat on them." He noted that if they got "a break in the weather we might get something we could be proud of and get a chance to get our investment back . . . plus ten percent." (Ford was planning to shoot in October 1948.) In closing, Ford told Bellah to take his ideas "for what it's worth," adding that he was going on the *Araner* to do some fishing and some "thinking about the story. I'm delighted at the idea of our working together."[6]

Bellah's draft (dated August 27, 1948) opens in Brittles' quarters as he dresses for his final days of duty. Sergeant Hochbauer enters to give the latest news, which includes the birth of a new boy; that the stage to Sudro's Ford has halted service; and that Corporal MacKenzie was shot by "one of Broken Wrist's hyenas." Major Allshard informs Brittles during a meeting that he needs to know if Broken Wrist and his young men have taken authority away from Pony That Walks. Brittles suggests that he may have to go into their camp to find out, which will anger the Indian Administration. "I'll answer the letter," Allshard states. "You get me the information." The major also informs Brittles that his wife and her guest, Olivia Dandridge, will accompany the column to Sudro's Ford to catch the train east.

Leaving headquarters, Brittles passes Soapsud Row, greeting some of the married women, before passing the post cemetery. Brittles does not visit the graves of his wife and two daughters, only speaking to his wife from a distance. "Good morning, Mary," he says. "We're moving out shortly. I'll be back in six days. You mustn't worry, my darling. Just the regular routine relief. I love you my dear—more than ever."

Prior to the troop moving out, Brittles walks by some of the men and their mounts. He warns them that women will be accompanying the column and they need to "clean up your talk from now out. *And watch that word.*" Trooper Nikirk begins to curse at his horse ("You lob-nobbed, slab-ribbed son—") before Sergeant Donahue (the Irishman) blurts out, "Watch them words!" Another trooper anonymously shouts, "Watch them grammar!" but Donahue does not respond to it. Following this, Bellah included a scene of Donahue and another trooper carrying two china chamber pots to the wagon. "No dialogue. (Necessary for a belly laugh)" read the direction. Needless to say, this was dropped before the script was submitted to the PCA.

As the column makes its way toward Sudro's Ford, Cohill notices that Pennell has placed the wagon ahead of the pack mules that carry extra ammunition. He orders Pennell to get the pack mules in front of the wagon before Captain Brittles sees the mistake. As Pennell apologizes, Cohill cuts him off, stating, "Never apologize, Mister Pennell. It's a mark of weakness!"[7]

Bellah then inserted several brief scenes featuring various characters that dissolved from one to another: A couple of troopers discuss the death of Brittles' wife and daughters, which led to his three years of hard drinking; Olivia accuses Cohill of using his authority to keep Pennell at the rear of the column. He says he is doing it to "kick the romance out of him" unless she stops playing her "pretty little game" with Pennell. Brittles rides up and orders Cohill to relieve Pennell; Pennell informs Olivia he plans to resign his commission and head east to get a job. When she asks him when he made this decision, Pennell replies it was the night he asked her to marry him; Mrs. Allshard tells Brittles not to worry about Pennell and Cohill in regard to Olivia. "I don't like any of it, Abigail," he replies. "They're *my* boys and I've raised them right. I don't like a soft-mouthed filly in the corral. She's not the breed. Not the Army breed."[8]

Bellah inserted narration to play over a lap dissolve sequence "for pictorial background and time passage."[9] (Some of this narration was used in the film.)

> The dog-faced soldiers, the professionals, the 50-cent-a-day faces, riding on the rim of Empire. The hats change and the blouses change, but the faces themselves never change very much . . . the Regular Army *is* Cohill and Brittles, and Sergeant Donahue and all the rest, and where ten or twenty of them gathered together, that place became the United States . . . Leaving their bones to bleach and the echo of their passing—only a cold word in a dusty book of history.[10]

As Sergeant Tyree informs Brittles that there's a large buffalo herd ahead of them, the patrol from Sudro's Ford rides in. One trooper, Quayne, has been wounded from an attack by Comanches. After examining him, Dr. O'Laughlin says he has to amputate his right arm. In this draft, O'Laughlin is accompanied by his civilian servant, McCrimmon, who carries a banjo and never says a word. In a handwritten note, Ford has the character playing "Wearin' of the Green," and the Irish troopers are "wrathful." He penned a line for one trooper saying, "Ya think bejesus they'd sing the right words over now, wouldn't ye?" He also wrote an alternate version with Quincannon, O'Feeney, O'Laughlin, et al., singing one chorus of the real words, "For there's a bloody law of the wearing of the green." While Ford briefly considered using the McCrimmon character, as well as the dialogue he had written, he discarded all of it.[11]

Cohill again confronts Olivia over Pennell, telling her that he is not the man for her, before he forcefully kisses her. She slaps him in return. Bellah then inserted another series of vignettes: Brittles asks Donahue where he's hiding his whiskey bottle, which the sergeant denies despite threat of a court-martial; Olivia relieves Mrs. Allshard who has been nursing Quayne in the back of the wagon; Donahue pulls a whiskey bottle from the captain's water jug on a wagon and then puts it back; Brittles takes a drink from his water jug, but fails to find the whiskey bottle; Cohill is riding with the column as he looks in at Quayne, seeing Olivia nursing him. "No dialogue necessary as their eyes meet."[12]

Tyree arrives at the Coleman ranch to find it burned out, with the husband, wife, and son dead. He spots the daughter hiding in the bushes, naked, "scuttling like a wild beast." Tyree rides back to inform Brittles, who has Dr. O'Laughlin accompany him back to the ranch. O'Laughlin manages to find the girl, wrapping her in a blanket as she laughs hysterically. Examining the girl, the doctor informs Brittles her wounds are fatal. (The PCA would flat-out reject the material about the young girl.)

In the wagon, Quayne, delirious and in pain, mistakes Olivia for his mother. "Hold me, Mom! I'm afraid!" he repeats over and over as his voice weakens. At first Olivia cannot handle this moment, but she summons the strength to comfort him as he dies in her arms. ("She's a woman now, in a woman's sorrow" notes the script direction.) When the column reaches the Coleman ranch, Pennell attempts to shield Olivia from the dead bodies, but she has changed. She lashes out at him, calling him a quitter, and refuses to marry him. The burial of the Coleman family and Corporal Quayne follows, with Brittles speaking a few words before handing it over to Dr. O'Laughlin. There is a note in the script to show "a snatch of ritual" regarding a military burial. Cohill asks permission to take a squad and go after the Indians, but Brittles refuses, reminding the young officer, "An order is an order. And glory is but the painted smile of a jade of the streets. This job of ours out here is marriage." When Cohill apologizes, Brittles admonishes him, adding that apologizing is a sign of weakness.

The column arrives at Sudro's Ford, which has a spur track for the transcontinental railroad, where Olivia will take the train to return to the East.[13] As they wait for the train, scout Ben Oldroyd rides in with the body of the US paymaster, and Dr. O'Laughlin takes the body to a nearby shed to perform an autopsy. The train, badly shot up by Indians, slowly limps into the station, with only the conductor and Senator Brome Chadbourne aboard. Bellah drafted a wordy scene, running three and a half pages, between Senator Chadbourne and Brittles, which allowed Bellah to insert background information about Brittles' drinking after the death of his wife and daughters, and the subsequent trial board. (None of this verbose dialogue adds anything of importance to the sequence.)

As they finish talking, Rynders, the Indian agent, rides in, claiming he's on his way back to Fort Starke. Mentioning the attacks by the Comanches, Brittles wonders aloud where they are getting their Henry rifles, but Rynders quickly discounts the story as being just fiction. Completing the autopsy, Dr. O'Laughlin shows the slug he removed, belonging to a Henry rifle just like the Indians now have.[14] Brittles explains his plan to capture the Indians buying the rifles from the gunrunners, but Rynders objects to the military taking action, claiming this is the jurisdiction of the Indian agency. The captain insists he has the authority, and will take action in a few days after the men and horses are rested.

Watching Rynders ride off, Brittles, knowing the Indian agent believed his plan, quickly orders the troop to move out. Olivia, who has decided to stay out west, and Mrs. Allshard are placed at the rear of the column for safety. Mrs. Allshard warns Olivia that this will be a hard ride, but the young woman indicates she is ready for the task. Pennell, brooding over Olivia's affection, accuses Cohill of going behind his back and taking Olivia away from him. As words get heated, Brittles stops their bickering.

Bellah incorporates the sequence from "The Big Hunt" where Rynders and the gunrunners are discovered selling rifles to the Comanches in Jackknife Canyon. It is Brittles who fires his gun, which startles the buffalo herd, and they stampede to the rim, falling on and killing Rynders, the gunrunners, and some Comanches. Brittles then orders Cohill's troop to follow Broken Wrist to determine his plans. Thanking Brittles for all he taught him, Cohill knows he will likely never see him again. Brittles shakes his hand, saying, "Good luck, Flint."

The remaining column returns to Fort Starke, where Brittles hands in his final report to Major Allshard. Finding Sergeant Donahue, the captain asks him to come to his quarters later in the evening, then pays a visit to his family's graves. As he tells his wife that he will be leaving tomorrow and heading west, a bugler playing "Taps" is heard in the background. Donahue arrives at Brittles' quarters and they share a drink, as Brittles displays the coat and derby he will wear as a civilian. He inveigles Donahue to try on the coat and hat, as Corporal Krumrein and three other troopers walk in. Brittles orders them to arrest Donahue for drinking on duty and not being in uniform, instructing he be held in the guardhouse for thirty days until his retirement. Naturally, Donahue resists and there is a fight, until Mrs. Krumrein ushers Donahue to the guardhouse. (Bellah's script direction reads "The FIGHT—but good. Wrecking the place.")

The following morning during Brittles' last troop inspection, Corporal Krumrein presents him with a silver watch. There is an insert shot of the watch, showing the inscription: "To Captain Nathan Brittles, Cavalry, United States Army. In grateful remembrance of his service. From C Troop. *Lest We Forget*. Good luck." (Ford scrapped the insert shot and pruned the inscription. Instead, he has Brittles read it aloud: "To Captain Nathan Brittles, From C Troop. *Lest We Forget*.")

Knowing that Broken Wrist and his tribe, along with the Kiowa and Arapaho, are heading toward Fort Starke, Brittles says good-bye and rides out of the fort. Arriving at Cohill's camp, he learns Pony That Walks has lost his authority to Broken Wrist. Writing an order, he hands it to Cohill and rides off with Tyree and another trooper into the Indian camp.

As Brittles walks up to Pony That Walks, an arrow is shot between his legs. The captain picks it up and breaks it before throwing it at the brave. Brittles asks Pony That Walks if his young men will be foolish and fight. "Young men are always foolish men," the old chief replies. He points to Broken Wrist, who is telling the young warriors they have two branches on the trail: one is slavery (referring to a reservation as "the barren ground"); the other is death ("a warm blanket"). Hearing this, Pony That Walks tells Brittles that the young men "have not the wisdom of our years." Brittles bids his friend good-bye, saying he is going to a faraway land. The old chief reminds him that they will once again cross trails, as they have "walked in friendship since youth."

Later in the evening, as the young warriors gather to perform a war dance, Brittles leads C Troop into position and they stampede the pony herd into the night. With this action completed, Brittles suggests the troop follow the tribes back to their reservations before he rides off. A courier arrives, carrying Brittles' appointment as chief of scouts, with a rank of lieutenant-colonel. Cohill sends Pennell and two troopers after Brittles and have him return to the fort. Bellah has written a small note in the script to Ford about a potential scene at post headquarters between Brittles and Allshard ("The 'You've got my chair, I believe, major' scene if you want it."). It's likely he and Ford discussed an idea for Brittles returning to the fort, stating to Major Allshard that he is now sitting in Brittles' chair. From there, the script has Brittles reading a proclamation that promotes Donahue to the scout detachment with a rank of captain. "You can't *do* it to me, Captain darlin'!" Donahue wails. Brittles corrects him, stating that it's an order. The script then has a brief note: "Kiss Cohill and Olivia off and out."

* * *

Bellah's script is overly verbose, as he attempts to jam in as much material as he can from his two stories, as well as background information about the main character. His short stories are leaner (especially when describing a character), but in this script draft his tight writing style gets away from him. A couple of scenes are long-winded, slowing down the pacing of the entire script. Such sequences might work better in a novel, where a writer has the freedom to expand more with dialogue and description, but writing dialogue for a movie script requires an entirely different style and talent.

Bellah's second draft, dated September 11, opens with Tyree stopping the runaway stagecoach of the US paymaster "within the shadow of Fort

Starke," as Tyree tells the gate sentry they won't get paid for another three months. As the coach is running wildly, Bellah inserts narration stating that with Custer's massacre, "every tiny outpost on the frontier" lives "in the shadow of death."

He has also replaced Hochbauer with Sergeant Donahue in delivering the latest news to Brittles as he finishes dressing. This sets up the sergeant taking a drink from the whiskey bottle in the olla (water jug) and Brittles' reaction to his breath, which Bellah notes establishes "their long service friendship and the continuing drinking gag."

The demise of Rynders in this draft was debated by Bellah, with a note suggesting either killing him during the pony stampede through the Indian camp, or in an earlier scene when Brittles spots a large buffalo herd "in accordance with last conference."

The final scene has Brittles returning to the party at Fort Starke where the officers' wives present him with a buckskin jacket, complete with the shoulder bars of his new rank and his Medal of Honor pinned on the front. Cohill introduces Olivia as his wife (at least two weeks have transpired since the Indian pony stampede), and Brittles leaves to visit his family's graves. He tells his wife he is back; "I shan't be leaving you again—they'll let me stay now . . . until . . . time for Lights Out." Olivia approaches, surprising Brittles, who apologizes as he tries to explain why he visits the gravesite. She reminds him, "Never apologize, Nathan; it's a mark of weakness."[15]

Much of what Bellah and Ford had developed in those drafts does make it to the screen, although Bellah's script needed a lot of polishing to make it flow smoothly.

To do this, Ford hired Laurence Stallings and Frank Nugent.[16] Gone were the scenes of the buffalo stampede and the train limping into the station after an Indian attack. (Those two scenes, if filmed, would have heavily increased the film's budget.) One weakness in Bellah's script was creating a believable budding romance between Cohill and Olivia. According to Dan Ford, Stallings expanded and fine-tuned the romantic triangle between Olivia, Cohill, and Pennell. He also embellished the scenes of Brittles at the family gravesite and his receiving the silver watch into compelling emotional moments. One of Nugent's most important contributions was taking Bellah's brief narration and using it to coalesce the entire story.[17] Only Stallings and Nugent received credit for the screenplay, with Bellah given "story by" billing.

As Ford held talks with Stallings and Nugent, he also wrote his own story points or dialogue for potential scenes. While none of his material was included in the final script, this illustrates that Ford's fingerprints are all over both Bellah's draft and the final shooting script, but he needed writers to flesh out his vision and ideas to bring them to life. Years later, John Wayne noted that Ford "used writers so well. He dug everything out of them."

Ford had written a brief bit of dialogue between Brittles and Mrs. Allshard where he expresses his frustration in not being able to stop Red Shirt and his men. "Dad-blast it, Abby! If I didn't have you and that dad-blasted filly—" he says before Mrs. Allshard interrupts, warning him to watch his language. Brittles apologizes, to which Mrs. Allshard replies, "Never apologize." Brittles goes on to grumble that he "could stop this dad-blasted Indian war right now if I didn't have you and that—young lady around!" In another brief scene, Ford composed an encounter between Brittles and Mrs. Allshard regarding her matchmaking plan for Olivia. The captain calls Abby a "cantankerous, stubborn old—" when she cuts him off. "Old! Old! Well, Mr. Captain Nathan Brittles, I am eleven years younger than you—if you please!" Brittles is frustrated at her "dad-blasted matchmaking" with one of his younger officers. "Look here Nathan," Mrs. Allshard replies, "I'm going to marry that girl to a cavalry man if it's the last thing I do. Dad-blast you!" Neither of these scenes was incorporated into the script.[18]

Ford also suggested cutting certain scenes, such as one with Brittles and Cohill discussing the Indian tribe's actions as the troopers and wagon are crossing the river. Ford noted the scene should "be cut for speed," just showing the cavalry move to the river. He also dumped a brief moment between Tyree and Quincannon after the Indians have killed Rynders. Tyree relates how the Indian agent made a mistake of whipping a warrior who happened to be Red Shirt's brother, and got off "mighty lightly," while the Indians were more thorough with the other gunrunners. Quincannon nods, saying, "Did ye ever think to notice, Sergeant Tyree, that the more whiskey an Injun drinks, the more it brings out the Irish in him?"[19]

Ford sketched out an idea of getting the cavalry to cross the river, writing the "column runs smack dab into big Indian concentration. Brittles can't fight 'em—he runs for the river." Ford has Brittles telling Cohill to "buy me time" as "rash young braves dash by yelling taunts at soldiers—careful maneuver to gain the river." He also has written the following note: "Winchesters? Could Brittles rearm his men with rifles? After leaving fort—trick it some way." In any case, none of these ideas came to fruition.[20]

* * *

How much does the October 16, 1948, shooting script by Stallings and Nugent differ from the released film? In some cases, Ford has either dumped entire scenes (prior to filming or in the editorial room) or whittled down scenes and/or dialogue to the bare minimum.

A perfect example of Ford's adroitness can be found in the first pages of the script. It opens with a wide shot, four hours after the battle of the Little Bighorn. The description states "the stricken field of Custer's last stand on the Little Bighorn stretches out into the distance toward a ridge whose crest was never gained . . . All along the gentle slope lie the grotesquely-sprawled figures of slain troopers—half stripped, scalped, some pin-cushioned with Sioux lances." The direction describes the camera panning over the horrific scene of dead men and horses as we hear buzzards circling above. The camera comes across an oil-skin wallet, its contents ripped open, showing a few pages of a love letter. The breeze riffles the pages before they blow away, revealing a tintype photo of "a sweet-faced woman." The camera ends on a shot of a trooper's hand clutching a broken saber as the narrator "begins his commentary in a natural, casual, Western manner."[21]

> Custer is dead . . . He lies here on the battlefield of the Little Bighorn this afternoon of June 25, 1876 . . . among two hundred and twelve officers and men . . . horse soldiers of the regular army . . . empire builders . . . guardians of a continent.

There are additional shots of dead soldiers and a few dead Indians as the narration mentions how the troopers were using single-shot carbines against Winchesters, as well as commenting on General Crook fighting "to a standstill" on the Rosebud Creek. The camera finds a bugler lying on his instrument, with only the bell of a bugle showing "7th CAV U.S.A." as the narrator states that with the annihilation of Custer's command, ten thousand Indians led by Sitting Bull, Crazy Horse, Gall, and Crow King prove the white man has no magic. The last sentences are spoken over a scene of several medicine men watching smoke signals.

The action then shifts to a buffalo herd as the narrator intones that a great sign from the heavens has come with the buffalo returning. (The script direction suggests "allow 10 shots," adding "It is hoped the cinematographer may be fortunate enough to find a herd of buffalo so disposed along the landscape as to suggest the enormity of the herd which once roamed the western plains.") During this part of the narration, six Indian leaders are watching the buffalo herd as one stands with both arms raised ("as if in benediction to the distant herds"), while another gathers a handful of earth and "tosses a little dust to the four winds." Shots of smoke signals go on as the narrator mentions various tribes uniting to drive the white man out. The script direction details another scene of two tribes of Indians standing on opposite sides of a stream, "dressed in wide disparity, depending on the director's selection of topography and tribal haunts." This was followed by a scene featuring Indians performing a war dance.

Ford pared everything down. Gone are the shots of the Little Bighorn battlefield. Instead, he opens the film with the 7th Cavalry guidon waving against a red sky as smoke billows. The narration has also been condensed to provide enough of a story setup, announcing "Custer is dead. Around the bloody guidon of the immortal 7th Cavalry lie two hundred and twelve officers and men." As the narration continues, there is a group of scenes showing a lone cavalryman being chased by two Indians, a soldier tapping out a telegraph message, a stagecoach dropping a bundle of newspapers that people grab, and a Pony Express rider galloping into a station to make a quick change of horses, while the narrator states "one more such defeat as Custer's, it would be a hundred years before another wagon train dared to cross the plains."[22] (The sets of the

Western town and the Pony Express station were part of the town built in Monument Valley for Ford's *My Darling Clementine* in 1946.)

A large party of Indians rides past the camera (dressed as nondescript Plains Indians) as the narrator comments that various tribes are ready to launch a war against the US Cavalry. The film dissolves to a runaway stagecoach "pulled by crazed and lunging beasts, going hell for leather under streaming lines." As the coach rattles away, two cavalrymen (Sergeant Tyree and Trooper Cliff) spot the runaway and chase after it. Tyree ("a lance-straight figure and the air of a born horseman") brings the coach to a halt, dismounts, and opens the passenger door as a man in a major's uniform falls out. Trooper Cliff says it is Cheadle, the paymaster, with Tyree adding that they won't get paid for another three months.[23]

Ford and Bellah had a disagreement about this scene, as the writer stated it should be a paymaster's wagon. Ford insisted it would be a stagecoach. Bellah went to the trouble of drawing what a paymaster's wagon would look like, but Ford was adamant. "I told him, 'For christsake, Mr. Ford, it's gotta be a paymaster wagon.' He said no, it would be a stagecoach. So, I said 'shit' and walked out," Bellah recalled. (There was a pool circulating around the Argosy office on how long it would take before Bellah was thrown out of the office by Ford. It did not happen.) After completing his script draft, Bellah left to continue a lecture tour of the United States and Canada.[24] Bellah would not work with Ford again until he and Willis Goldbeck wrote the screenplays for *Sergeant Rutledge* (1960) and *The Man Who Shot Liberty Valance* (1962).

Both the script and film show the raising of a flag as the bugler blows "Reveille" at the fort (shot in front of Goulding's Trading Post), before cutting to the outside of Brittles' quarters, then dissolving to a three-frame tintype on a table of Brittles' wife and daughters. (Ford added narration over this scene: "And wherever the flag rises over some lonely Army post, there may be one man. One captain fated to wield the sword of destiny.") Inside the quarters the script notes there is an olla and a wall calendar, but the script direction specifically states the "calendar's month should not be visible." Brittles is described as "a man of war, some fifty-five years old, lines mark it strongly but they are the effects of weather and no interior quarrel of the human spirit. His cavalryman's mustache could strain a quart of coffee through its gray filaments."

Sergeant Quincannon (changed from Donahue in Bellah's script) enters, greeting him with news of the birth of a child; that the stagecoach stopped running to Sudro's Wells; and the death of Private MacKenzie. As he does this, Quincannon reaches into the olla and pulls out a whiskey bottle and downs a drink before replacing it. (Ford uses this piece of business to set up another scene later in the film.) Brittles walks up and smells the sergeant's breath, commenting he "smells like a hot mince pie." Quincannon feigns innocence, claiming he took the oath to stop drinking at Chapultepec.[25] Brittles mutters, "Beats me where you hide the stuff," before turning his attention to the calendar where he marks off a day, commenting he has six more days before his retirement.

During the sequence where Brittles and Major Allshard examine the paymaster's stagecoach, the script had a brief scene featuring Mrs. Allshard and her niece, Olivia. Stepping out on the balcony, Olivia asks what is happening, as Mrs. Allshard says it doesn't concern them and ushers her back inside. Ford dumped the dialogue, preferring to just show Olivia come out on the second-story balcony to watch before being guided away by Mrs. Allshard. The shot is simple, yet demonstrates Mrs. Allshard's attempt to shield her niece from the harshness of the frontier.

In the script draft, this sequence ends by the coach, with Major Allshard requesting that Rynders, the Indian agent, come to his office in an hour. Rynders arrives at the outside of Allshard's office, noticing the major, Brittles, and Tyree waiting for him. Dr. O'Laughlin steps out of the office holding the bullet that killed the paymaster—a bullet from a Winchester rifle, and the same caliber that killed Private MacKenzie the previous day. Rynders is quick to dismiss any theory that the two dead men were killed by any Indians in his area, or from rifles sold to them. When it came to filming this scene, Ford changed the location to inside Allshard's office, but it was cut from the final print.

While the script has Allshard sharing a dispatch about the death of Custer with Brittles and other officers, Ford chose to make it a more intimate moment. Inside Allshard's office, the major hands Brittles the missive, and he begins to read aloud the names of the men who were killed. Ford then cuts to Brittles walking into the post's cemetery. Opening a camp stool, he sits down and places flowers at the foot of the graves of his wife and children. Taking a dipper from a bucket, he waters the plants bordering the grave (the script suggested periwinkles) as he begins to talk to his wife, Mary.

Ford cuts to a close-up of Mary Brittles' headstone as a woman's shadow begins to rise in front of it. Brittles turns to see it is Olivia, who has brought some flowers.[26] (Ford will use a similar shot in *The Searchers* [1956], when Scar's shadow comes over young Debbie hiding in the family graveyard.) The script contained a different set of direction for this scene, with Brittles walking to the stockade gate where a corporal presents him with a water bucket, gourd, and a camp stool. The script indicated the corporal's actions were routine when Brittles approached. Wagner, the blacksmith, walks up with "a sheath of summer's best hollyhocks" and gives them to Brittles. Ford did shoot this scene at the fort set, but discarded it. Instead, he re-shot the scene, now happening at night, featuring Brittles walking to the family gravesite, alone.

In Bellah's draft, Brittles admonishes the men to watch their language as they are about to move out. Ford chose to have Quincannon give the orders, and react to the trooper yelling "Watch them grammar!" looking "in vain for the offender." (As the column moves out, the script notes that the fort band plays "She Wore a Yellow Ribbon"; however, in the film, we never see a band, just hear the melody and lyrics.)

The script detailed a note relating to the cavalry riding out of the gate: "It is hoped the location, terrain, and light may suggest the effect of a rising sun which will gild the landscape onto which Brittles is leading his troop. But if the weather proves cloudy or rainy—and no changes can be made to the shooting schedule—this and the preceding scenes preparatory to the troop's departure can be constructed as being made in the gray light of a false dawn. No plot point would be affected by such a change."[27]

As the troop rides out, the script's narration begins, "So here they are . . . the dog-faced soldiers . . . the regulars, the fifty-cent-a-day professionals . . . riding the outposts of a nation." The narration continues, talking about each character (Quincannon, Tyree, Cohill, Pennell, and

Brittles) in an individual shot, ending as the fort gates close. Ford wisely eliminated the narration, which would slow the film's pacing, choosing to let the musical score play over the entire sequence, giving the scene a heroic feel. (Ford did use some of the narration at the end of the film.)[28]

As the cavalry column moves toward Sudro's Wells, a dust cloud is left behind them. The script direction notes: "CAMERA PANS slowly to discover a smaller dust cloud" moving tangent to the cavalry column. This is Rynders driving a buckboard wagon, as a freight wagon (the gunrunners) comes out from behind a butte to greet him. The camera does a whip pan to feature Tyree ("taking advantage of the available cover"), watching them before returning to his horse and riding away.[29] Ford deleted all of this, preferring to have Tyree galloping up to Brittles and reporting that he'd trailed Rynders to where he met two men in a wagon.

Later in the script, the wounded Corporal Quayne, with an arrow over his heart, lies in the wagon, as Dr. O'Laughlin rides up to plead with Brittles for them to stop so he can perform surgery. Brittles at first refuses, but eventually agrees to have the troop dismount and walk slowly. The script describes the troopers' walk as "a funeral march"; the scene "shrieks with silence—a suspenseful silence like that in a quiet room with a noisy clock." Instead of a clock sound, the script suggests the noise would come from the sound of boots and horses' hooves moving along the soft ground, the clinking of canteens, and a squeak of a wagon's wheel in need of grease.

There is a listing of several short vignettes to show the passage of time as the surgery takes place: the troop column walking slowly; the wagon driver with a grim look on his face; troopers moving rocks out of the way of the wagon's wheels; Mrs. Allshard assisting the doctor by removing Quayne's bloody shirt and tossing it out of the wagon; troopers glancing at Quayne's shirt on the ground as they stoically walk on; the wagon's wheels slowly moving; "portrait studies" of Brittles, Quincannon, and others; and O'Laughlin tossing bloody water from a basin as some troopers watch. Brittles is finally hailed to the wagon where the doctor tells him that Quayne will "live to make sergeant." Brittles shouts out that the corporal will be fine and orders the troop to mount and walk.

Ford stays with the basic idea of this sequence, but adds his own touches that make this a memorable sequence. The most impressive touch was Ford's decision to film wide-angle shots of the troop and wagon slowly moving during a thunderstorm that came up unexpectedly while filming. (Some call this an example of Ford's "Irish luck.") The sudden storm is a perfect example of Ford taking advantage of an unexpected event and making good use of it. (He once said, "There's no problems, only opportunities.") Ford includes a few shots of the troopers walking their horses along as lightning strikes and thunder rolls, as well as a shot of the wagon's wheels moving slowly.

One of his wonderful touches is when Mrs. Allshard offers Quayne a glass of whiskey. Despite his pain, the soldier gallantly says, "After you, ma'am, if you please." Mrs. Allshard pauses for a brief moment, then drains the glass before pouring another for Quayne. Gulping down the liquor, he begins to sing a portion of "She Wore a Yellow Ribbon" while another soldier administers the ether. Mrs. Allshard joins in singing to bolster both her strength and Quayne's, but as he slips into unconsciousness, her singing trails off. As the doctor begins his work, she says, "Oh, easy Mikey."

Later, as Brittles talks to the doctor at the back of the wagon, Mrs. Allshard comes out, tossing out bloody water from a pan before sitting down on the tailboard. "Thanks, soldier," Brittles says to her, patting her on the head before galloping off. Mrs. Allshard smiles briefly, then grabs the pan as if she may get sick. This is an example of Ford using a touch of humor to soften the sentimental moment.

Ford included a few embellishments to the script's Sudro's Wells sequence. Instead of Brittles seeing something off camera and ordering the troop to charge as it was detailed in the script, Ford uses a wide shot of the troop moving along when a trooper gallops in to report to Brittles, but we cannot hear what is said. Brittles, the bugler, and this trooper gallop up to a rise and stop, and the captain removes his binoculars for a better view. Ford inserts a point-of-view shot from the binoculars showing Tyree and his small detachment holding off a party of Cheyenne Dog Soldiers.[30] Brittles then orders a group of troopers forward and they charge into the burned-out stage stop, chasing off the Indians.

Tyree reports that Ma and Pa Sudro are dead, while their two children were found safe in the smokehouse. The sergeant leads him to examine Trooper Smith, who after complimenting Tyree's actions ("In the best tradition of the cavalry"), calls out "Captain Tyree! Captain Tyree!" When Tyree replies, there is no response. Gently laying Smith on the ground, Brittles softly says, "Afraid he can't hear you, Captain." At the graveside service, Brittles mentions Trooper Smith was really Brome Clay, a Confederate general. As "Taps" sounds over his grave, two former Confederate soldiers salute, as do all the troopers. (In the film, Ford has Dr. O'Laughlin read a passage from the Bible before Brittles gives his speech.)

There was a feud between Ford and Bellah over the scene of the Confederate officer's burial, as this piece appeared in another one of Bellah's short stories that Argosy had not purchased. Ford claimed he had tried to contact Bellah to make a deal but could not get in touch with him. Bellah reportedly said, "Why don't you be quite frank—in addition to you being on a budget, you're a crook."[31]

With the stage at Sudro's Wells destroyed, Brittles has no choice but to go back to the fort. The script details a scene where troopers are building up squad fires with a lone sentry figure standing out prominently, while other troopers appear to be asleep under their blankets. A Cheyenne Indian, watching the sleeping cavalry troop, shoots an arrow at the single sentry. The body falls into the fire and begins to burn. Running to the dead body, the Cheyenne discovers it is not a soldier, but Olivia's dressmaking dummy. The script then details several shots of Brittles, Cohill, Pennell, Olivia, and others as they make their way back to the fort in the darkness. Tyree rides up and speaks with Brittles (there was no written dialogue), and Brittles asks for Pennell to join him. Tyree guides them to a ridge where they dismount and watch Rynders and his interpreter selling rifles to Red Shirt and his men. (The interpreter's character was named Lee Bradley. Bradley, a Navajo, was a liaison/interpreter for the Navajo tribe on many of Ford's films.)

There is a note in the script that states: "Director suggests this scene be shot at *night* at a site near the permanent camp location, generator lights to be augmented with flares."[32] Filming in Technicolor at this time required a greater amount of illumination, especially for any exterior night scenes. (This is why the majority of exterior night scenes in this period were filmed on a soundstage or studio backlot.) To illuminate a location like Monument Valley in 1948 would have required an additional number of lights and technicians to properly accomplish such a task, even if it was staged near the company's permanent camp. (The supplementary lighting equipment and manpower would have also meant a significant increase to the budget.) Lighting and generator equipment in the 1940s were much more cumbersome than today's apparatus, not to mention the fact that modern film stock does not require as much light for exposure, thus allowing productions to film nighttime exterior scenes anywhere.

The entire sequence of the dress dummy shot with an arrow was cut by Ford. Instead, as the troop moves through the night (on a soundstage set), Tyree rides up to Brittles with news of the Indian agent selling rifles. Brittles tells the bugler to have Pennell join them. Dismounting, they see Rynders on the back of a wagon as his interpreter says Red Shirt claims fifty dollars per rifle is too much. Rynders states he knows he has the money from the paymaster's box, and it is fifty dollars or no deal. Angered by his comment, Red Shirt shoots an arrow into Rynders, as other Indians break open the boxes of rifles and ammunition. One of the gunrunners is shot in the back by an arrow, while the interpreter is thrown over into a blazing fire as he screams in pain. Brittles, Tyree, and Pennell watch the events. (In the script, Pennell's reaction to the killing is of one who is "learning something.") Brittles borrows Tyree's knife to cut a piece of tobacco, and offers him some, which Tyree declines. ("No, sir. I don't chew and I don't play cards.") Brittles notes that chewing tobacco is a nasty habit, adding, "Been known to turn a man's stomach." As he finishes the sentence, over the continued screams of the tortured man, Brittles looks at Pennell. Taking the bait, Pennell says, "I'll take a chaw if you please, sir." Returning to their horses, Brittles asks Pennell if he is still thinking about resigning. "No, sir," Pennell replies. (The script has Brittles asking Pennell this question, but the young lieutenant does not reply.)

The script's version of Brittles' last day at the fort opens with Brittles dressing to review the troops. In his quarters there is a suit box lying on the plank table with a "claw hammer pepper-and-salt suit" along with a "high-crowned, flat top hard hat." The script suggests other evidence that Brittles spent the night separating his military gear from personal items. As Quincannon enters, Brittles tells him to give his saddle to Pennell and sell his other items. The sergeant asks about the olla, and Brittles plucks out the whiskey bottle. Quincannon feigns surprise, asking how long he knew it was there. "Ever since the battle of Bull Run!" Brittles replies, before drawing a line through the calendar.

Leaving the quarters to do his final inspection, Brittles tells Quincannon to try on his suit. Stepping outside, he sees the troop mounted and at attention ("every man shined and polished"). Quincannon brings out the captain's dress coat, which Brittles quickly changes into before mounting his horse to join the troop. After telling the troop he knows their performance under the new commander will make him proud, Pennell asks Tyree to present him with the silver watch, which Brittles turns over, to read the inscription. The script noted he "somewhat sheepishly takes out his spectacles to peer closer." Brittles thanks the men, tells Pennell to proceed on his mission, and gallops off.

Ford opens this scene with Brittles asleep in a chair at his desk, holding the framed photo of his family, as Quincannon enters. He gives instructions to sell the items and put the money in the troop fund, and to give Mrs. Allshard his extra saddle. ("Be easier on her disposition.") After Brittles reveals Quincannon's whiskey bottle, he goes over to the calendar and crosses off the week, before tearing off the month and placing it in the burning stove, commenting, "There's that." Quincannon tells him to wear his jacket with his Medal of Honor ("The men will like it, sir"), and before walking out, Brittles tells the sergeant to try on his civilian suit.

Exiting his quarters, Brittles sees the troopers lined up and rides over to deliver his speech. (Instead of Tyree, it is Corporal Krumrein who presents him with the watch.) Brittles is touched, and sniffs as he takes out a pair of glasses to read the inscription before telling the men to proceed on their mission. Ford cuts to a shot of Allshard, his wife, and Olivia watching before Mrs. Allshard, overcome with emotion, walks away. As the major vainly searches his pockets for a handkerchief, Olivia offers him her lace hanky, which he takes. As the troopers move out, Pennell offers Brittles a smart salute, and the captain, emotionally overcome, slowly straightens himself and returns the gesture. Riding past Major Allshard and Olivia, he gallantly waves his kepi hat. Olivia sits down on a step, looking for her hanky, which Allshard hands her. Ford again cuts the script's material to the bone, keeping what he instinctively knew would make the scene play well.

Immediately after this scene, the script has Quincannon in the dress suit ("The big ape is stuffed bursting into Brittles' suit and is now trying the hat at different angles on his head"), pretending to be addressing a lady in a mock monologue when Brittles walks in. The captain asks for a side view, then tells him to go to the sutler's store and order a similar suit, giving him some money to have a few drinks while he's waiting. The sergeant "starts to salute, awkwardly comes in contact with the derby, tips it, and practically stumbles out."

As he walks to the store, Brittles tells Sergeant Hochbauer to arrest Quincannon for being out of uniform and drinking on duty. When Quincannon enters, he demands a drink, yet the script has no dialogue between him and the bartender. Hochbauer enters with six other men and tells Quincannon he is under arrest. Protesting that Captain Brittles gave him permission, Quincannon refuses to submit to arrest and the fight begins. The script included a camera angle outside the doorway of the sutler's store as "four men in rapid succession are shot out like cannon balls, head first, feet first, sideways." A cast-iron stove comes flying out of the doorway, followed by one of the men with his head stuck in the elbow of the stove's pipe, blindly swinging away. Quincannon eventually tumbles, and by now there is nothing left of Brittles' suit as Mrs. Allshard runs in and stops the fight. Quincannon claims his arrest is treachery as she marches him to the guardhouse.

While Ford used the basic layout of the scene, he eliminated things like Quincannon's mock monologue and protesting his arrest, yet added other touches. As Brittles comes back into his quarters, he sits down looking at his watch for a moment before Quincannon emerges from the dressing area in the suit. Brittles tells him to order a duplicate, handing him a few coins to get a drink. Quincannon says nothing, dumbfounded by the generosity. At the door a sudden confidence comes over him as he pulls the lapels of the coat and puts the walking stick under his arm and exits. Strutting down the parade grounds, he nods at other soldiers who stare in disbelief, and when Sergeant Hochbauer tells him he's out of uniform, Quincannon replies, "I am in the proper uniform. The uniform of a retired gentleman," before bounding up the stairs of the sutler's store.

Brittles orders Hochbauer to arrest Quincannon, and assembles several men to help him (stuntmen Fred Kennedy, Fred Graham, Frank McGrath, Mickey Simpson, and Bob Rose). Entering the store, Quincannon bangs his walking stick on the counter, telling Connelly, the bartender, to give him an Irish whiskey. Hochbauer marches in with his men, and asks Quincannon if he'll come along peaceably. "Laddy," the sergeant replies, "I've never gone any place peaceably in me *life*." Setting his drink down, Quincannon hauls off and hits Hochbauer, knocking him backwards. The fight is on! One soldier goes tumbling, as another (Fred Graham) throws a few punches before getting knocked down.[33]

Wagner, the blacksmith, comes up and gets whacked, as the bantam Fritz stands on a chair and smacks the sergeant, who tosses him over the bar with one hand. Quincannon turns to Connelly, remarking, "Ah, Connelly, the old days are gone forever." The soldiers mount another attack, mostly hitting each other as Connelly gets into the act by whacking a few of them with a broom. As four of them rush to the bar, Quincannon stops them with an offer of a toast. ("Men! Now we want no unpleasantness. A toast first, and the guardhouse after—if you're able.") Raising his glass, Quincannon toasts Captain Brittles on his retirement. Draining the liquid, all of them throw their glasses through a closed window, except for Connelly—who tosses a nearly full bottle of whiskey. Thanking the men for a "very pleasant moment," he punches Heinze in the face before walking away. The troopers limp after him, but Quincannon stops at the doorway, hitting Hochbauer, who sails down the steps. Other troopers fly out the door, before Quincannon calls out for them to join him in another drink. ("Come have a little somethin' before you go.") He places one trooper in a chair at a table, giving him a glass of whiskey. As the man drinks it, he falls backwards in the chair, out like a light. Mrs. Allshard and Dr. O'Laughlin rush in, with her ordering Quincannon to the guardhouse. Walking down the steps, she admonishes the beaten soldiers for "picking on one man."[34]

As Brittles leaves, Major Allshard assures him that Quincannon will remain in the guardhouse for two weeks until he retires at his proper rank. Walking away, Mrs. Allshard and Olivia (wearing a yellow ribbon in her hair) stop to say good-bye. As he mounts his horse, Olivia asks if he thinks Cohill is all right. The script direction notes that "if Brittles hadn't changed his mind about heading to California, the girl's entreaty tips the scales to his decision." He replies he doesn't know, but tells her to hold on to her yellow ribbon. (Some historians believe the custom of a woman wearing a yellow ribbon dated back to the Civil War, although others state there is no evidence to support the claim.) He "rides away briskly, and with no backward glance," as Quincannon, from the guardhouse window, cries out to Brittles that "it's mutiny, sir . . . treason!" Riding out of the gate, Brittles turns and salutes the flag. The script notes that he slows down a "trifle" as he passes the post cemetery, almost as if he is going to stop, but he doesn't. Once past the cemetery, he gallops away.

Again, Ford follows the script to a point, but deleted Quincannon's cries of treachery and Olivia asking about Cohill. In the moment between Allshard and Brittles, Ford slightly changed the dialogue, with Allshard giving his word that Quincannon will "retire as top soldier." Mrs. Allshard stops him, saying, "Good-bye is a word we don't use in the cavalry. Till our next post, dear." She hugs him and kisses his cheek, as Olivia asks if she can "haul off and kiss you too, Captain?" They hug and Brittles mounts his horse, walking out of the fort, riding past Dr. O'Laughlin, who says, "May the road be kind to ya." Outside the gate, Brittles salutes the colors, with no shot of him passing the post cemetery.

Following this scene in the script, there were a series of vignettes in the Indian encampment featuring several tribes ("suggested by the varied clothing worn by the differing bands") partaking in a war dance at night. Shots included individual braves racing their horses through the encampment shouting and firing their guns in the air, Red Shirt greeting another tribe riding in, and handing them rifles taken from Rynders. As this chief raises the rifle in the air, "the SOUNDS of PANDEMONIUM rise to a new CRESCENDO" before dissolving to Cohill and Pennell watching the encampment from a distance. Brittles rides in to greet the young officers, who inform him about the war dance, suggesting they strike first. Brittles advises them he was not sent by the major, then writes out a written order that he gives to Cohill, before he and Tyree ride to the Indian camp.

Inside the camp, Brittles greets his old friend Pony That Walks, who says his young men do not listen to him and many lodges will be empty and squaws will soon sing the death song. He invites Brittles to come with him and hunt buffalo, but the captain declines, saying he must go far away. The old chief gives him his pipe as a gift before Brittles and Tyree leave. The script direction notes the war dance continues as Brittles leads the charge of cavalry through the camp and scatters the pony herd. Accomplishing this task with no casualties, Brittles hands Cohill his saber and rides off. The script then details the cavalry following the Indian tribes walking, while Pony That Walks rides alongside Tyree, who addresses the chief as "General," and asking how he likes the McClellan saddle. Pony That Walks shouts, "Hallelujah!"

Ford condensed the montage of the Indian sequence, opening with a stunning shot of Indians riding in single file along a ridge with a portion of Monument Valley behind them as gray clouds darken the sky. It is a shot only Ford could capture on film, a Charles Russell painting come to life. As the Indians ride along, Ford brings in the narration to set the stage for the upcoming sequence.[35] He features various shots of the Indian village as women beat drums, men sing, and a large group of mounted warriors, led by Red Shirt, march through the encampment. Ford then cuts to Brittles arriving at Cohill's encampment and giving him the written order. Arriving in the Indian camp, Brittles walks toward Pony That Walks as Red Shirt shoots an arrow between his legs. He stops, picks up the arrow, breaks it, and spits on it before flinging it back at the warrior.

In the scene between Brittles and Pony That Walks, Ford begins with a wide shot, showing them standing opposite each other before cutting to individual medium shots of the two men. When the old chief says they are too old for war, Brittles replies, "Yes, we are too old for war. But old men should stop wars." Ford uses a close-up for this moment, capturing Brittles' weariness and determination to see that his last act as an army officer is successful. The old chief can do nothing, but urges Brittles to come with him and hunt buffalo and "smoke many pipes." The captain declines, and the two old friends bid each other good-bye.

From this scene, he cuts to Brittles leading the entire troop through a small gully, lining up in two columns. The cavalry successfully charges through the encampment, stampeding the pony herd into the darkness. (Ford eliminated the tribe performing a war dance.) As the bugler sounds "Recall," Brittles looks at his watch, noting that he's been a civilian for two minutes. "It's your army, Mr. Cohill," he says, saluting the officer, and riding off. Ford reverts to a wide shot, keeping the bugler (blowing "Recall") in the left foreground as Cohill and Pennell take up the center of the camera frame, watching their former captain riding over a ridge.

Brittles rides alone through Monument Valley as the narration once again comes into play. During a story conference, Ford had written his own version of the narration: "So, Nathan Brittles rode west into the setting sun. Towards the Santa Fe Trail—seeking—seeking what is there to seek when we're old. Revives memories—memories of a job well done." Ford noted the narration is broken off suddenly with "Ben Johnson riding like hell towards camera. Telegraph sequence."[36]

The version of the narration in the film is similar to Ford's idea, as we watch Brittles make his way through Monument Valley. ("So, Nathan Brittles, ex-captain of Cavalry, U.S.A., started westward for the new settlements in California. Westward toward the setting sun, which is the end of the trail for all old men.") The narration continues, stating the army wasn't finished with Brittles and sent "a galloper after him. That was Sergeant Tyree's department." (This last line was a reference to Brittles asking Tyree's opinion; the sergeant would reply, "That ain't in my department.")

Tyree gallops away from camera into the vastness of the valley, before the scene cuts to both Brittles and Tyree riding in silhouette against a red sky. Stopping him, Tyree hands him a telegram "from the Yankee War Department." Brittles learns he's been appointed as chief of scouts with a rank of lieutenant-colonel, endorsed by Generals Sherman and Sheridan, and President Grant. The two men ride off to return to Fort Starke. (Ford eliminated the sequence of the troopers following the Indian tribes and Tyree and Pony That Walks riding together.)

Returning to the fort, the script has Brittles escorted by Quincannon (in full dress uniform) to the assembly hall, where he is greeted by the entire troop and their wives. Allshard approaches, telling him he's two days overdue. As Brittles offers an apology, Allshard grins, reminding him, "Don't apologize. It's a mark of weakness." Olivia and Cohill tell him he may be surprised to learn they are engaged, but Brittles replies that everyone above the rank of second lieutenant at the post knew it. Pennell offers that there will be a time when he is first lieutenant, as everyone chimes in with, "In ten or twelve years!" Olivia asks if he will stay for the dance, but Brittles excuses himself. Knowing what he means, she hands him the flowers she has been wearing on her dress as he walks out.

Hochbauer walks up to Quincannon, who hands over his saber, but the officer refuses. Ordering the troopers to escort the sergeant back to the guardhouse, Hochbauer slips a pint of whiskey into the sergeant's waistband. Smiling and patting the bottle, Quincannon tells Hochbauer he hopes the man "will be a soldier yet." Brittles walks out the front gate toward the post cemetery, as the corporal of the guard gives him his camp stool. "Brittles takes it, and our last sight of him is walking up the line—toward the cemetery silhouetted in the evening sky."

Ford adjusted some material in this last sequence. Gone is Brittles being led by Quincannon into the assembly hall. Instead, Tyree opens the doors of the hall, and as they step in, Quincannon greets Brittles ("Welcome home, Colonel darlin'!"). Brittles leans in to smell his breath, as Mrs. Allshard takes his arm and they walk up the aisle to applause from the officers and their wives. Greeting Cohill and Olivia, the dialogue remains the same as in the script, with the only change being Brittles telling Olivia he has to "make my report, first."

Thanking everyone, he heads for a side door where Wagner (the blacksmith) hands him the camp stool, and Olivia gives him her flowers. Exiting, the band (which we never see) softly plays "She Wore a Yellow Ribbon" as Cohill and Olivia begin to dance with others. Pennell remains by the door, watching Brittles. As the music continues, the scene dissolves to Brittles walking to the family gravesite alone, at night. The shot dissolves to show the entire cavalry troop, Brittles in the lead, riding past the camera as the narrator concludes, "So here they are. The dog-faced soldiers. The regulars. The fifty-cents-a-day professionals, riding the outposts of a nation. From Fort Reno to Fort Apache, from Sheridan to Starke, they were all the same. Men in dirty shirt blue and only a cold page in the history books to mark their passing. But wherever they rode, and whatever they fought for, that place became the United States."

* * *

The completed script was sent to Joseph Breen at the Production Code Administration for approval. In an October 19, 1948, letter to Breen, Ford noted he would "be most interested in your reaction to the material."[37] Seven days later, Breen wrote to Merian C. Cooper that the basic story "seems acceptable under provisions of the Production Code." He went on to remind Cooper that the "greatest possible care" had to be taken in selecting and photographing the dresses and costumes of the women, noting that the Code "made it mandatory that the intimate parts of the body—specifically the breasts of a woman—be fully covered at all times. Any compromise with this regulation will compel us to withhold approval of your picture." He also asked Cooper to contact Mel Morse at the American Humane Association "with respect to all scenes in which animals are used."[38]

Breen took exception to certain scenes in the script that would "have to be handled with care so as to avoid the impression of excessive gruesomeness, as well as to avoid possible deletions by political censor boards. We refer, specifically, to such items as Rynders slashing the Indian across the face with the whip, and the action in scenes 240, 243, and 246." The script had Rynders spotting a young brave (Red Shirt's brother) making a grab for one of the rifles in an open box. The Indian agent "with a teamster's skill" lashes the face of the Indian, leaving a red welt on his face. Scene 240 was Rynders being killed by an arrow as blood widens on his white shirt, while scene 243 featured Hench, one of Rynders' goons, being chased by an Indian who finally corners him and slams a lance into his body as two young warriors count coup on him.[39] The concern over scene 246 had to do with the interpreter being continually thrown on the fire.

In the film, as Rynders is hit with an arrow, he grabs at the shaft with his left hand as some blood trickles out over his fingers. As he slumps down, Rynders' other hand covers the bloody one. Filmmakers during this period not only had to be very selective when it came to using blood on an actor, but also, how a character was shot with an arrow. During this period, a stuntman (or in this case, actor Harry Woods) wore a thick, heavily padded piece of balsa wood under their costume. An experienced archer would then shoot the arrow at his target (the padded balsa wood piece) and the performer would act as if being hit. Harry Woods held a small sponge soaked in Max Factor's Technicolor blood in his left hand and squeezed it over the arrow as he fell down.

Today, filmmakers have eliminated the need of a professional archer to show a person being hit with an arrow. One way is to attach the arrow (minus the deadly tip) to a monofilament wire. One end of the wire is attached to a harness under the actor's costume, while the other end is in the hands of a special effects man who "shoots" the arrow shaft using an air gun. The arrow flies into the scene (the wire is undetected by the camera) and the actor acts as if he's been hit, grabbing the shaft. Another way is to feature the actor with his back to the camera, and we hear the sound effect of the arrow hitting as the actor turns to the camera, showing the imbedded arrow. This is done by having a plate with a spring (similar to a mouse trap) with the arrow shaft already attached, facing downward. The plate is attached under his costume with the arrow outside. As the actor takes the hit, he releases the spring (either by a wire or touch of a finger) and the arrow swings upward into place, giving the desired effect.

After the death of Rynders, as the Indians break open the boxes of rifles and ammunition, we see another gunrunner (played by Peter Ortiz) running toward the camera. We hear the sound of an arrow hitting Ortiz's back as he takes the hit, then slowly turns and falls to the ground, showing the arrow in his back. (For this shot, the arrow shaft was already attached to a harness under his costume, thus eliminating the need of an archer.) The interpreter character is the one thrown onto the fire several times, although he does a quick tumble over the flames (fully clothed) before being quickly thrown again.

On October 25, Cooper replied to Breen, noting "that all of the points raised by you either have been taken care of insofar as the script is concerned, or will be taken care of during the course of actual photography and production of the photoplay, to the end that the finished picture will be acceptable under the provisions of the Production Code."[40] Katherine Cliffton, Argosy's story editor, sent Breen a letter on February 4, 1949, with the lyrics from three songs the production contemplated using. The songs were "The Girl I Left Behind Me," "Oh Bury Me Not on the Lone Prairie," and "For His Lover Who Was Far Away." Four days later Breen replied that the lyrics "seem to meet the requirements of the Production Code," but PCA's final judgment "[would] be based on the finished picture."[41]

* * *

When it came to casting the role of Captain Nathan Brittles, the accepted story is that Ford wasn't so certain John Wayne was right for the role. Reportedly, it wasn't until he saw an advance screening of Howard Hawks' *Red River* that he changed his mind, adding, "I never knew the big son of a bitch could act." According to the August 18, 1948, issue of *Hollywood Reporter*, it was announced that Charles Bickford "was in talks" to play Captain Brittles. Bickford had a prickly personality, especially with certain directors, and one can only imagine what would have transpired if he had worked with Ford. In many cases, these announcements were more for the sake of publicity than reporting the actual truth. Many studios would mention an actor's name in an upcoming production, but this was just a ploy by the studio publicity department to keep the upcoming production in the newspapers and magazines. While Ford may have toyed with the idea of using another actor, it is very doubtful he thought of anyone else but Wayne for the role. Henry Fonda, who had made six films with Ford, lacked the emotional warmth needed for the character of Brittles, and even if Ford had wanted Fonda in the role, the actor had begun a long Broadway run in *Mister Roberts* in February 1948.

With Wayne cast as Brittles (he was paid $100,000),[42] Ford brought in Victor McLaglen to play Quincannon. (McLaglen, who won an Oscar playing Irishmen, was of Scottish descent and born in Kent, England.[43]) Ford cast Mildred Natwick as Mrs. Allshard, George O'Brien as Major Allshard, John Agar as Cohill, and Ben Johnson as Tyree. The majority of the supporting cast was made up of Ford's stock company: Arthur

Shields (*Dr. O'Laughlin*), Francis Ford (*Connelly, the Bartender*), Tom Tyler (*Corporal Quayne*), Don Summers (*Corporal Krumrein*), William Steele (*Trooper*), Fred Kennedy (*Trooper Heinze*), Mickey Simpson (*Wagner*), Bob Rose (*Fritz*), Ray Hyke (*Trooper McCarthy*), Cliff Lyons (*Trooper Cliff*), Fred Graham (*Sergeant*), Fred Libby (*Sergeant*), Michael Dugan (*Sergeant Hochbauer*), Frank McGrath (*Derice, the Bugler*), and Jack Pennick (*Sergeant Major*).

For the role of Red Shirt, Ford cast actor Noble Johnson, while Chief John Big Tree was given the role of Pony That Walks.[44] Ford picked actor Irving Pichel to do the narration, who had previously supplied the adult narrative voice for Ford's *How Green Was My Valley* (1941) and his 1943 documentary, *December 7th*. Other actors in the cast included Rudy Bowman as Trooper John Smith (the former Confederate general), Paul Fix as Rynders' interpreter, and a young man recently discharged from the US Marine Corps, Peter Ortiz, as one of Rynders' goons.[45] Actor Forrest Tucker was set for the role of Rynders, the Indian agent, but was replaced by Harry Woods. The probable reason for his replacement appears to be a scheduling conflict, as Tucker was working on another film, *Montana Belle*, that started in late October 1948, the same time Ford's film was in production. (*Montana Belle* wasn't released until 1952.)

On all of his films, Ford would find work for performers he knew from his days at Universal or Fox. For this production Ford had a list of names for potential bit or extra parts that included Elmo Lincoln (the first actor to play Tarzan in a 1918 film), Ruth Clifford, Gertrude Astor, Jim Mason, William Farnum, Mae Marsh, Harry Tenbrook, Dot Farley, and Steve Clemente.

Harry Carey Jr. was given the role of the callow Lieutenant Pennell. Shortly before his father's death, Dobe (a nickname because his hair color resembled that of adobe bricks) asked him why he wasn't working for Ford. His father replied that the director wouldn't hire him, but stated that once he was dead, Ford would hire his son. True to his father's prophecy, Ford cast him as the young bank robber in *3 Godfathers*. "It was a baptism by fire," he recalled years later. "Ford was just brutal to me. I was in the barrel every day, no matter how hard I tried not to be. One day he walked past me muttering loud enough for me to hear, 'I should have gotten Audie Murphy.' I tell ya, he shook any confidence I had to its core. But he got things outta me [performance], I never thought I was capable of doing."[46] Having survived Ford and the Death Valley location, the young actor felt he was ready for anything Ford could toss at him this time.

For Joanne Dru, who was cast as Olivia, this was her third film. Dru was not required to do a screen test, but visited Ford in his office to "talk with him, and that was it." (Ford rarely, if ever, did screen tests for his films.) Dru was a close friend of his daughter, Barbara, who begged her father to be Dru's stand-in on the film. Ford reportedly refused, claiming the two girls would drive him nuts, but he eventually relented. (Barbara had to stand on boxes to bring her up to Joanne's height.) The two girls had a grand time together on location, and Dru loved Ford, who she affectionately called "Papa." "It was instant love with us. He never gave me a bad time. Papa was warm and sweet. He'd tease me, he had a fantastic sense of humor. He was truly an original, there was nobody like him. I related to him like a father," she recalled. When it came to directing, Ford "didn't really give much direction, and only stopped you if you were doing something wrong."[47]

* * *

The budget for *She Wore a Yellow Ribbon* was $1,851,290.20, with a thirty-three-day shooting schedule, considerably lower in both categories compared to *Fort Apache*.[48] For Argosy Pictures the logistics of bringing a film company into Monument Valley was now a well-executed operation. One call to Harry Goulding started the process on his end, while another call went out to Anderson Boarding Supply and Company to set up their tents, showers, and toilet facilities.[49] Cars, trucks, and small planes were arranged for transporting personnel and equipment to Monument Valley.

Ford had written a note to himself: "Col. Tim McCoy, Technical Advisor," same as he did on *Fort Apache*, but he chose to rely on Philip Kieffer as military advisor, as well as playing an officer in several scenes.[50] When it came to stunts, Ford's "Iodine Squad" was summoned to work by Cliff Lyons, who coordinated the stunts and also appeared as one of the troopers. For doubling in brass, Lyons was paid $500 a week for seven weeks as stunt coordinator, and $300 a week for five weeks as an actor. Along with Lyons came Frank McGrath, Fred Graham, Post Park, Fred Kennedy, Slim Hightower, and Bob Rose. All played troopers in the film (a few occasionally doubling as Indians), earning an acting salary of $300 a week, plus an additional weekly $300 as stuntman. When any of them performed a stunt, they were given a "stunt adjustment," such as Fred Graham earning an additional $400 for the fight scene in the sutler's store, while diminutive Bob Rose got $200 for being tossed around in the fight. Post Park, who handled the blind driving of the runaway stagecoach, earned an extra $1,450.[51]

Any time Ford returned to Monument Valley it was a windfall for the Navajo tribe. It meant a few weeks of steady work, good pay and good food, and working with a man who dearly loved them. One day when Ford arrived on the set, the Navajos broke out singing "Happy Days Are Here Again" in their native language. "I took it as a great compliment," he recalled.[52] All 221 Navajo extras were paid $6.60 an hour for an eight-hour day for nearly four weeks. Those using their own horses in the film made an additional $1.50 an hour for an eight-hour day, with hay and feed provided by the company.

For the visual look of the film, Ford wanted to capture the color palette found in the paintings of Frederic Remington and Charles M. Russell. "It wasn't exactly [just studying] Remington, it was also Charlie Russell. Matter of fact, it was more Charlie Russell than Remington," he said years later. With Remington's work, Ford seriously studied his cavalry paintings and sketches, paying attention to the wardrobe and the faces. "I tried to get his [Remington] action in the picture," Ford recalled.[53]

The decision to shoot in Technicolor required renting the specific camera from Technicolor, as well as using the three-strip Technicolor film. Argosy rented three cameras at $90 each per week, while 240,000 feet of Technicolor film stock cost $35,920. (Winton Hoch, the director of photography, was paid $4,863 for six weeks.) Set construction, both on location and at RKO-Pathé Studios, totaled $44,585. The price of the sets varied from the front and inside of the fort set in Monument Valley ($19,320), the interior set of Brittles' quarters (on a soundstage,

$681), the fort cemetery (on a soundstage, $7,541), the exterior of the Indian encampment ($2,196), to the interior of the wagon (for Quayne's surgery, $100). The prop department had their hands full, manufacturing breakaway lances, preparing the stagecoach and army wagon for location work, as well as painting 400 arrows and 100 spears for the Indian extras. Once again, military material was needed, such as 50 McClellan saddles, 50 canteens, rifle boots, saddle pads, and blankets for seven weeks, totaling $1,725. They also rented a stagecoach ($400), an army wagon ($100), and a buckboard ($100) for four weeks. Rubber-tip arrows (550), 50 bows, 20 quivers, and 46 shields were also needed for six weeks ($380).[54]

The makeup and hair department supplies ran $1,164, while wig rentals (mainly for stuntmen and extras) cost $1,956. When it came to the cast wardrobe, costumes for Joanne Dru were the most expensive, totaling $1,642, with Mildred Natwick's wardrobe ($1,245) a close second. (An additional set of costumes was made for the stunt doubles of Dru and Natwick for the riding sequences.) John Wayne's wardrobe cost $925, while costumes for Harry Carey Jr. and Ben Johnson amounted to $625 and $450 each. Chief John Big Tree's wardrobe cost $175, and most of the stuntmen's trooper uniforms ran $75 each. Rental fee for cavalry uniforms, overcoats, gauntlets, and gun holsters and belts (all primarily for extras) totaled $3,135. For the final scene in the assembly hall, 27 women's party dresses, jewelry, and fans were rented for $1,087. The total amount for the Indian wardrobe cost $10,612, which accounted for 50 "full dress" costumes ($65 each), 200 additional Indian clothing items (buckskin shirts and pants, $30 each), 61 breastplates ($1,735), and 100 blankets ($5.40 each).[55]

In any Western, livestock is an essential part of the film. Clarence "Fat" Jones was one of the leading suppliers of horses, mules, wagons, and various pieces of equipment.[56] He began providing horses for the film industry dating back to 1912, when his stables were in the Edendale (now Silverlake) area of Los Angeles. By the 1920s, he had moved his stables to North Hollywood, where it remained an active rental facility until his passing in 1963. From his stables, Fat Jones supplied ten cast horses ($500 a week for six weeks), two falling horses ($220 for three weeks), and twelve work horses ($360 a week for three weeks). The pride of Fat Jones Stables was Steel, a chestnut horse that looked gorgeous on screen, with three white feet (left fore and the two back hind) and a white blaze down the center of his face. This was the horse Ben Johnson rode in the film.[57] Argosy also rented horses from ranches in Utah and Flagstaff, as well as eleven dogs (fifty cents a day for seventeen days). The total for hay and feed during the four weeks of location work came to $3,489.

A large herd of buffalo was needed, for when the column sees the shaggy beasts. While most people do not associate buffalo with the arid region of Arizona, evidence shows that the animal's range did include areas of northern and eastern Arizona.[58] The company made arrangements to use the buffalo herd at House Rock Valley, which required rounding up the herd ($5 a day for four days, $7,000), and using 350 buffalo in the film ($5 a day for three days, $5,250).[59]

* * *

Once again, cast and crew left from Union Station in Los Angeles for an overnight train ride to Flagstaff, Arizona. From there, Ford, Wayne, Hoch, and a few others took a small charter flight to Monument Valley, while the majority of the cast and crew had to endure a long drive on mostly dirt roads. For Harry Carey Jr., this was his first time going to Monument Valley, and he recalled the drive was "almost impossible in good weather and if it rained? Forget it!"[60]

Ben Johnson recalled the first time he arrived at Goulding's, just before evening.

> We drove up in this car and got out and I heard someone holler way across—you could just barely hear them. And then immediately after kind of an echo, there's one that hollered way back over here. In about thirty or forty minutes, right down below—like a quarter of a mile—a fire starts up and the Indians start singing and dancing. When this sound starts bouncing against the back wall and out into this valley, it was the most eerie sound. It sounded like a bunch of coyotes. If I could've had a recording of that it would be priceless. It just makes the hair stand [up] on the back of your neck. It's really something. And that sticks in my mind more than anything else in Monument Valley.[61]

Life on location can be fun or boring, depending on where one finds oneself. Today, when filming in Monument Valley, cast and crew members are put up in hotels or motels either in nearby Kayenta or at Goulding's. On location, cast and crew will work six days a week, often putting in ten- to fourteen-hour days (depending on the script and schedule). Sundays are usually spent doing laundry, catching up on sleep, or taking a tour of Monument Valley sites.

It was a lot different in 1948, beginning with the accommodations. The Anderson Company set up tents for cast members and crew to sleep in with a Navajo blanket on the dirt floor and kerosene heater to ward off the October chill. Crew members would sleep four to a tent, while tents for many cast members held two each. A few cabins were built up by Goulding's Trading Post for some of the actors, which Harry Carey Jr. called "nothing more than a glorified hogan."[62] None of the tents had a bathroom, so lavatory and shower facilities had to be shared, with the toilet being a port-a-potty, and the shower, a washhouse consisting of a five-gallon drum with holes punched in the bottom, filled with cold water from a hose. No one took a long, luxurious shower.[63]

On location, Ford turned to actor Arthur Shields to coach Harry Carey Jr. in nailing down his character. Shields, brother of actor Barry Fitzgerald and a veteran of Dublin's famed Abbey Theatre, was the *only* person Ford ever allowed to coach another actor on his set. "Shields told me something I've never forgotten. He said the role I had was the hardest one to play. He said, 'You're not as handsome, you don't get the girl, and you won't stand out in this picture by playing another nice guy. You have to be a guy outta West Point who is a stuck-up, rich, spoiled prick.' He laid it all out for me. Right then it all just clicked for me. I had planned on playing Pennell as a nice guy," he noted.[64]

* * *

Monday, October 25, and Tuesday, October 26, Ford, Wingate Smith, Winton Hoch, and Cliff Lyons scouted locations. Principal photography began on Wednesday, October 27, with Ford filming the runaway stagecoach and Tyree and Trooper Cliff stopping it.[65] He spent the rest of that day shooting all of the chase sequence between Tyree and the Indians.

Watching Ben Johnson outrun the Indians is one of the highlights of the film, illustrating what Dan Ford so eloquently stated—that the actor was "poetry on horseback." Johnson said others were better actors than he was, but nobody could ride a horse as well as him. It wasn't bragging; it was a fact. Ford *loved* watching Ben ride. In this film and in *Rio Grande*, he did not miss a chance to show off Ben's horsemanship. "Ford always liked to watch me ride a horse . . . He always had me chasing Indians or running from them or something," Johnson said.[66]

As the chase begins, Ben Johnson mounts his horse, with the Indians in close pursuit, and gallops off to the right of the camera frame. Ford kept the entire chase going from right to left, while one beautiful shot in this sequence has Tyree and the Indians galloping toward the camera, with the rock formation Agathlan (also called El Capitán) in the distance. Shot as the sun was setting, the trailing dust, kicked up by the riders, is highlighted by the descending sun's rays.

Cutting from that shot, Tyree comes across a small chasm. Stopping for a brief instant, he wheels his horse back and then urges him forward. The horse jumps across the chasm easily, bringing the Indians to a halt, not willing to take the risk. It is a wonderful shot, except there was no chasm for Johnson and Steel to jump over. It was movie magic by means of a matte shot.

Matte shots, originally called glass shots, combine two separate images, usually by blocking (or masking) off an unwanted area of the camera frame while photographing the desired space. In this case, the bottom section of the frame was masked off, only exposing the upper half of the frame, showing Tyree and his horse jumping. (A hurdle was placed in the masked-off area to make the horse jump.) The matte painting was created at the studio by matte painters—some of the most gifted artists in cinema—and then photographed and optically combined with the footage from Monument Valley in post-production. (In a second matte shot, showing the Indians riding up to the edge of the chasm, the camera was positioned at a low angle shooting upwards, with the bottom of the frame masked off.)[67]

The following day, October 28, was spent at Goulding's Trading Post filming scenes of Brittles coming out of his quarters, looking at the stagecoach, and examining the Indian arrow. Again, a bit of movie magic and camera angles allowed Ford to cut corners and save time. At Goulding's property, the trading post served as the exterior for the fort headquarters; the potato cellar was the exterior of Brittles' quarters; and a building was constructed to serve as the exterior of the sutler's store. Since all the actors and crew were living right there, it was an easy location, without having to move cast, crew, and equipment to another site. The exterior of the fort grounds and front gate were built in front of Sentinel Mesa, to the left of the road that now takes visitors into Monument Valley. Again, camera placement did the trick to hide the fact that the two sets were almost four miles apart.[68]

Sunday, October 31, Ford covered additional scenes at Goulding's, including Brittles' reaction to the wagon accompanying the column, Olivia and Cohill in front of the headquarters with their embrace interrupted by Mrs. Allshard, and Ross thinking Olivia is wearing the yellow ribbon for him. The next day was spent out in open country (southwest of Goulding's), filming scenes of Tyree's report of spotting Rynders and the gunrunners, Olivia complaining to Cohill about walking their horses, and Tyree and Brittles watching the Arapaho tribe on the move, forcing them to change course. That day alone, Ford completed eleven scenes in the script within a ten-hour day. Throughout the course of production, Ford worked at an intense clip. An example of Ford's economy in filming is demonstrated in the scene where Brittles and Tyree are watching the Arapaho tribe on the move. Ford never once uses a close-up in the sequence, relying on either master shots, medium long shots, or two-shots. (Ford preferred using close-ups for a dramatic story point.) By using these camera angles, Ford only had to reposition his camera three times, adjusting the camera lens for the desired angle (i.e., master or two-shot), thus saving considerable time in finishing the scene.

November 2 and 3 were spent shooting scenes of Pennell telling Cohill he will resign, Mrs. Allshard complaining she never got to see one of her gardens grow, and the troop looking at the buffalo herd. The following day, November 4, the company set up location by the East Mitten Butte in the valley, filming the sequences involving Corporal Quayne's patrol running from the Indians, and Quayne reporting to Brittles before seeing the doctor. Ford managed to cover six and five-eighths script pages (and at least twelve setups) in less than nine hours.

* * *

"Shot under protest."

In later years, Ford loved to recall how his cameraman balked at filming the thunder-and-lightning scene in *She Wore a Yellow Ribbon*. Ford said that Winton Hoch filed a complaint, saying the scene was shot under protest. With a slight smile, he added that Hoch won the Academy Award.[69] It's another example of Ford enhancing a story to make it sound better than the truth. Hoch always rebuffed Ford's version, but not vigorously. However, in one interview years later, Hoch claimed he never shot anything under protest, adding, "The old buzzard [Ford] would never sacrifice a good story for want of a few facts."[70]

Whenever he was asked about this scene, Harry Carey Jr. adamantly stated that Hoch never wrote a letter of protest. He concurred that the weather went from bad to worse, as clouds rolled in, making it hard to photograph anything without using an enormous amount of artificial light for any shot. Lighting an outdoor wide shot to look natural was impossible in such weather, especially with the three-strip Technicolor stock. (Ford was filming wide shots of the cavalry moving through open country, and Dr. O'Laughlin begging Brittles to slow down for the surgery as the storm moved in.)

As the clouds darkened and lightning began to flash, Ford decided to call it a day. When the cast members and extras began to head toward the cars to take them to Goulding's, they were suddenly ordered back to mount up. Some called it Ford's Irish luck, but more than likely he was struck with inspiration and wanted to take advantage of an opportunity. Harry Carey Jr. heard Ford ask Hoch if he thought they could film a shot of the troop moving along. The cinematographer believed it was awfully dark, but would shoot it if Ford wanted to. Giving him the order to shoot, Ford told Hoch to open up the aperture on the camera, adding that he'd take the rap if the shot didn't come out.[71] Ford later told his grandson, Dan, that the shot wasn't even scheduled, but it made the sequence.

* * *

Whenever he was filming in Monument Valley, Ford always hired a Navajo medicine man known as Hosteen Tso, which meant either "Mr. Big" or "Mr. Fat." Ford took to calling him Fats, and with Lee Bradley acting as interpreter, he would explain to the medicine man that he wanted some puffy clouds in one area, and some long, streaky ones in another area of the sky. "The old man sat up on top of the mountain and, by God, here come the clouds!" Harry Carey Jr. recalled. One day Mildred Natwick happened to overhear Ford describe to Fats how he wanted a few scant clouds in the sky after lunch. The actress giggled at Ford's request, which the director quickly halted with a harsh look. She recalled the medicine man went up on the hill, and sure enough, the clouds Ford requested showed up for the afternoon's work.

The day before the thunderstorm, Fats was asked what the weather would be like the following day. He replied he didn't know. When asked why, he replied, "Radio's broke."[72]

* * *

Ford loved his stunt crew, but he was a hard disciplinarian. "He made the stunt boys go on the wagon, especially Slim Hightower and Fred Kennedy," remembered Harry Carey Jr. One stuntman Ford had little control over was Frank McGrath. "McGrath, you couldn't do anything about," Carey said. "He drank a quart a day. He'd play cards at night with the old man [Ford] and he'd be insulting [him] and [he'd] kick him under the table and call him a 'mean old bastard.' The old man wouldn't say a thing, but the next day he'd be on his ass . . . he'd really work his ass off."[73] Ben Johnson remembered McGrath as a "great little guy and very capable," but he was "his own worst enemy" because of his drinking. Yet Ford put up with him, despite threatening to never hire McGrath again. (McGrath's usual reply was, "Go ahead, DeMille wants me.") Despite the needling they gave each other, Ford truly liked the man and his work. Stuntman Chuck Hayward observed that if Ford suspected anyone had imbibed the night before, the following morning he'd be up in their face, adjusting a bandana or hat to get a whiff of their breath.

"If they were caught, Ford picked on them mercilessly throughout the day," he said.[74]

* * *

Saturday, November 6, was spent filming the sequence at the Sudro's Wells set, while Monday and Tuesday, November 8 and 9, Ford moved the company to the San Juan River for scenes of the troop crossing the river and Cohill kissing Olivia good-bye. (This amounted to ten pages in the script.) Regarding the river crossing, the script contained a notation that "It is the director's intention actually to ford the river with the troop as spectacularly as possible, making full use of all the various talents of the company, featuring small, unsung bits of strength and prowess which the occasion would provide."[75] Several Mormons were used as cavalry troopers, and the two days along the river were very cold. At one point, Ford caught one Mormon man taking a swig of whiskey, claiming it was for "medicinal purposes."[76]

The following two days, Wednesday and Thursday, were spent at the fort set, filming the company's departure, the paymaster's stagecoach coming through the gate with Tyree's patrol behind it, and Cohill stopping Pennell and Olivia from going on the picnic.

It was during this last scene that Harry Carey Jr. said he was almost killed.

From the first day of filming, he felt pretty good as he managed not to be in the barrel with Ford. That changed with this scene, where he had to drive his buckboard out of the gate at a good clip. Setting up the shot forced him to back up the wagon at a slight angle, and when it came to filming the scene, one of the front wheels caught under the wagon and ruined the shot. Ford started in on him. "Oh, Jesus, Dobe! You lived on a ranch. Just back them up!" he said. Another take is ruined, and Ford's comments got Carey "hot under the collar." Ford's actions were deliberate, as he wanted young Carey's character to be mad at the end of the scene, where he's been embarrassed in front of the girl.

> Finally, I got the buggy backed up right, and now my temper's really boiling. Of course, ya can't say a word to the Old Man, but I had to let

my temper out *somewhere*. I had a buggy whip and when I went off, I *whipped* the horses, shouting "Haaaa!" We *flew* outta there, let me tell you. I was really mad, which is what he wanted for the scene.

What I didn't realize, because I was so damned mad, was the road went straight down and these horses were flying! By now we are out of the shot and I stood up with my feet against the buggy and pulling back on those lines trying to slow the horses. Cliff Lyons happened to be on this buckskin horse and saw what was happening. He galloped out, grabbing that right-hand horse, and just stopped the team. I thought I was a goner, but old Cliff saved my life.[77]

* * *

One scene with Victor McLaglen caused Ford some frustration.

Having worked for the director since *The Fighting Heart* in 1925, Victor McLaglen was used to Ford and his motives. By now, nothing Ford said bothered McLaglen. A biting comment rolled off the actor like water on a duck's back. While he would never admit it, Ford loved McLaglen and put up with him, even when he'd fall asleep in his set chair and begin snoring. Ford would loudly ask if someone could please wake up Victor, before going back to work.

"Jack knew how to use Vic better than anybody else," John Wayne once stated. When it came to filming Quincannon addressing the troop that women would be traveling with them and to watch their language, a happy accident occurred. One of the Navajo dogs had laid itself out in front of the troop, sunning itself without a care in the world. Ford saw the dog and got the idea that McLaglen should say something about it. As they filmed the scene, McLaglen bends down and pets the dog, saying, "Nice dog, cocker spaniel." (Ford wanted him to say "Irish setter.") Harry Carey Jr. said he thought Wayne was going to have a stroke from trying to stifle his laughter.[78] Two takes later, Ford got what he wanted when McLaglen pets the dog and says, "Nice dog, Irish setter."

* * *

The scene of Brittles receiving his silver watch was filmed on Friday, November 12. Recalling that scene years later, Wayne reflected on his character's emotions. "It was an emotional reaction rather than a studied response to given lines in a scene. It was a scene that I could imagine—and I did imagine [that] I couldn't cope with it any more than Brittles did in that scene. Pappy was very conscious of each personality, each actor's sensitivity. He knew the pain he was using when he put me in that scene. So, he knew that my reaction would be simplistic and deeply moving. Which I think it was."[79]

After completing this scene, Ford filmed the troop returning from the failed mission. The script describes their arrival as "a spent little force with none of the smartness it possessed short days before when it so proudly started out." The weather began to turn cold as they lined up the shot, with a biting wind that only added to the visual appearance of a worn-down cavalry column. As the men walk in, spattered in mud, other soldiers and family members watch in silence. Unlike their leaving the fort with the spirited playing of "She Wore a Yellow Ribbon," the return uses the same theme, but played softly, echoing the slow movement of the men and horses.

Saturday, November 13, the company returned to Goulding's Trading Post, with Ford filming the exterior scenes of Quincannon (in civilian clothes) walking to the sutler's store, the soldiers flying out of the store during the fight, and being marched out by Mrs. Allshard. By the afternoon, Ford was shooting the sequence of Brittles bidding good-bye to Allshard, his wife, Olivia, and Dr. O'Laughlin. Sunday, November 14, was spent filming all the scenes of the Indian encampment (in Rock Door Canyon), including the meeting between Brittles and Pony That Walks. Ford once again sought Arthur Shields' help in coaching John Big Tree with his dialogue, as he believed the man could not read or write English. "He [Shields] would repeat the lines and Big Tree would repeat them," Ford recalled, adding that Big Tree "was good in the scene."[80] The late afternoon was devoted to filming the cavalry stampeding the pony herd through the encampment.

Monday, November 15, marked the company's last day in Monument Valley. This included Brittles riding into Cohill's camp and giving him the written order before he and Tyree head off to the Indian camp. In the script, the scene takes up three and three-quarter pages. Under normal circumstances such a sequence would take about three to four hours to cover, with various camera angles. Again, Ford's economy in filming wasted little time. Opening with a wide shot of Brittles riding in, he cuts to a medium-wide shot (keeping seven actors and two horses in the frame) for the scene's dialogue, before cutting back to a wide angle, showing Brittles and Tyree riding out. Ford also shot images of the vast Indian group making their way across the land, and a traveling montage shot of Brittles after he left the fort.

While the cast and some crew members headed back to Los Angeles, Ben Johnson remained behind, traveling with the company to House Rock Valley (northeast of the Grand Canyon). It was there that Ford shot footage of the large buffalo herd, as well as shots of Tyree riding into them. As Tyree rides through, one can see a "spotted buffalo" with a white patch on the hindquarters and back legs. Such an animal is not the rare white buffalo, but very likely is a *cattalo*, a hybrid offspring of domestic cattle and an American buffalo.

Resuming filming at RKO-Pathé Studios on Tuesday, November 23, Ford spent the day leisurely shooting Brittles at the family gravesite. The rest of the week (Thursday was Thanksgiving, an industry holiday) was spent filming numerous scenes that included Brittles returning to the post dance, Quincannon's fight in the sutler's store, the funeral of the Sudros and Trooper Smith, Quayne's operation in the wagon, Brittles breaking up the fight over Olivia, Rynders' death in the Indian camp, and Brittles, Tyree, and Pennell watching.

Monday, November 29, Ford covered all the scenes in Allshard's office, notably Brittles stating his mission was a failure, and requests to go help Cohill. With that completed, Ford moved over to Brittles' quarters, filming the opening scenes. The following day, November 30, Ford finished the remaining scenes in the captain's quarters and wrapped principal photography. *She Wore a Yellow Ribbon* completed filming in thirty-one days (not counting travel days), and brought the production in $581,290.20 *under* budget.[81]

* * *

The film now moved into post-production, where such things as editing, adding sound effects and matte shots, creating the opening credits, and scoring the film were handled. Richard Hageman once again was chosen to score the film, at a salary of $8,000, while Jester Hairston was hired as choral director ($200), providing his own choir to sing the film's title song during the opening credits and within the film.[82] In later years, Ford recalled that he came up with the title for the film based on the song. Whether this is true, or just more of Ford's Irish blarney, is a matter of conjecture.

> I have no musical education. My liking, my taste has always been negro spirituals or cowboy country music. I can't carry a tune very well, but one tune I remember my Uncle Mike used to sing was "She Wore a Yellow Ribbon" . . . I always remembered that. Later on in life I had the idea that's a hell of a title for a picture—a cavalry picture.[83]

(The script's original working title, *War Party*, came from one of Bellah's stories. However, both of Bellah's drafts, as well as the one by Stallings and Nugent, used the title, *She Wore a Yellow Ribbon*. Other potential titles were considered, including *Brittles U.S.A.*, *Forward*, *Buffalo Hunt*, *The Great Herd*, *War Dance*, *Yellow Scarf*, and *Long Knife*.[84])

The origin of "She Wore a Yellow Ribbon" is not very clear-cut. Songwriter George A. Norton copyrighted his song "(Round Her Neck) She Wore a Yellow Ribbon" in 1917, at the time of America's entry into World War I. However, according to author Kathryn Kalinak, an 1838 minstrel song, "All Around My Hat," is considered to be the antecedent of Norton's 1917 song.[85] The origin of that song is believed to date back to 1820s England, but when it was played in America, it was adapted with a dialect for minstrel shows. The lyrics of the 1820s song begin, "All around my hat I will wear the green willow / And all around my hat for twelve-month and a day / And if anyone should ask me the reason I'm wearing it / It is all for my true love who is far, far away." The lyrics in Ford's film open with " 'Round her neck she wore a yellow ribbon / She wore it in the winter and the merry month of May / When I asked her why the yellow ribbon / She said 'It's for my lover who is far, far way.' " (Some historians believe the American minstrel version of the song, minus the minstrel dialect, might have been sung in the ranks of the US Cavalry, but evidence supporting this is nebulous.)

Richard Hageman, who believed "She Wore a Yellow Ribbon" was in the public domain, found a copy in a musical book of military and soldiers' songs in RKO's music department library. Author Kalinak speculates the book Hageman used was likely Edward Dolph's *Sound Off! Soldier Songs from the Revolution to World War II*, as Argosy's researcher, Katherine Cliffton, had included the book in her research list.[86] With the film's release, Regent Music Corporation released sheet music as a tie-in to the film, and was a popular seller.[87] That is when George A. Norton and Jerry Vogel Music stepped in, notifying all parties that the song was indeed still under copyright, and they planned to file suit. Aside from it being a military song, it also became popular with many colleges in the 1920s, including Williams College in Massachusetts, using altered lyrics. RKO and Argosy used that college's version as its defense, and the threat of a lawsuit disappeared.[88]

Hageman's score opens with an energetic rendition of "She Wore a Yellow Ribbon" before the chorus begins singing the opening lyrics, then diverting to "The Girl I Left Behind Me." As the narrator mentions Custer's death, "Garryowen" is played in the background before switching to a composite of music that leads into an upbeat tempo of "Bury Me Not on the Lone Prairie." As we see images of Indians on the screen, Hageman reverts to the stock Indian motif he had previously used in *Fort Apache*, then veers to a vibrant score, making ample use of horns and strings to match the action of the runaway stagecoach.

When Brittles and Allshard review the names of the dead in Custer's company, Hageman reprises "Garryowen," this time with a soft, melancholy theme that carries over to Brittles visiting his family gravesite. As we see the headstones of his wife and children, a trumpet softly plays, then dissolves into a wistful theme with a strong use of strings and the occasional harp.

As the troop leaves the fort, Hageman launches into "She Wore a Yellow Ribbon," with accompanying chorus, in a lively, heroic melody. This version of the song is in stark contrast to the scene when the cavalry troop returns after Brittles' failed mission, where Hageman offers a somber, low-key rendition in muted notes by the string and horn sections. For the scene of Brittles reviewing the troop for the last time, Hageman chose "Battle Hymn of the Republic," starting off in soft tones as it slowly builds. Brittles bids the troop farewell, and Hageman launches into a hearty rendition of "The Girl I Left Behind Me" (with a choral accompaniment) before merging into the melody of "She Wore a Yellow Ribbon" as Pennell stops and salutes Brittles. Pennell rides out of the fort, and the score softly fades as Brittles enters his quarters, looking at his watch.

The traditional "Irish Washerwoman" becomes Quincannon's theme as he walks to the sutler's store in civilian clothes. It is played in a lighthearted, jaunty melody, using strings and a flute to match the sergeant's stride. When the soldiers enter to arrest him, Hageman starts off with "You're in the Army Now," before returning to "Irish Washerwoman," then mixing the two songs throughout the fight sequence.

At the end of the film as Brittles leaves the dance to "make my report," Hageman returns to "She Wore a Yellow Ribbon" again, this time using strings and muted horns in a slow melody as we see him at the family gravesite. Cutting to the cavalry riding through the countryside, the score launches into a hearty mixture of "She Wore a Yellow Ribbon" and "You're in the Army Now," before returning to "The Girl I Left Behind Me" as Hageman makes generous use of horns and strings to create a heroic finale.

* * *

"It's not often that a careful character study with a western background comes along," commented *Variety*. "Such a picture is 'She Wore a Yellow Ribbon,' and it sets a mark that will be hard to match. It is another of John Ford's classics of the early west, told with the distinctive craftsmanship that is his trademark. It rates the box office payoff it will surely get. The thoughtfully developed story is told in magnificent Technicolor hues that perfectly set up the sweeping display of action against the western backdrop." The trade magazine went on to note the menace by the Indians, that they are "never seen in actual conflict, a development that makes 'Yellow Ribbon' different from the usual western plotting." They commented that Wayne "does a standout performance as the rugged captain, making it exciting and emotionally sound. The other standout among the stars is Ben Johnson, a comparative newcomer but a young man with a personality that grabs a strong hold on the audience. He is Wayne's scout and at home in the saddle or with a dialog line . . . Ford and his associate, Merian C. Cooper, have given the film showmanly wise production framing, displaying care in every detail."[89]

Bosley Crowther of the *New York Times* noted that "Mr. Ford has superbly achieved a vast and composite illustration of all the legends of the frontier cavalryman . . . And, best of all, he has got the brilliant color and vivid detail of those legendary troops as they ranged through the silent 'Indian country' and across the magnificent Western plains . . . His action is crisp and electric. His pictures bold and beautiful. No one could make a troop of soldiers riding across the Western plains look more exciting and romantic than this great director does. No one could get more emotion out of a thundering cavalry charge or an old soldier's farewell departure from the ranks of his comrades than he . . . Mr. Wayne, his hair streaked with silver and wearing a dashing mustache, is the absolute image and ideal of a legendary cavalryman. A newcomer named Ben Johnson is likewise vivid as a trooper from the South . . . Bulwarked with gay and spirited music and keyed to the colors of the plains, 'She Wore a Yellow Ribbon' is a dilly of a cavalry picture. Yeehooooo!"[90]

The industry trade paper, *Hollywood Reporter*, stated, "There can't be any doubt that 'She Wore a Yellow Ribbon,' filmed under the magnificent direction of John Ford, from a splendid drama by James Warner Bellah, with a perfect cast, beautifully photographed amid the unique backgrounds of the great plains, is the finest outdoor picture produced in Hollywood for a long time . . . Winton Hoch and associate Technicolor director Morgan Padelford rate the highest possible praise for the beautiful and effective photography of the unique and colorful backgrounds and the fast-moving action . . . The picture is a sure-fire bet for success in every exhibition location."[91]

Cue magazine felt the film had "a tendency to linger awkwardly over sentimental scenes and low-comedy—an old weakness of director John Ford, who even so, knows how to jam action into his large-scale westerns."[92] The *Los Angeles Times* observed that Ford "outdoes himself in the pictorial results," creating a movie with "tremendous outdoor effects, and fair plot and circumstances." Observing Wayne delivered a "surprising portrayal" as Brittles, the newspaper gave approbation to all the cast—and even included the scenery. "Ford seems to make his scenery act in this production," the review added.[93]

The box office popularity for *She Wore a Yellow Ribbon* was strong, and by January 25, 1951, the film had posted earnings of $2,530,142.77. In Canada, the film had taken in $97,583.79, with the total earnings of both countries coming to $2,627,726.56. (Total foreign earnings amounted to $133,301.07.)[94]

* * *

One big fan of this film was General Douglas MacArthur, who was known to screen the film on a monthly basis. Ford once speculated that MacArthur's famous speech to Congress in 1951, where he says, "Old soldiers never die—they just fade away," may have been influenced by the scene where Wayne's character says, "Old soldiers, Miss Dandridge, how they hate to give up."[95]

Lux Radio Theatre, sponsored by Lux Soap, was another radio anthology show that adapted films for a one-hour format on the CBS radio network. *She Wore a Yellow Ribbon* aired on March 12, 1951, with Wayne reprising his role as Captain Brittles. Mel Ferrer played Cohill and Marla Powers essayed the Olivia Dandridge role. While the performance basically followed many of the film's story points, because of time constraints it omitted others, such as Quincannon's fight with the soldiers in the sutler's store.[96]

* * *

Coming to the end of a long career is often hard for many to accept. While most look forward to retirement to pursue personal interests, the loss of spending decades doing a much-needed and loved job leaves a void no personal hobby can truly fill. Those who have risen through the military ranks understand the meaning of service and duty to country. While one may not always agree with their orders, a soldier's job is not to question the directive but to carry it out to the best of one's ability.

Captain Nathan Brittles faces an uncertain life as his day of retirement draws closer. With his wife and children deceased, his only family is the US Army. For forty years he has braved shot and shell, from the Mexican-American War and the Civil War to the solitary forts of the Western frontier. Because his knowledge is vast and keen, the men under his command respect him. To the junior officers he mentors, he is a surrogate father figure and a man to emulate. The military is all he has known, coming fresh off his father's farm to join the army. Now a mandatory rule of retirement at a certain age is forcing him out, even though Brittles has "enough leather on the saddle" to still be useful. It is a bitter pill he is forced to swallow. However, like a true soldier, he is determined in his last days to do what he has done for four decades—follow orders, teach younger officers, and maintain the peace with Indian tribes.

Unlike Colonel Thursday in *Fort Apache*, Brittles is not a martinet. Like any good commander, he leads by example, and his officers and soldiers trust his judgment and leadership. We also see a gentler side to Brittles, whether it is his concern for a wounded officer or visiting his family's gravesite. The time he spends at the graves of his wife and two young daughters not only illustrates his love for them, but his loneliness. As he shares his feelings about his upcoming retirement, it is obvious Brittles will not only leave behind the army, but his family as well.

During his final patrol, Brittles has to contend with a rivalry between Lieutenants Cohill and Pennell over Olivia Dandridge, Major Allshard's niece. Cohill, who comes from a military family with seven years' experience, is scheduled to take command of the troop after the captain's retirement. However, dealing with Olivia Dandridge, he often lets his emotions overtake him. Lieutenant Pennell, on the other hand, is a diamond in the rough. The son of a wealthy railroad magnate, his appointment to West Point was not something he sought. His lack of field experience manifests itself when Brittles announces the column will change direction to avoid conflict with a large Indian party. Cohill remarks that this move will cost them half a day of travel, with Pennell quickly adding, "The ladies may miss the stage, sir!" Brittles and Cohill shoot a disgusted look at the young officer, who quickly realizes his mistake. Offering an apology, Brittles cuts him off with a brusque, "Oh, shut up!" When Brittles and Tyree observe Rynders selling the rifles to Red Shirt, Pennell is chosen to accompany them. It is this scene that marks the moment of his character's epiphany. Pennell accepting Brittles' dare to chew tobacco demonstrates he is no longer a callow rich kid, but a man serious about his position and military career. At the end of the movie, as the dance resumes and Brittles walks to his family's gravesite, Pennell stands alone at the door, watching. To be an officer like the captain is now Pennell's aspiration.

Brittles is hampered when it comes to keeping rifles out of the hands of Red Shirt due to his orders to escort Olivia and Mrs. Allshard to the stagecoach stop at Sudro's Wells. He is too late when he arrives at Sudro's Wells, as the Indians have not only attacked the stage stop, but also killed Ma and Pa Sudro and left trooper John Smith mortally wounded. Looking at the area, Brittles pats his gun holster, commenting to Tyree, "It's about time I did retire." His mission is a failure.

Olivia apologizes to Brittles, admitting that this was all her fault, but he reminds her to never apologize, as it's a sign of weakness. Olivia protests, noting this was his last patrol, and she is to blame for its failure. "Only the man who commands can be blamed. Rests on me. Mission failure," he states as he kicks a wheel of the burning stagecoach in frustration, causing the entire carriage to collapse. He gently pats Olivia on the back before slowly walking away, attempting to lighten the moment by commenting, "Well, we missed the stage, Miss Dandridge."

Olivia, the spoiled daughter of an army officer, has enjoyed the comforts of Eastern civilian life. Those luxuries clash with the hardscrabble existence on the frontier that offers few, if any, creature comforts for a young woman. Major Allshard's comment that she is not "army enough to stay the winter" only illustrates that she is incapable of withstanding a hard winter with few amenities. Because of her pampered upbringing, Olivia inadvertently delays Brittles' chance to stop the Indians from gaining the rifles, leading to the deaths of Ma and Pa Sudro, and two children becoming orphans. Witnessing what her presence has caused awakens in her not only a responsibility but, like her aunt, Abby Allshard, a willingness to become a woman of the frontier and accept its beauty and harshness.

Returning to the fort, Brittles reports to Major Allshard that he failed to get the ladies on the stagecoach and failed to stop the gunrunners. "Failed at everything. Leave the army a failure," he says bitterly, before requesting permission to take the troop out after a short rest and relieve Cohill and his two squads. The major refuses, adding that Pennell will need all the daylight he can get to reach Cohill. Brittles explodes over the order of sending "that babe in the woods" to aid Cohill. Despite his retiring the next day, Brittles begs the major to give him that one day after forty years of being a good soldier. Allshard refuses, stating that Cohill and Pennell will have to run their chances, just like they had done. "That's what we get paid for," he reminds Brittles, who reluctantly understands. "Old soldiers, Miss Dandridge," he says to Olivia before walking out the door. "Someday you'll learn how they hate to give up. Captain of the troop one day, every man's face turned toward ya. Lieutenants jump when I growl. Now, tomorrow, I'll be glad if the blacksmith asks me to shoe a horse."

Nathan Brittles is a soldier without an army. A man without a purpose.

Walking out of his quarters on his last morning, Brittles sees Lieutenant Pennell and the men formed at attention before moving out. His reaction is pride mixed with sadness. When he is given the silver watch and reads the inscription, Brittles chokes up. Using the cover of removing his reading glasses to gain his composure, he softly mumbles his thanks to Pennell and the men. Summoning up his old demeanor, he orders Pennell to proceed on his mission, yelling good luck to the troop as he gallops off. It is a spirited leave-taking, suppressing his true feelings. As Brittles dismounts, his eyes are red, his body slower in its movements, drained from the emotion he has been hiding. Watching the troop leave the fort, he lightly touches the saber on his saddle, cradling the watch and its case in his left hand. Pennell, the last to ride out, turns to Brittles and salutes. Brittles stands at attention and returns the salute, his hand slowly falling as Pennell rides away.

Brittles will not go into retirement quietly. He has a few final hours left in the army, and will use them to correct his failure. Galloping into Cohill's bivouac, he hands the younger officer a written order ("might come in handy at our court-martial") before he and Tyree ride into the

Indian camp. It is a bold move, but Brittles sees it as a chance to stop a bloody war by attempting to reason with his old friend, Pony That Walks. The old man admits he has no power over the young warriors, who are emboldened by the death of Custer and the return of the buffalo, adding they are too old for war.

Brittles launches an alternate plan, leading the troop to charge into the sleeping Indian village and stampede the pony herd. Accomplishing his task, with no injuries to the troopers or the Indians, Brittles tells Cohill and Pennell that the lack of horses will force the Indian tribe to walk back to the reservation. "Walkin' hurts their pride. You watching will hurt it worse," he says. Looking at his new silver watch, it is two minutes past midnight. "Been a civilian for two minutes. It's your army, Mr. Cohill. Good luck," he says, saluting the younger officers before riding off.

However, the army has not written off Nathan Brittles. With the endorsement of President Grant and Generals Philip Sheridan and William Sherman, Brittles is appointed chief of scouts with a rank of lieutenant-colonel.[97]

Brittles has returned home—to his family and the army.

* * *

"When we did *She Wore a Yellow Ribbon*, he [Ford] gave me a cake with one candle on it," Wayne recalled to Peter Bogdanovich. "You see, I was just part of the family. He never thought of me as an actor, and then he saw *Red River*, and he wanted to top it, and he did. He gave me that part in *Yellow Ribbon*, where I play a sixty-five-year-old guy . . . I think it's the best thing I've ever done." (Wayne was forty-one when he shot the film.)

And the significance of the candle?

"Actor. I had finally arrived," Wayne replied.[98]

Makeup artist Don Cash used old-fashioned makeup techniques to age Wayne to a man of sixty-five. Aside from graying Wayne's temples and the actor's own mustache with Max Factor's hair whitener, a section of gray hair was sewn into the front of his toupee. To complete the rest of the look, Cash relied on the traditional application of highlights and shadows to subtly suggest aging. As good as an age makeup can be, it is the actor who must convince the audience that he is an older man. From little touches like rubbing his arthritic knuckles against the cold or stretching out his left leg before leaving his quarters, Wayne indicates an advancing age without exaggerating the point.[99] His Captain Brittles can be a stern taskmaster, such as when he admonishes Cohill and Pennell for almost coming to blows over Olivia. ("The officer to whom I'm surrendering command of this troop in two more days, should have so little grasp of leadership as to allow himself to be chivvied into a go at fisticuffs, while 'Taps' still sound over a brave man's grave. God help this troop when I'm gone!") His words and demeanor are enough to shame and intimidate the two younger men, who realize he's right.

Yet Wayne also shows us a softer side to Brittles, notably at his wife's grave. He plays this moment perfectly, as speaking to his deceased wife illustrates the character's warmth and loneliness. There is nothing contrived about this intimate moment, and when it came to filming this scene, Wayne said Ford gave "me plenty of leeway. He kept the noise to a minimum on the set, and we quietly went in and shot the scene." Wayne said that Ford watched his work to make sure this sequence "didn't get overly sentimental."[100]

Another moment that is beautifully played by Wayne is when he receives his silver watch. This scene demonstrates Wayne's subtle ability to infuse his character's emotion without becoming mawkish. Exiting his quarters, the smile on Brittles' face slowly fades when he sees the assembled troop, realizing this is his last time to review the cavalry. He turns slightly, his back to the men as he buttons his jacket, as well as checking his emotions. Addressing the troop, Brittles is all business, yet this demeanor changes when he is presented the watch. He glances around, with a touch of embarrassment, before taking out a pair of glasses to read the inscription. ("To Captain Brittles. From C Troop. Lest We Forget.") As he starts to read aloud, Brittles sniffs, and you sense he is holding back tears. As he reads "Lest we forget," Wayne's voice lightly quivers, and he sniffs again before clearing his throat. Wayne stated that Ford, especially in this scene, would try to inject a bit of lightness into a sentimental scene, "to take the edge off." By having Brittles reach for his glasses and look around to see if anyone was watching, Ford gave the scene a brief touch of humor before hitting the audience with Brittles' emotional moment. Ford once commented that when it came to a sentimental scene, one should "play it straightforward. Don't be ashamed of it."[101]

John Wayne gives one of his finest performances as Captain Brittles. He can be affable at times, yet there is an underlying sense of loneliness and heartache throughout. The latter is evident in the scene where he marks off the week in red crayon on his last day, before committing that month's calendar page to the fire burning in the woodstove. The gesture displays the man's resignation to his fate, frustrated that his age is forcing him out of a job he can still perform.

Wayne would receive his first Oscar nomination for Best Actor for his performance in *Sands of Iwo Jima*, released the same year as *She Wore a Yellow Ribbon*. Wayne once mistakenly stated that he had been nominated for his work in Ford's film, not the war film. Perhaps it was wishful thinking on his part, as his Brittles performance was much more nuanced. Wayne was very proud of his performance in this film, later stating that his work "turned out to be, I think, the best acting job I've done." More than twenty years after the film's release, John Ford simply stated, "I still think it's Duke's best performance. He was great in it."[102]

Victor McLaglen's Quincannon is the epitome of a burly Irish sergeant in the US Cavalry. (Nugent's brief description of the character was "half-horse, half-alligator.") McLaglen adroitly displays his talent for comedic situations, most notably when he asks, "Whose dog is this?" or his escapade in the sutler's store.

Ben Johnson is nothing short of perfect as Tyree. Despite this being his first major role, Johnson delivers his dialogue with an easygoing style, something that would serve him well in his fifty-three-year career. When it came to directing Johnson, Ford treated him gently, and he was never "in the barrel."[103]

As the rival officers, John Agar and Harry Carey Jr. play their parts equally well, given the limited material they had to work with. Joanne Dru supplies the right amount of annoying coquettishness in teasing both young officers who vie for her affection. Yet, her character does come around to understand what it means to "be army." Everyone else in the film, from Mildred Natwick and George O'Brien to the smaller parts, provide solid performances. Despite the fractious relationship with his older brother Francis, Ford commented that his brother's performance "always paid off."

She Wore a Yellow Ribbon is a visual feast of Technicolor at its best. While audiences were familiar with Monument Valley from Ford's previous films, this time he unveils the location in all its beauty, with the rich hues of the land and its sunrises and sunsets. (Ford not only knew the valley well, but also what times of day were optimal to photograph certain locations.[104]) Winton Hoch was one of the premiere Technicolor cinematographers who never photographed a film or television show in black-and-white during his thirty-seven-year career.[105] His efforts in this film paid off, as he won the Oscar for best color photography, the film's only nomination.

Many historians and critics over the years have discussed Ford's use of broad humor in his films, with some feeling his affection for this style of comedy often hurt or detracted from his work. Critics are divided over the fight sequence between Quincannon and the soldiers in the sutler's store. A majority feel the fight is too broad and overextended, hurting the film's tempo, while others believe the entire scene works and doesn't impair the film's pacing. (It is possible that Ford felt this sequence was another way of "taking the edge off" the emotional scene of Brittles receiving his watch and subsequent departure.) Ultimately, it is left to the viewer to make the final decision, and the lion's share seem to enjoy the sequence, adroitly enhanced by Hageman's score.

The only gag that lacks a strong payoff comes at the end of the brawl when the blacksmith, Wagner (Mickey Simpson), slowly walks backwards (holding his sledgehammer) and sits on a bench with a stunned look. Unlike the others who literally get punched out the door, Wagner's actions fall flat in comparison. Originally, Wagner was supposed to get hit by Quincannon and fall headfirst into a barrel of flour, but Ford changed the action to Quincannon taking a swing at Wagner, who walks back slowly and just sits down without moving. Had there been a shot of Wagner being hit and then walking backwards, this likely would have translated better than it does.

She Wore a Yellow Ribbon is unlike other Ford films that had a well-rounded plot with a definitive beginning, middle, and end. Instead, with this film Ford has created a lyrical cinematic ballad with various vignettes (the Indian uprising and the romantic triangle) around the main thread of an aging military officer's remaining days. Wayne once said that Ford "told his feelings through people," and it is certainly true in this film. While it contains many light moments, the underlying theme is one of change, the old making way for the new. However, the tradition of the army will remain despite the passing seasons. Throughout the film Ford uses moments to subtly remind the viewer of this, whether it's Brittles crossing out another day on his calendar, his joy at sharing the sight of buffalo with younger officers, or receiving his silver watch. They all add up to a sense of time rapidly moving on. It is never easy for one who has devoted several decades to their job to step aside and relinquish it to a new generation. The character of Captain Nathan Brittles allowed Ford to present a compelling argument that experienced older individuals are still an important asset to any industry, and pushing them aside is unthinkable.[106]

With *She Wore a Yellow Ribbon*, Ford once again celebrates the honor and courage of the cavalry in a far-off Western fortress, but also reminds the audience of the importance of the man who leads them.

SHE WORE A YELLOW RIBBON

Argosy Pictures–RKO Radio Pictures. *Released:* October 22, 1949. *In production:* October 26, 1948, to November 30, 1948, thirty-one days. *Producer:* Merian C. Cooper. *Director:* John Ford. *Screenplay:* Frank S. Nugent, Lawrence Stallings, based on the short stories "War Party" and "The Big Hunt" by James Warner Bellah. *Cinematographer:* Winton Hoch. *Second Unit Cinematographer:* Archie Stout. *Editor:* Jack Murray. *Assistant Editor:* Barbara Ford. *Art Director:* James Basevi. *Set Decorator:* Joe Kish. *Musical Score:* Richard Hageman. *Musical Director:* Lucien Cailliet. *Choral Director:* Jester Hairston. *Sound:* Frank Webster, Clem Portman. *Sound Effects:* D. Pat Kelley. *Assistant Director:* Wingate Smith. *Second Assistant Director:* Edward O'Fearna. *Second Unit Director:* Cliff Lyons. *Production Manager:* Lowell Farrell. *Wardrobe:* Michael Meyer (men's), Ann Peck (women's). *Makeup Artists:* Don L. Cash, David Sadler, Joe Bonner, Abe Haberman, Ed Voight. *Hairstylists:* Anna Malin, Joan St. Oegger, Lillian Shore, Katherine Duter, Rudy Filper, Annie Hodges,

Mandlee McDougall. *Body Makeup Artists:* Myrna Gade, Helen Taylor. *Props:* Jack Golconda. *Set Dressing:* Joseph Kish. *Camera Operator:* Harvey Gould. *Dolly Grip:* Tom Clement. *Still Photographer:* Alexander Kahle. *Special Effects:* Jack Caffee, Daniel Hays. *Special Photographic Effects:* Jack Cosgrove. *Second Unit Camera Operator:* Charles Boyle. *Gaffer:* Robert Campbell. *Wardrobe Researcher:* D. R. O. Hatswell. *Script Supervisor:* Meta Stern. *Military Technical Advisor:* Major Philip Kieffer, US Army (Ret'd). *Set Accordionist:* Danny Borzage. *Armorer:* Barlow Simpson. *Running Time:* 104 minutes. *Budget:* $1,851,290.20. *Domestic Rental Gross:* $2,530,142.77. Rereleased in 1955. *Working Title: War Party.*

Filmed at RKO-Pathé Studios, Culver City, California. Goulding's Trading Post, Monument Valley. Mexican Hat, Utah.

Cast

John Wayne (*Captain Nathan Brittles*), Joanne Dru (*Olivia Dandridge*), Ben Johnson (*Sgt. Tyree*), John Agar (*Lt. Flint Cohill*), Harry Carey Jr. (*Lt. Ross Pennell*), George O'Brien (*Major Mac Allshard*), Victor McLaglen (*Sgt. Quincannon*), Mildred Natwick (*Mrs. Abby Allshard*), Arthur Shields (*Dr. O'Laughlin*), Noble Johnson (*Red Shirt*), Chief John Big Tree (*Pony That Walks*), Tom Tyler (*Cpl. Quayne*), Michael Dugan (*Sgt. Hochbauer*), Harry Woods (*Karl Rynders*), Rudy Bowman (*Trooper Smith, aka General Rome Clay, CSA*), Paul Fix, Peter Ortiz (*Gunrunners*), Francis Ford (*Connelly, Bartender*), Frank McGrath (*Cpl. Derice, Bugler*), Mickey Simpson (*Sgt. Wagner*), Fred Graham (*Sgt. Hench*), Fred Kennedy (*Trooper Badger*), Don Summers (*Cpl. Krumrein*), Ray Hyke (*Trooper McCarthy*), Bob Rose (*Fritz*), Cliff Lyons (*Trooper Cliff*), Fred Libby (*Sergeant*), William Steele, Dan White, Al Murphy (*Troopers*), Jack Pennick (*Sgt. Major*), Philip Kieffer, Jack Tornek, Post Park (*Officers*), Billy Jones (*Courier Trooper*), George Sky Eagle (*Chief Sky Eagle*), Evelyn Moriarty, Ruth Clifford (*Party Guests*), Irving Pichel (*Narrator*).

Stunts

Fred Graham, Frank McGrath, Fred Kennedy, Cliff Lyons, Bob Rose, Bryan "Slim" Hightower, Billy Jones, Post Park, Allen Lee.

Longtime assistant director and John Ford's brother-in-law, Wingate Smith, said he would never approach John Ford with a question if he was sitting in his director's chair by himself, as it meant he was working out a scene in his head. *Courtesy Lilly Library, Indiana University*

Merian C. Cooper looking at Willis O'Brien's creations for *King Kong*.

John Ford adjusts the hat strap on Henry Fonda while a wardrobe man uses a pounce bag to apply dust to the actor's costume.

John Wayne, stuntman Frank McGrath (dressed as an Apache), and Henry Fonda during a break in filming the climax for *Fort Apache*. *Joseph Musso Collection*

The tent city erected for cast and crew just below Goulding's Trading Post. *Joseph Musso Collection*

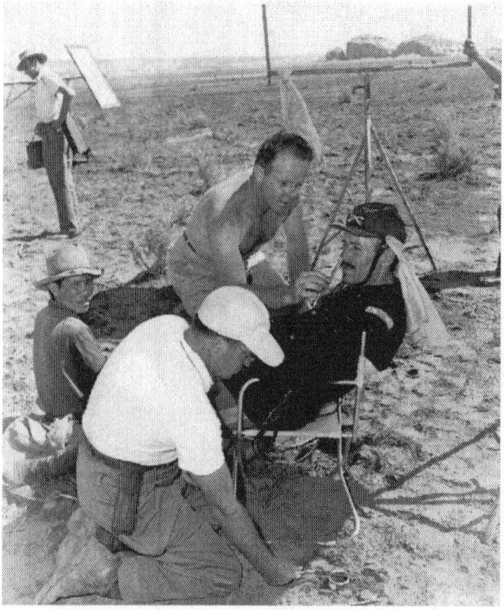

Makeup artists Emile LaVigne (kneeling) and Webster Phillips touch up Henry Fonda's mustache. LaVigne is using a Sterno can to heat a curling iron, which will then be used to style Fonda's mustache. *Courtesy Lilly Library, Indiana University*

Philip Kieffer (left), John Wayne, and Grant Withers (right) during a break in Monument Valley. Kieffer served as the military technical advisor on all three of Ford's cavalry films, as well as playing an officer. *Photo by Wilbur Braden, Courtesy Denise Slosar Collection*

Ford directing the scene between Colonel Thursday (Henry Fonda, back to camera) and Cochise (Miguel Inclán, center). Bob Many Mules stands behind and to the left of Cochise, and the two Stanley brothers stand to the right.

The exterior of Goulding's two-story trading post stood in for the Hassayampa stage stop in *Fort Apache*. Ford would use the trading post as the fort headquarters in *She Wore a Yellow Ribbon. Courtesy Lilly Library, Indiana University*

Whether on location or on a soundstage, John Ford always had a tea break in the late afternoon. Here, several cast members enjoy the respite on a soundstage at RKO-Pathé Studios in Culver City. Note the backdrop of the fort set in the background. Left to right: Anna Lee, Movita, Pedro Armendáriz, Irene Rich, and Shirley Temple.

Deleted scene of decorating Colonel Thursday's quarters. The chair, donated by Dr. Wilkens (Guy Kibbee), has collapsed under him as Mrs. Collingwood (Anna Lee, left) and Mrs. O'Rourke (Irene Rich, right) watch. Philadelphia (Shirley Temple) attempts to help the doctor, as Sergeant Beaufort (Pedro Armendáriz, in front of the fireplace) looks on. *Joseph Musso Collection*

Wayne, Ford, and Ben Johnson filming at Goulding's Lodge for *She Wore a Yellow Ribbon*.

Ben Johnson (left), Wayne, Ford, and assistant director Wingate Smith at Goulding's Lodge during the filming of the stagecoach sequence for *She Wore a Yellow Ribbon.*

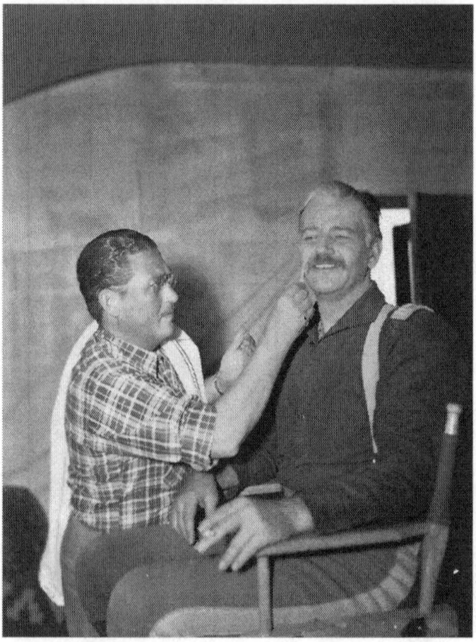

Makeup artist Don Cash applies hair whitener to Wayne's mustache to help age his character. *Joseph Musso Collection*

Navajo tribal members prepare to ride out to location from the company's tent city.

Lining up a shot of a large number of Indians riding past camera.

Deleted scene where Major Allshard (George O'Brien, left), Captain Brittles (Wayne), and Dr. O'Laughlin (Arthur Shields, right) examine the bullet from the dead paymaster as Indian agent Rynders (Harry Woods) looks on.

Another deleted scene where Wagner, the blacksmith (Mickey Simpson), presents a small bouquet of flowers for Brittles to place on his family's grave.

The land in any John Ford Western was as important as any performer. For his first Technicolor film shot in Monument Valley, Ford wanted to capture the color palettes found in the paintings of Frederic Remington and Charles M. Russell. This is one of the more stunning moments he captured on film, with the exception of the thunderstorm sequence.

When it came to riding a horse, no one could top Ben Johnson. Ford added the sequence of Tyree being chased by Indians because he loved watching Ben ride. The horse he is riding, Steel, is the same one he rode to win the rodeo world championship in team roping in 1953.

John Ford wanted to do a benefit show for the Military Order of the Purple Heart, and someone suggested a tabloid version of the stage play *What Price Glory*. Ford chose to mount the play in its entirety with an all-star cast. Rehearsals were held at the Masquers Club in Hollywood. From left to right: William Lundigan, Mike Ross, Gregory Peck, Harry Carey Jr., Ward Bond, Maureen O'Hara, Pat O'Brien, James Lydon, John Wayne, Larry J. Blake, and Jim Davis. Ford is seated in the audience on the far right with a cap on his head. Director Ralph Murphy stands in front of the stage.

Ford always preferred to have a camera mounted on a wooden tripod, harkening back to his days making silent movies. Here he is setting up a shot at White's Ranch in Moab, Utah, for *Rio Grande*. Songwriter/actor Stan Jones (right, in uniform) waits for the camera setup.

Stuntman Frank McGrath doubled for J. Carrol Naish as General Sheridan. *Joseph Musso Collection*

Lunch break in Professor Valley outside of Moab, Utah. Sitting at the table, from left to right: Claude Jarman Jr., Victor McLaglen, Steve Pendleton, Philip Kieffer, John Wayne, Ben Johnson, and Harry Carey Jr. (partially obscured).

Rio Grande marked Patrick Wayne's acting debut. He was hired by his godfather, John Ford, who paid him ten dollars a day to play one of the children in the fort. Working on this film was very special for Patrick, as he got to spend so much time with his father.

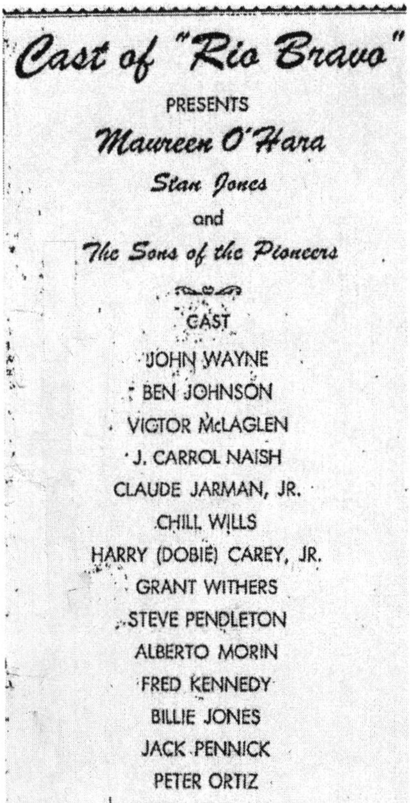

Cast of "Rio Bravo"

PRESENTS

Maureen O'Hara

Stan Jones

and

The Sons of the Pioneers

CAST

JOHN WAYNE
BEN JOHNSON
VICTOR McLAGLEN
J. CARROL NAISH
CLAUDE JARMAN, JR.
CHILL WILLS
HARRY (DOBIE) CAREY, JR.
GRANT WITHERS
STEVE PENDLETON
ALBERTO MORIN
FRED KENNEDY
BILLIE JONES
JACK PENNICK
PETER ORTIZ
DON SUMMERS
DON HATSWELL
LEE BRADLEY and his NAVAJOS

IN A BENEFIT SHOW FOR THE
MOAB LIONS CLUB CHRISTMAS FUND

Three Nights

MONDAY, TUESDAY, WEDNESDAY
June 26-27-28
8:00 p.m.

High School Auditorium
MOAB, UTAH

Prices: Adults, $1.00; Children Under 15, 50c

NO TICKETS WILL BE SOLD AT DOOR FOR MONDAY AND TUESDAY SHOWS

Reserved Tickets for These Nights Will Be on Sale at Booth on Main Street Saturday, Monday and Tuesday

Advertisement in the Moab *Times-Independent* newspaper for the benefit show Ford staged while on location. Tickets sold out for all three nights.

Rex Allen (left) watches as John Wayne and Shug Fisher (of Sons of the Pioneers) perform in front of a live audience in Moab for Allen's CBS radio show. *Joseph Musso Collection*

Stuntman Cliff Lyons making the transfer from his horse to the wagon, with Essie White (wife of George White) doubling Maureen O'Hara. Just behind the bench seat is a stuntman handling the lines, known as "blind driving." *Courtesy Moab Museum*

Stuntman Fred Kennedy grabs on to the pole held by stuntman Chuck Roberson. The camera is behind Kennedy's back, and as he grabs the pole and falls down it appears he was stabbed with a spear. *Courtesy Lilly Library, Indiana University*

The cinematic chemistry between Wayne and Maureen O'Hara was captured so beautifully in this scene with few words of dialogue. *Courtesy Lilly Library, Indiana University*

Intermission

I had nothing to do with it.

—JOHN FORD

DURING THE MAKING OF *SHE WORE A YELLOW RIBBON*, FORD MENTIONED that he wanted to do some form of a benefit show for the Military Order of the Purple Heart. Someone on the set suggested staging a tabloid version of the World War I stage play *What Price Glory* by Maxwell Anderson and Laurence Stallings (one of the writers for *She Wore a Yellow Ribbon*).[1] Ford decided to stage the entire play, including the profanity spoken by various characters, featuring an all-star cast supported by well-known character actors. Harry Carey Jr., who appeared in the production, remembered Ford asked him to have his neighbor Gregory Peck call him. "I went to Peck's house after I left Ford's office and I said, 'Jack Ford wants you to call him.' You have to remember that he was the biggest star in pictures at the time, along with John Wayne. Peck got like a little kid and called Ford and was put in the play. He thought Ford wanted him for a picture."[2]

For the leading roles of the quarreling Marines, Flagg and Quirk, Ford chose his favorite whipping boy, Ward Bond (making his theatrical debut), and Pat O'Brien, while Maureen O'Hara was chosen as Charmaine, the French girl, whom the two officers fight over. Harry Carey Jr. felt O'Hara was not suited for the role of Charmaine. "She looked so fresh and beautiful," Carey noted, "and the humor of the play centers around the fact that she [Charmaine] was a hooker and these two guys fall in love with a beat-up dame. Maureen was *anything* but beat-up."[3] The rest of the cast included John Wayne (also making his theatrical debut), Forrest Tucker, Ed Begley, George O'Brien, Wallace Ford, Robert Armstrong, Harry Carey Jr., Larry Blake, Charles Kemper, Jimmy Lydon, Jim Davis, Luis Alberni (who appeared in the original Broadway play), Fred Graham, and, in a rare solo performance without his comedy partner, Oliver Hardy.

All Hollywood studios agreed to cooperate with the stage production, adjusting the work schedules of their stars and supporting players in order to attend the nightly rehearsals. Pat O'Brien claimed only somebody like Ford could have gotten the project off the ground, with all the parties involved donating their time and effort. None of the actors took a salary, the sets were designed and built for free, and all of the costumes were donated by Western Costume. Auditions and rehearsals were held at the Masquers Club, a bastion of Hollywood history until it met the wrecking ball in 1985. The club, formed in 1925, was an actors' meeting place, similar to the famous New York actors' club, The Lambs.[4] Although he supervised the production, Ford did not direct the play; that task was left to Ralph Murphy, who had experience as a stage director before moving into films in the early 1930s.[5]

Harry Carey Jr. remembered, "Ford never once interfered with Murphy. Not a word. He'd sit out in the audience and never said a word, but was at every rehearsal. Murphy gave a little speech before we went on, sort of a pep talk. He would turn to the Old Man and ask if he wanted to say anything, but he never did. As far as direction, he would always claim he knew nothing about stage direction. He loved the stage. He was fascinated with it."[6]

The final dress rehearsal was held on February 21, 1949, at the Masquers Club, before an audience of 450 invited guests, including more than 80 paraplegic war veterans and their wives, and Secretary of the Navy John Sullivan. Before the performance, James Stewart explained how the play's proceeds would be used to help the disabled veterans. The following night, February 22, *What Price Glory* opened in Long Beach. The next day cast and crew left from the Glendale train station for three Northern California cities (San Jose, Oakland, and San Francisco) before returning to engagements in Pasadena and Los Angeles.

Audiences were enthralled by seeing so many stars on one stage at one time. "The audience went wild when the whole cast came down in one [line] to take a bow," recalled Larry Blake. Harry Carey Jr. echoed those remembrances. "The audience would just applaud when Ward [Bond] and [Pat] O'Brien came onstage. When [John] Wayne made an entrance, they'd just gasp. With Greg Peck it was like Frank Sinatra. He was such a heartthrob; the girls would just start squealing when he came onstage." Film historian and biographer John McCabe said James Cagney told him that Oliver Hardy supplied the biggest laughs of the whole play. "It was the funniest thing I think I have *ever* seen," Cagney recalled. "Roland Winters and I had to hang onto each other, we were laughing so much."[7]

After their presentation at the Pasadena Civic Auditorium, the final performance was scheduled for the Philharmonic Auditorium in downtown Los Angeles. However, the company faced a problem that befell the producers of the original stage version: the profanity used by the characters. The governing board of the Philharmonic Auditorium insisted that all shows must conform with its religious standards, and suggested the play stick to the 1927 film script, which Ford flatly refused. (Ironically, the 1927 silent film gave audiences a shock when they read the actors' lips as they hurled profanities at each other.[8]) The controversy did not end there. Jimmy Fidler, a well-known gossip columnist and host of a popular radio show in Los Angeles, attacked not only the charity presentation of the play, but the Masquers Club and Ford personally for the use of profanity, and urged his listeners to boycott the production. This brought a stinging reply from actor Alberto Morin, himself a distinguished war veteran and member of the OSS in World War II. As a member of the play's cast, Morin publicly chided Fidler's remarks as "fatuous, smug, and hypocritical." As the company prepared for the March 1 Pasadena date, they were still without a theater in Los Angeles. The Paramount Theatre on Hollywood Boulevard was offered to the production, but the dressing rooms were deemed too small.[9] Finally, an agreement was made to stage the final performance at the famous Grauman's Chinese Theatre on Friday, March 11.

The play was very successful, earning over $47,000, but according to Harry Carey Jr., all of the money disappeared shortly after the final performance at the Chinese Theatre. "The guy who handled all the money for the production ran off with all the receipts," Carey recalled. "People asked Jack if they should go after the fella and Jack said, 'No. He'll be looking over his shoulder the rest of his life.' "[10] (The Military Order of the Purple Heart association wound up receiving $4,202.84—$54,217.70 in 2023 dollars—which Carey believed came out of Ford's own pocket.)

There had been discussions about taking the play to New York or Washington, DC, for a week, but nothing came of it. A substantial reason for the play disbanding was due to many of the actors having conflicting schedules, while another reason might have been related to Ford himself. Between the problems with the Philharmonic Auditorium and the theft of the box office receipts, Ford appeared to have lost interest. "By the time we hit the Chinese Theatre," Larry Blake recalled, "Ford's enthusiasm had waned. Everyone else really wanted to continue, but he wasn't as keen on it [the play] as he was originally."[11]

* * *

Merian Cooper wanted to make one more ape film.

He pitched a story to RKO about a young woman, Jill (Terry Moore), living in Africa who raises a baby gorilla she names Mighty Joe. The ape grows to gargantuan size (much like King Kong), and a showman, Max O'Hara (played by *Kong* alumni Robert Armstrong), thinks he'd make the perfect attraction in his jungle-themed restaurant in Los Angeles.[12] Of course, Joe goes on a rampage, destroying the restaurant, and is finally caught and sentenced to be killed. Jill, with the aid of Gregg (Ben Johnson) and O'Hara, helps Mighty Joe escape. As an orphanage burns, it is Mighty Joe who saves the children, proving he is no menace to society. Jill, Gregg, and Mighty Joe happily return to Africa in the final fade-out.

Mighty Joe Young (1949) was Argosy's fourth film under their RKO agreement. Willis O'Brien and his young protégé, Ray Harryhausen (working on his first film), were hired to handle all the stop-motion effects, with live-action filming taking place between December 1947 and March 1948. Released in July 1949, the film did reasonably well, earning $3.25 million worldwide, but it wasn't enough to relieve Argosy's financial albatross with RKO and the banks. While John Ford was credited as presenting the film along with Cooper, he had nothing to do with the production. Hardly enthused with Cooper's adolescent fantasy story, whenever Ford was asked about the movie in later years, he sharply stated, "I had nothing to do with it."[13]

Having read a book about the Boers' desire to seek an area in South Africa they could call their own, Patrick Ford mentioned it to his father as a potential project. While his father found the subject interesting, he also recognized that the reality of turning the xenophobic Boers into caring characters shot down any possibility of making the story into a movie.[14] Still intrigued with the basic idea, Ford and his son discussed fashioning the story into the Mormons' search for their own land.[15] Patrick Ford and Frank Nugent developed the script, titled *Wagon Master*, which follows two young cowboys (Ben Johnson and Harry Carey Jr.) who hire on to lead a wagon train of Mormon settlers to the San Juan Valley of Utah. Along the way, they encounter a stranded medicine show and confront the murderous Clegg family before getting the Mormons to their beloved valley.

Wagon Master (1950) would be Argosy's last film under their RKO contract. Once again, the company turned to Bankers Trust for another loan in the amount of $650,000. In order to secure the loan, Argosy had put up all their films as collateral. (The only exception was *3 Godfathers*, which MGM owned.)

Budgeted at $999,370, Ford's shooting schedule was a tight thirty days, split between locations in Moab, Utah, and interior work at RKO-Pathé Studios. *Wagon Master*, although well received by many critics, performed modestly at the box office, earning roughly $1 million. One of the film's drawbacks—from a box office and marketing point of view—*Wagon Master* offered no major stars for marquee attraction, thus relegating it to "B" picture status in theaters. (Ben Johnson, Harry Carey Jr., and Ward Bond were the leads.) RKO promoted the film by relying on Ford's name, just as they had done with *The Fugitive*. Movie posters and newspaper ads trumpeted the film as "John Ford's lusty successor to *Fort Apache* and *She Wore a Yellow Ribbon*." Unfortunately, *Wagon Master* did nothing to ease Argosy's heavy debt.

Like other filmmakers who chose the independent route, Ford and Cooper came to realize that artistic freedom came with a very high price tag. By the early 1950s, according to RKO's accounting books, *She Wore a Yellow Ribbon* had earned $4 million worldwide, including a 1955 reissue release. Argosy's profit turned out to be a paltry $13,000.[16]

Rio Grande

You have chosen my way of life. I hope you have the guts to endure it.
—Lt. Col. Yorke (John Wayne)

Wagon Master concluded Argosy's contract with RKO. The studio, which Howard Hughes purchased in 1948, never made overtures to strike a new deal, nor did Cooper and Ford express interest in remaining there.

Cooper did reach out to Louis B. Mayer at MGM about possibly setting up shop at the Culver City lot, but Mayer declined. With nothing on the horizon, Ford went back to work at 20th Century-Fox. In order to get the studio to loan out Henry Fonda for *The Fugitive*, Ford had promised Darryl F. Zanuck he would make a picture for him. Zanuck handed him the script to *Pinky* (1949), centering around a light-skinned Black woman who passes as white and works as a nurse. Jeanne Crain played the lead role, with Black actress Ethel Waters playing her grandmother. A week into filming, Ford left the picture, with the studio claiming Ford had become ill and his absence necessitated a replacement. The truth was that Ford did not like working with Ethel Waters, and couldn't use his usual directorial tactics to get a performance out of her. It didn't help matters that Waters held an unconstrained dislike toward the director, and white men in general. Zanuck replaced him with Elia Kazan, and a few weeks later assigned Ford to direct *When Willie Comes Marching Home*, a wartime comedy with Dan Dailey.

Meanwhile, Argosy Pictures drifted aimlessly.

* * *

Republic Pictures had established itself as Hollywood's dominant "B"-picture studio, producing numerous Westerns (featuring a few singing cowboys), crime melodramas, and serials, with stars like Roy Rogers, Dale Evans, Gene Autry, Monte Hale, Rex Allen, Allan "Rocky" Lane, and John Wayne. Lacking the critical prestige of the major studios, Republic made up for it at the box office, understanding what appealed to their core audience and giving it to them in bulk. Republic budgets were lean, ranging from $50,000 for a quickie seven-day shoot to $200,000 for a fourteen-day production. The studio's backlot of Western streets, city and residential blocks, jungle and lake, as well as several stages, was in constant use. One makeup artist claimed the only days off he had were Sundays, Fourth of July, Thanksgiving, and Christmas.[1]

Herbert Yates was a salesman for the American Tobacco Company before associating himself with Hedwig Laboratories, a film-processing company for the emerging film industry. In 1924, Yates began his own film-processing business, Consolidated Film Industries (CFI), becoming one of the industry's busiest film labs.[2] While running his processing lab, Yates had his eye on the production end of the film industry, and eventually merged six Poverty Row companies into one company—Republic Pictures—in 1935.[3] Mascot Pictures had leased space on the recently built Mack Sennett Studio lot in Studio City, with an option to buy the property. Once the merger was completed, Mascot executive Nat Levine transferred the lease to Yates, who purchased the property.[4]

Like other smaller studios or production companies, Yates had always longed to compete with the major studios. He once asked John Wayne what it would take to get John Ford to work at Republic, which resulted in Wayne mentioning to Merian Cooper that Yates was interested in talking about a possible deal. The producer went to meet with Yates, who brushed him off, not knowing Cooper's background in the business. "Yates called Ford and asked who the hell he sent over. Ford hung up on him," Wayne recalled.[5] Wayne drafted an agreement that gave Argosy 15 percent of the box office *gross*, and no restrictions on the budget, which Yates signed.

A group had gathered at Ford's home on Odin Street in Hollywood to play bridge, and Wayne pulled Ford aside to show him the deal, signed by Yates. Ford glanced at it, wadded up the paper, and said, "Let's play bridge."

"He never answered me. Not a goddamned thing!" Wayne related years later. "When they [Cooper and Ford] went back over there, he [Yates] beat 'em down to where they didn't have anything. God, it was sad!" Listening to the audio recording of the interview conducted by Dan Ford, one can hear the frustration in Wayne's voice, emphasized by his hand pounding the table. Wayne always believed that Ford never mentioned the deal to Cooper. "If he had, he'd [Cooper] have been sitting on Yates' doorstep the next morning," he said. For the rest of his life, Wayne believed Ford resented him making a deal on his behalf. Ford's "Irishness" got the better of him, blinding his judgment on a strong deal.[6]

* * *

Argosy and Republic Pictures officially signed a nonexclusive contract on January 4, 1950, which called for the company to deliver no more than three films, all directed by Ford, over the next two years. Yates stated in a press release that the agreement "was no sudden decision," adding that he and Argosy had been "thinking about the merger for a long time." In later years, Ford claimed the reason they left RKO and signed with Republic was for "a better deal. More money, more liberty, more freedom." The reality was that no other studio was knocking on Argosy's door with a more lucrative contract. (By now, Argosy had trimmed much of their staff and let lapse any options on other scripts and books.)

The agreement stipulated that no project could exceed a budget of $1.25 million and could run no longer than 111 minutes, as Yates firmly believed no audience would sit through a film longer than two hours. The contract did allow Ford to maintain final cut approval, something he had lost at RKO on *Wagon Master*. However, Republic reserved the right to change anything for foreign distribution or make any cuts the Production Code Administration deemed necessary. Unlike the deal Wayne had gotten for Ford, Argosy would only get 50 percent of the *net* profits. The studio would fully fund and maintain ownership of the pictures. (Not having to worry about funding a film was the only bright spot in this deal for Argosy.) The contract also stipulated that either party could cancel the agreement after the first picture, so it was incumbent on Ford to make the first film a winner at the box office.

One of the main reasons Ford agreed to the Republic deal was that he would finally be able to produce his dream project, *The Quiet Man*. However, Yates was notoriously tight with a dollar, demanding Ford's first film be a Western; if it was successful, then he could go ahead with *The Quiet Man*. Yates believed the box office profits from the Western would cover the cost of Ford's Irish film, which he had little faith in.

* * *

Setting up offices at Republic, Ford chose another story by James Warner Bellah for their first project. "Mission with No Record," another cavalry story set in the Southwest, focuses on Colonel Massarene, a ramrod officer who tolerates no soldier that slacks in his duties, including his son, Donald, who failed mathematics and was dismissed from West Point. The son joined the army the next day as a regular, winding up at his father's post. Father and son have not seen each other for nearly fifteen years, the result of his wife leaving him over his devotion to military duty.

The area under Massarene's command has been hit hard by raids from the Apache, who cross over into Mexico for sanctuary. Washington politics forbids the military to cross the border and attack the marauders. General Sheridan gives Massarene a personal order to cross the Rio Grande River and go after the Apaches. "I'm tired of hit and run and diplomatic hide and seek," the general states. "Cross the border and burn 'em out, and to high hell with the Department of State!" Sheridan assures the colonel that he and President Grant will take personal responsibility in Washington, adding that the colonel is to "smash 'em" like Colonel Mackenzie had done.[7]

The cavalry moves out, with only Massarene and Lieutenant Topliff knowing the details of the mission. Arriving at Corinth Wells, they find homes burned and women's bodies lying in the front yard. A young girl, "her mind gone completely," pleads for a drink of water and someone to "tell me a funny story." Massarene orders Lieutenant Cohill to take up the pursuit, but the Apaches have already crossed the Rio Grande. Massarene and the rest of the troop arrive at the riverbank in the evening, and inform the soldiers they will cross the river and go into Mexico. "I'm burning everything in my path," he states. Massarene assures them he is operating under orders from General Sheridan, and they do not need to worry about "the consequences of tonight's work."

The attacks come down "like an avalanche from darkness, leaving nothing behind but the wail of savage women" as the soldiers burn seven villages. The last attack takes place at a Mexican chapel, where the Apaches have taken refuge. As one soldier's horse is shot out from under him, young Massarene rides up to rescue him, hauling him up onto the back of his horse before his horse is shot down. The two men land on the steps to the chapel, and Massarene's son fires his pistol, while his other arm is severely wounded. The colonel grabs the reins of a free horse and charges toward the chapel where his son and the other soldier climb onto the horse and gallop off. As they escape, the colonel is shot but stays in the saddle. With the attack a success, the cavalry heads back to the Rio Grande, with Massarene, his son, and Topliff the last to cross back into the United States. The colonel orders that Major Allshard take over command and his son see the surgeon about his arm. Young Massarene salutes his father who returns the gesture.

* * *

Instead of relying on Frank Nugent for this project, Ford turned to James Kevin McGuinness, a native Irishman, who first worked with Ford on *The Black Watch* (1929), and scripted the narration for Ford's *The Battle at Midway* (1942) documentary.[8] By 1931, McGuinness was supplying screenplays and original stories for MGM (*Tarzan and His Mate*, 1934; *China Seas*, 1935; *Men of Boys Town*, 1941), eventually moving into a producer's chair. A vehement anti-Communist, McGuinness was a member of the Motion Picture Alliance for the Preservation of American Ideals (MPA), a group founded by conservatives who were against any communist or fascist infiltration into the film industry, or America. Some believe McGuinness's strong political beliefs and ties to the MPA led to his dismissal at MGM by late 1949. This could be why Ford chose to reach out and help a friend when he needed the work.

McGuinness changed the name of the lead character from Massarene to Lieutenant-Colonel Yorke. In a one-page biographical sketch McGuinness details Yorke's military career, from his West Point graduation in 1858 to serving in the 6th US Cavalry under Colonel Robert E. Lee. In 1860, he married Genevieve (last name was left blank), who came from New Orleans, but remained in the South until after the war. Following the war, the Reconstruction years—and the Carpetbaggers—"only increased" the differences between Yorke and his wife. Through the influence of Mrs. Yorke's family, their son, Phillip Kirby Yorke, entered West Point.[9] McGuinness's script, written under the title *Rio Bravo*, added an important aspect to the film which was missing from Bellah's story: the relationship between Yorke and his estranged wife, Kathleen. McGuinness also included the characters of Pennell, Cohill, and Collingwood in the script, but they were not used in the film. (The characters of Cohill and Pennell do appear in Bellah's short story.)

Ford made numerous changes to McGuinness's script, more so than the previous cavalry films, by eliminating or trimming scenes and dialogue. In a few cases, Ford shot a completely different scene than what was in the script. During the editing process, Ford inserted scenes in a different part of the film from where they had appeared in the script.

McGuinness's description of the film's opening main titles sequence presents "picturesque shots of the cavalry column on the march. Background music sung by the Sons of the Pioneers." Ford does use various shots from the film of the cavalry on the move during the opening credits, but discarded the idea of using the Sons of the Pioneers, preferring to rely on Victor Young's score. As the "Directed by John Ford" credit appears, a bugler (Frank McGrath) rides up in front of a towering rock monument blowing the "Guard Mounting" call. (If this shot of the bugler looks familiar, it should; it was originally used in the opening credits of *Fort Apache*.)

McGuinness describes Colonel Kirby Yorke as "the personification of command—face grim and lined with fatigue; uniform dusty, but sits his saddle erect."[10] As the column returns to the fort, the script notes that the troopers in the first squad (composed of the Sons of the Pioneers) are "singing softly—much less volume than under the main titles—to keep up their own spirits and to pass the dreary time." After dismissing the troopers, Sergeant Major Quincannon informs the colonel that General Sheridan is waiting in the tent, before asking permission to join the troopers at the sutler's store. Yorke reluctantly consents, and Quincannon promises not to "abuse the privilege."[11]

Ford dropped the Sons of the Pioneers singing and all of the dialogue between Yorke and Quincannon; instead, Yorke walks to his tent when he sees the general's horse. Inside the tent, Yorke and Sheridan share some coffee as he relates the capture of Natchez, while most of his band crossed the Rio Grande River into Mexico. Yorke comments that three of his soldiers were killed, staked facedown on anthills. Sheridan acknowledges that he has the dirtiest job in the army, but the colonel replies he is not complaining, as he gets paid for it. "Maybe you should. I don't know," Sheridan says. Looking at his cup, Yorke comments that army coffee isn't as strong as it used to be. "I'll make a note of it," the general replies. "Maybe someday, it will get better and stronger." Learning from the general that his son failed at West Point comes as a surprise, leaving Yorke lost in thought for a brief moment, as he hasn't seen his son in fifteen years.

Both the script and the film segue to the introduction of new recruits who form a line in front of the fort's headquarters. The script has Quincannon calling out their names as Yorke observes them. When Jeff Yorke acknowledges his name, the script notes that Yorke's facial reaction reveals "he knows that this is his son," and includes reaction shots of Yorke and Jeff looking at each other, "holding their emotions in check." As Yorke tells the new recruits they face a life of hardship, the recruits show "great concern," realizing this undertaking "is more serious than anything they ever bargained for." Ford followed most of this material, adding veteran soldiers singing "You're in the Army Now" (from 1917!) as the recruits walk to their positions in front of Yorke's headquarters.

When Quincannon begins calling out names, Ford cuts to the interior of headquarters, showing Yorke and two captains examining a map before the camera returns to Quincannon, who calls out "Yorke" (in a deep echo). The camera pans to see Jeff as he replies (also in a deep echo), "Present, sir." Ford then cuts to the reaction of Yorke and his officers, as the colonel walks out to address the recruits.

After being dismissed by Yorke, the script details a US marshal stopping Quincannon and the recruits on the parade grounds, asking if there's anyone in this group from Texas. Boone introduces himself, saying, "Yes, sir, I'm from Texas! Name of Boone. Daniel Boone." The marshal hesitates, commenting that the name sounds kind of familiar, but says he's looking for a man named Tyree. The marshal is ushered off to the sutler's store as Quincannon tells the recruits, "Horse thieves we don't have here. Horsemen we'll make out of you yet." (Ford moved this scene to right after Tyree and Boone show off their skill at Roman riding.)

Both the film and the script have Jeff reporting to Yorke's tent, where his father states they haven't seen each other in fifteen years. "So I've been told, sir. I have no clear memory," Jeff replies. Yorke tells his son, "You have chosen my way of life. I hope you have the guts to endure it." Asking to speak, Jeff says he is not at the post to call him "Father," but came as Trooper Jefferson Yorke, adding, "That is all I wish to be."

As Jeff is dismissed, the script has Jeff walking out of the tent, where Quincannon asks the boy what got him called on the colonel's carpet so quickly. "I got born, Sergeant," Jeff replies. Ford trimmed a few lines of dialogue between Yorke and Jeff, eliminating the part between Quincannon and Jeff. Instead, he has Yorke walk over to where his son is standing and compare his height against his son's by making a pencil mark on the tent roof.

The script's version of the riding lesson begins with Tyree, Boone, and Jeff each jumping their mounts over a three-rail hurdle. For the next demonstration, Quincannon chooses Jeff to ride alongside him, as they run their horses and jump the hurdle. Tyree and Boone follow the example, and riding back to Quincannon, "they rise—Roman-fashion." (The script does not contain any Roman-riding sequence, which leads one to wonder if McGuinness's comment inspired Ford to create one.)

Ford's version of this sequence starts with troopers racing their horses around the track before jumping a six-foot hurdle. Quincannon then has a trooper mount two horses, standing with a foot on the back of each to demonstrate Roman riding, then asking Tyree if he'd like to give it a try. Boone and Tyree look at each other, run to the horses, and take off, standing on the backs of galloping horses and clearing the jumps. (Here is where Ford inserted the scene with the US marshal looking for Tyree.) Quincannon looks directly at Jeff, asking if he'd like to try Roman riding. Jeff quickly accepts the challenge, and notices his father watching as he walks to the horses. Hesitating for a moment, Jeff jumps on the mounts and gallops away, but coming to the hurdle, takes a hard fall to the ground.

Directly after the riding lesson, McGuinness wrote a scene involving an argument between Jeff and the overbearing German, Heinze. Mocking Jeff as the sergeant's pet, Heinze also speaks dismissively about the American cavalry, and Jeb Stuart and Sheridan ("Sheridan and Stuart—schoolboys playing at cavalry!"). Jeff asks Heinze to apologize, but the German just spits at him. Picking up a bucket of water, Jeff dumps it over Heinze, who challenges him to a fight.

Walking to the end of the picket line, they square off as Quincannon serves as referee. The script notes "Jeff is no match physically to the burly ex-Uhlan," as he gets knocked down three times.[12] Quincannon asks Jeff to call off the fight, but the boy refuses to give in. The contest of fisticuffs resumes until Yorke walks into the middle of it, questioning if this is a friendly boxing match. "Yes, sir, Colonel. Extremely friendly. A scientific test of skill," Quincannon replies. Jeff, Tyree, and Boone agree that it is a friendly match, while Heinze says nothing. Yorke is unable to "conceal a momentary flicker of pride" that his son is taking a beating "without whimpering." Telling them to carry on, he walks away.

The fight resumes and Jeff is knocked out. Quincannon, ordering Tyree to take Jeff to the hospital, walks over to Heinze and tells him it's the right hand he should be watching. Placing his left hand on Heinze's shoulder, Quincannon draws his right fist back and hits the German "with all the weight and knowledge of twenty-five years of barroom brawling." Heinze is knocked out cold, as Quincannon calls out, "Another man fer the sick tent."

As in the script, Ford goes to the fight after the Roman-riding scene. However, he has changed things, mainly eliminating the dialogue between Jeff and Heinze. Instead, this scene opens with Heinze landing backwards into a large bucket of water. Jumping up, Heinze and Jeff square off and the fight is more of a free-for-all scrimmage. Quincannon, stopping the fight, asks what started things, but Jeff refuses to speak. Tyree points to Heinze, saying the soldier "spoke real derogatory about the boy's pappy." Boone chimes in that Heinze called Jeff "the teacher's pet of a chowder-headed Mick sergeant. What's that mean, doc?" When Quincannon asks Heinze if he meant it, Ford has the two men deliver their dialogue at a clipped pace, providing humor to the moment.

Quincannon: "*Didja* say that?"

Heinze: "Yes I did."

Quincannon: "Ya did, *didja*?"

Heinze: "Yes I did."

Quincannon: "*Didja* mean it, *didja*?"

Heinze: "Yes I did."

Quincannon sets the fight for later that night. Then repeats to himself what Heinze said, only getting the words mixed up ("Chowder-faced . . . ") until he asks Boone to repeat it. Looking at Heinze, he asks the soldier one more time, "And ya meant it, *didja*?" He replies, "Yes, I did."

Ford cuts to the fight in progress, with Jeff getting the worst of it. The fight comes to a halt as Yorke walks in demanding to know what is happening. Quincannon says it's a soldiers' fight and refuses to answer what caused it. Both Jeff and Heinze also refuse to answer. Realizing he will not get any further, Yorke tells them to carry on, and strides out.

As Quincannon says they should continue the fight, Jeff turns to Heinze and the two men smile and shake hands. "Sorry, soldier," Heinze says, and Jeff apologizes.[13] Dr. Wilkins escorts Jeff to the hospital as Quincannon walks over to Heinze and, as in the script, hits Heinze, toppling him over.

Ford added a scene that takes place the following morning in the barracks. As Jeff wakes up, a bandage over his left eye, he sees Heinze, Tyree, and Boone smiling at him, proud of Jeff for proving his mettle. Yorke walks by the window and looks in just as Dr. Wilkins shoves a spoon into Jeff's mouth, with Jeff complaining, "Why, that's castor oil!" Ford concludes the scene with Yorke's reaction of mixed emotions.

When it came to introducing Kathleen Yorke, the script has her arriving with several supply wagons. Seeing a woman sitting on the seat of the first wagon, Dr. Wilkins exclaims, "Holy salt specific mackerel—a woman!" Yorke and Quincannon also look, the sergeant with "a look of apprehension" as he "blesses himself, as though in fear." Informed by Wilkins that unauthorized women are not permitted at the post, Kathleen states she has a signed letter from General Sheridan. Yorke steps in to handle things, and Kathleen "freezes" when she sees her husband. Walking to his tent they pass Quincannon, who Kathleen calls an arsonist, leaving the man "frozen in awe and fear."

Ford eliminated Wilkins entirely, as well as adding a few other modifications. We see Kathleen sitting next to the driver, Corporal Plunkett, who points to the colonel's quarters as he stops the wagon. Captain Prescott informs Kathleen that her visit is unauthorized. As Kathleen announces she is Trooper Yorke's mother and has a pass, Ford added a touch of humor to the scene. Reacting to Kathleen's identity, Plunkett covertly spits out his tobacco wad into his hand.

As she gets off the wagon, Ford cuts to a shot of Yorke and Quincannon recognizing her, before returning to a close-up of Kathleen's reaction. As Yorke and Quincannon walk toward the wagon, the sergeant blesses himself. Walking to his tent, Yorke and Kathleen pass Quincannon, who bows slightly and greets her with, "Welcome home, darling." Remarking that Yorke still has that arsonist with him, Ford reverts to a reaction shot of Quincannon, who has no clue as to the meaning of the word, believing it to be something appalling. Yorke reminds her that anything Quincannon did was under his orders, "reluctantly, I may add." Looking at Quincannon, Kathleen dubs him the reluctant arsonist and walks into the tent.

Once inside his tent, the script describes Yorke awkwardly moving things around as Kathleen remarks he is "as nervous now as the day we got married." Yorke replies, "Then it was desire. Now it could be guilt." Kathleen gets to the point of her visit: She wants to buy Jeff's release from the army. Yorke refuses, informing her that the boy took an oath, and adding that she still expects special privileges. His reply strikes a bitter nerve in her, as she replies, "I know we lost the war and our privileges. You helped destroy them. But you can't ever destroy what is best.

There will always be ladies and gentlemen—they will always live by a higher code than their fellows. You do, too—although you call your code 'duty.' It's only a difference in words, Kirby. The principle is the same." He wonders aloud if that is a compliment or an insult; Kathleen replies that it's a little of each.

Ford dropped all of this conversation, and, as they enter the tent, goes directly to Kathleen announcing her intention to buy her son's release. She admits Jeff was ashamed of failing at West Point, and she promises to get him a tutor after he is released, but Yorke points out that Jeff took an oath and must fulfill his duty. "Ramrod, wreckage, and ruin! Still the same Kirby!" she snaps. Yorke, with a slight smile, replies, "Special privilege for the special born. Still the same Kathleen." He also cautions that the release requires his signature, something he will not grant. Both the script and film then have Yorke asking her to dine with him that evening, which she accepts.

After he walks out, Kathleen opens a music box, playing "My Gal Is Purple." Listening to the tune, her demeanor softens for a moment, lost in her thoughts. (In the film, the music box plays "I'll Take You Home Again, Kathleen.") As they eat dinner in silence, the regimental singers arrive to serenade the couple. (The script had them singing "My Gal Is Purple," but Ford chose "I'll Take You Home Again, Kathleen.") Ford added dialogue that indicates the song has an emotional bond for them. Listening to the singers, Yorke uncomfortably admits this song was not his choice. "I'm sorry, Kirby," she replies wistfully. "I wish it had been." As the group finishes, Kathleen and Yorke go back inside the tent where he takes a blanket and bids Kathleen good night. She apologizes for disposing him of his quarters. "I disposed you more forcibly fifteen years ago," he replies.

The script went on to have Kathleen state that Bridesdale, her family's plantation, was rebuilt after the war, and Jeff will have a home there when he wants it. "Fortunate Jeff," Yorke replies as he walks out. (Ford dropped Kathleen's comment about rebuilding Bridesdale and Yorke's reply.) Kathleen begins clearing the table as Quincannon arrives, stomping his feet to announce himself. He states that the wives of the noncommissioned officers have offered to help her in any way, including laundry. She refuses the overture, but asks Quincannon to take her to her son. The sergeant declines, citing he is on guard duty. "Women I've never seen, who owe me nothing, offer me everything," she fires back. "But you, Sergeant, you owe me three burned barns. Burnt to the ground. My home seared and scarred. Slave quarters set to the torch. Hundreds of acres of crops blackened and destroyed. Horses and cattle driven away." Her comments weigh heavily on Quincannon, who finally agrees to her request. "Thank you, Sergeant. I was sure you'd be as gracious as a laundress," she replies.[14]

Ford kept Quincannon's approach to the tent, but eliminated all the dialogue about the women wanting to help and Kathleen's request to see Jeff. Instead, as the sergeant announces himself, Ford cuts to a shot of Yorke climbing into a wagon to sleep before returning to feature Quincannon and Kathleen walking toward Jeff's tent.

As they head to Jeff's tent, the script shows the Apache prisoners singing by three campfires in the stockade. It describes Natchez looking over Kathleen "with unabashed appraisal. Even under that grim, fixed face the nature of his thoughts is obvious." Ford shows Quincannon and Kathleen walking past the Apaches, as he tells another sergeant to make the Apaches stop singing before they continue on to Jeff's tent. The script has Jeff sitting in the tent with Tyree and Boone as his mother enters, and he introduces them before they walk out.

Ford decided to have Jeff, Travis, Boone, and Donnelly (played by his soon-to-be son-in-law, Ken Curtis) singing "Aha, San Antone!" inside the tent before his mother arrives.[15] As his friends leave, mother and son face each other for the first time since his dismissal at West Point. Jeff asks her what kind of man his father is; "Lonely," she replies. "A very lonely man." Responding to Jeff's comment that his father is a great soldier, she says, "What makes soldiers great is repugnant to me." When Jeff learns of her intention to buy his release, he refuses. "I'm gonna work this out my own way," he says.

Following Jeff's rejection, McGuinness has Kathleen using a "mother's charm" to change the subject ("softly, winningly reminiscent") by talking about their home and how the trees were heavy with leaves and green hills. Admitting this was his favorite time of year back home,

Kathleen ("pressing her advantage") goes on to say how his horse "whinnies incessantly, grieving for you." Realizing she is trying to win him over to leave, Jeff says it would be quitting, even refusing her offer to study at VMI (Virginia Military Institute) to get an officer's commission.[16] (Ford eliminated all of this.)

When it came to the Apaches attacking the fort to rescue Natchez, Ford generally followed the script's action, but again made a few alterations. The script has Quincannon holding Natchez and the other prisoners at gunpoint, but is jumped as "the rescuing braves ride and seize their captive brothers, lifting them onto their ponies." Instead, Ford shows a group of Apaches riding up to the stockade wall and pulling it down to free their fellow tribesmen. Another piece Ford eliminated concerned Dr. Wilkins. Having previously complained about the various bureaucratic forms he was constantly required to fill out (something Ford cut out), as the Apaches set numerous fires in the fort, Wilkins throws armloads of paperwork into a nearby blaze. The script has three separate shots of the doctor's actions (obviously for a comedic touch), building to the last one, where he expresses a "whooping joy."

Ford added shots of troopers coming out of their tents and firing rifles, a confused bugler blowing "Reveille," torched hay bales becoming a blazing fire and causing frenzied horses to jump a fence, and young Margaret Mary (in the script the character is named Maria Theresa; for clarity, I will refer to the character's name in the film) yelling frantically and running into the arms of Quincannon. Ford also added Boone and Tyree guiding Kathleen away from the tent as Jeff and others return fire at the fleeing Apaches. One warrior is shot off his horse in front of them, causing Kathleen to faint.

Learning his wife is not in his quarters, Yorke gallops to Jeff's tent where he finds his son helping Kathleen to her feet. After he orders him to take his mother back to his tent, Ford cuts to a Navajo scout (played by Lee Bradley, Ford's trusted Navajo interpreter) identifying the dead Apaches from three different bands (Mescalero, White Mountain, and Chiricahua). Yorke realizes the tribes have united, and unless the cavalry can stop them there will be an all-out war. Back at Yorke's tent, as he readies for field duty, Kathleen asks if she is under arrest for being out of bounds. "No, but we can't have the colonel's lady fainting every time there's a little shooting," he replies. Leaving his tent, Kathleen calls after him, hesitating to express her feelings. Instead, she takes his dress clothes with the intention of cleaning them. Mounting his horse, they share a silent look before Yorke moves the troop out.

Following the troop's departure, McGuinness included two sequences that were refashioned by Ford. The first one has the cavalry reaching the Rio Grande to witness the aftermath of a fight between the Apaches and the Mexican Rurales on Mexico's side of the river. Yorke, accompanied by his bugler and Captain St. Jacques, rides into the middle of the river (the international border line) where he speaks with the Mexican lieutenant. Yorke details their army doctor to render medical aid for the wounded Rurales as he tells the Mexican officer that Natchez is a "scourge to your country and mine." He offers to place himself and his men under the lieutenant's command to attack Natchez and his band, but the officer says his orders are to protect the Rio Bravo side.[17]

"It's criminal," Yorke states. "We're hamstrung by civilians a thousand miles away from danger, while our people on both sides of the river are being plundered and murdered." Yorke adds that he hopes one day the soldiers will be allowed to pick up this imaginary line "which separates our friendly people" and drop it thousands of miles south of the river. "I will salute that day," the lieutenant replies, heading back to his side of the river. Yorke orders the troop to bivouac at the river before returning to the fort the following morning as the scene fades out.

Ford retained most of the material between the lieutenant and Yorke, but deleted the comments about being hamstrung by civilian politicians and the soldiers moving the border line. Instead, he has Yorke salute the lieutenant's fidelity to duty and returns to his men as the cavalry doctor crosses the river to render aid. The scene then dissolves to the regimental singers singing "My Gal Is Purple" by a campfire as Yorke walks alone on the riverbank. (Ford moved this sequence to follow the scene in the hospital where Dr. Wilkins explains to Quincannon the meaning of the word "arsonist.")

The other scene reshaped by Ford has Quincannon and Wilkins walking to laundresses' row, where the wives of the noncommissioned officers handle the fort's laundry. Quincannon asks the doctor the meaning of "arsonist," and, learning the definition, states, "Divvil a penny did I make out of it." He goes on to reveal how Yorke ordered him to burn down Bridesdale during the Shenandoah campaign, thus explaining Kathleen's anger toward him.

Tyree, Jeff, and Boone are helping Kathleen, who is washing clothes, when Quincannon asks if he can help her. "It's rather late for you to be pouring water on anything, isn't it, Sergeant?" she replies, as a lieutenant and the US marshal approach Tyree. Placing Tyree under arrest, he goes quietly to await the return of Colonel Yorke to sign the legal papers. As others watch, Kathleen castigates "Yankee justice" for arresting a kind lad, while promoting "arsonists to be sergeant majors!" The comment is too much for Quincannon, who drops his clothes to the ground and "frantically dumps buckets of water into an empty tub."

As Ford shot the laundry scene, he eliminated the dialogue between the sergeant and doctor about the definition of an arsonist. Instead, Wilkins and Quincannon approach Kathleen, who offers to take the doctor's clothes. The doctor suggests she wash Quincannon's clothes first, who hesitantly gives her everything but one item—his long johns. The sergeant holds them behind his back until she grabs them from him. Examining the long johns, Kathleen puts her hands through two large holes in the seat. "As a doctor, I would diagnose those as saddle sores," Wilkins comments.

Ford follows the script, with the marshal taking Tyree into custody, along with Kathleen's statement about Yankee justice and insulting Quincannon. However, Ford changes Quincannon's response, giving it a more humorous touch. Upset at her words, Quincannon grabs a bucket and throws it in the river. As he sits down on the pier, Margaret Mary scolds him. Ford then cuts to Yorke and his troop on the move, giving a sense of time and distance before returning to Wilkins in the hospital, whittling a stick. It is here that Ford has Quincannon ask Wilkins the definition of an arsonist, after which he laughs heartily before describing Yorke's order. Stretching out his right hand, he yells that this was "the black hand that did the dirty deed! I wish you'd knock it off with that stick!" Without missing a beat, Wilkins whacks the stick over

Quincannon's hand, breaking it in two, before resuming his whittling of the remaining portion.

Another sequence Ford modified was Yorke's return to the fort. The script had Yorke entering his tent alone, with no evidence of Kathleen using it as her quarters. Quincannon approaches, announcing Kathleen, who enters the tent. She is described as "dressed with extreme care for this visit"; her shoulders "shine alluringly in the candlelight." Noting she has not made use of his quarters, he reminds her, "They're yours by right. You're still my wife." Kathleen replies, "I believe the politer novelists refer to my situation as 'wife in name only.'"

Frustrated by her comment, Yorke tells her she must obey his orders as the commanding officer, or he will remove her from the post. Kathleen informs him that she has bought an acre of land outside the post limits where she could set up a tent if she chooses. Admitting she is "the most provocative woman" he knows, Kathleen points out that "he acted as though you believed it once upon a time." Yorke grabs and kisses her, and she "neither resists nor assists." He stops, yet holds on to her. "The law gives you what it terms 'conjugal rights' over me," she says, since they're still legally married. Yorke replies that he never had any rights, only privileges.

As they walk back to her tent, Kathleen states, "I could never understand why you buried yourself out on these lonely frontier posts—where even the greatest heroism is as unnoticed as another grain of sand on the desert." Yorke tells her if she was standing where he is and looking at her, she'd understand. Kathleen hints that letting Jeff go might bring her back to him. He admits he could say yes very easily, but he also knows that Jeff needs to "learn that a man's word to anything—even his own destruction—must be honored."

Ford follows the basic outline of this scene, having Yorke return to his darkened tent, drinking from the water jug before lighting a lamp. Turning around, he sees Kathleen illuminated by the lamp. As she rises from a chair, Yorke grabs her around the waist, wheeling her to him as they kiss. Kathleen is slow to respond at first, but her emotions quickly take over. (This demonstrates Kathleen's growing softness toward Yorke, while the script continues to show her rigidness in their relationship.)

He suddenly stops and apologizes, leaving Kathleen conflicted. As Yorke escorts her to her tent, she expresses regret that his duty led to destroying two beautiful things—Bridesdale and their marriage. Yorke acknowledges that a reconciliation would require more than the physical work that rebuilt Bridesdale. Kathleen says a good start would be to let Jeff go. Asking if that would get her to return to him, she softly replies, "If that were a condition." Yorke is tempted, but states that Jeff has given his word and must honor it, no matter the ramifications. As she walks away, Sheridan arrives and asks Yorke for a cup of coffee.

Unlike in the film, the script had Sheridan's arrival taking place the following morning when Yorke lays out his plans. He will strip the fort by sending the women and children to Fort Beauregard under escort, and every soldier will be issued repeating rifles. Yorke suggests crossing the Rio Grande and venturing into Mexico to wipe out Natchez and his warriors. Sheridan declares he's forbidden to issue such an order, even though Yorke is willing to be court-martialed. McGuinness then inserted a sequence where Quincannon informs Kathleen that the general has requested her presence at dinner.

The following scene takes place in Yorke's tent. The meal is already in progress as Sheridan toasts President Grant. He then requests Yorke to "favor them with a sentiment." Raising his glass, the colonel declares, "To the men who live with sweat, dirt, and blood. The men who daily save an empire worth more than Europe for the price of a pint of whiskey, who live with honor without ever using the word, and die in glory with the bitter curse of the fighting man on his lips. To the raucous, forgotten but unforgettable companions, to the troopers of the United States Cavalry."

Admitting that it's a departure from protocol, Sheridan asks Kathleen to offer a salutation. "To those who never taste either honor or glory, but also know lonesomeness, and weariness, anxiety, and tears. To those who serve unknown and unnoticed and who sometimes uncomplainingly go hungry because that pint of whiskey has been bought. To those who not only save an empire, but are already beginning to populate it, without ever missing laundering the flannelette diapers of new America. To the women I have recently learned to know and to respect greatly. To the wives of the United States Cavalry," she says.

The regimental singers gather outside the tent to sing for the general, offering "an old Irish patriotic song" in tribute to the land of the general's parents. (A note in the script states: "If some different song should be decided on than the one Mr. Ford has presently in mind, a different and suitable introduction will have to be written for the spokesman. The Sons of the Pioneers render the song."[18]) Tyree, in the stockade, sings along, causing Quincannon to ask how he knows the song. The young man replies that he learned it from his Irish mother, which spurs the sergeant to open the cell door. Quincannon advises Tyree it is not "fittin' a lad like you die at the hands of a stranger. If you ever should see me again, you'll be good enough not to see me." Scaling the stockade wall, Tyree grabs Yorke's horse and gallops away.

Ford not only changed some of the dialogue between Yorke and Sheridan, but also moved it to follow Tyree's escape. He deleted the brief scene between Quincannon and Kathleen and the wordy toasts of Yorke and Kathleen, as well as completely revising Tyree's escape. In the film, as Sheridan arrives at the fort asking for a cup of coffee, Ford cuts directly to the dinner, with Yorke toasting Sheridan's health. The general responds with a toast to the president, then asks Mrs. Yorke to provide one. Kathleen simply says, "To my only rival, the United States Cavalry." Yorke drains his glass and places it upside down on the table, a gesture which catches Kathleen's attention. Quincannon announces the regimental singers, who offer "Down by the Glenside."[19] (Ford felt that since Sheridan was Irish, this was a good place for the song.)

The song concluded, Kathleen and the other officers bid Yorke and Sheridan a good night, as the colonel tells Quincannon he will sign the marshal's papers. Dr. Wilkins, Tyree, and the marshal are engaged in a poker game at the hospital when Quincannon notifies the lawman that Yorke is waiting for him. With the marshal gone, Tyree explains to Wilkins and Quincannon the cause of his legal problems. A Yankee attempted to take advantage of his sister, and when he tried to stop him, the Yankee pulled a gun and "got himself killed." Wilkins, placing a whiskey bottle in front of Quincannon, says, "If that boy was one of my troopers, I wouldn't be so eager to see him get hung." Pouring himself a liberal dose, Quincannon says he will take Tyree to Yorke's quarters, "unless you're a blackguard, steal a horse, stay away for a few days." Slamming the door behind him, Tyree gallops off on Yorke's horse, as Yorke and the marshal watch.

After Tyree's escape, Ford then cuts to the scene between Yorke and Sheridan; however, it is the general who gives the orders to send the women and children to Fort Bliss and Yorke to cross the Rio Grande and go after Natchez and the Apaches. Yorke replies that he's waited a long time to get that order, which he didn't officially hear. Sheridan assures him that if he fails, the members who will make up his court-martial will be the men who "rode with us down the Shenandoah. I'll handpick them myself." The general pauses for a moment, wondering aloud, "What will history say about the Shenandoah?" Yorke replies that his wife could tell him about the area, including her destroyed plantation. Offering the general some coffee, he adds, "You'll find it stronger."

Ford then cuts to Kathleen ironing clothes at her tent, as Captain St. Jacques and another captain visit. Yorke, hiding a bouquet behind his back, suggests the officers tend to their tasks. He informs Kathleen she must leave the next day with the other women and children. Learning Jeff will be part of the escort, Kathleen says their son will hate it, "but I love you for it." Giving him his clean uniform, Kathleen asks him if he wants to kiss her good-bye. He tells her he never wants to kiss her good-bye as they embrace.

The major difference in this scene between the script and the film is Kathleen. At this point in the script her attitude toward her husband borders on spiteful; thus, when she asks if he wants to kiss her good-bye, the emotion of the scene falls flat. The script has Kathleen resisting his orders, declaring she will stay on the property she bought outside the fort's boundary. When Yorke threatens to force her to leave, Kathleen calmly replies she would escape and come back. As a final effort to get her to comply, Yorke says if she will go with the others, he will assign their son as part of the escort. Agreeing to his offer, Kathleen asks if he wants to kiss her good-bye. Yorke, with "a fierceness of regret" in his voice, replies he never wants to kiss her good-bye before walking away.

Kathleen has shown little warmth toward Yorke up to this point in the script, aside from her reaction to the music box and her not resisting his kiss in the tent. However, in the film, Kathleen's love for her husband, while conflicting with her Southern heritage and emotions, can be glimpsed in several scenes. Each one, as the film progresses, shows her character softening toward her husband, and the rekindling of her feelings for him. Thus, when Ford arrives at this scene and Kathleen asks Yorke to kiss her, along with his reply, it is far more believable.

As four wagons are ready to move out, the script notes: "Every so often a trooper rushes and throws kisses of good-bye to his wife, or children." Corporal Bell rides up to one wagon, giving his wife money with a promise to write. Kathleen shares the wagon bench with Mrs. O'Feeney, her baby daughter, and Corporal Plunkett in the first wagon.[20] As they leave, Kathleen looks back and waves at Yorke, who returns the gesture.

Ford opens this scene as the children are being escorted to a wagon. Quincannon lifts Margaret Mary (carrying her ever-present school bell) into the wagon as she reminds him to "be a good boy." Corporal Bell climbs up to the children's wagon where his wife (wearing a wide-brimmed straw hat) sits on the front seat and kisses her good-bye. As the lead wagon starts off, with Kathleen sitting next to the driver (there is no Mrs. O'Feeney and child), Yorke walks alongside, following them through the front gate, as the band plays "The Girl I Left Behind Me."

Following the wagons' departure, the script and film follow the basic outline for the following section, with some differences. The script has Tyree meeting up with Jeff and Boone at the rear of the wagon column on the trail. He warns them about a muddied water hole with fresh pony tracks, and Boone rides up to warn the lieutenant when the Apaches attack. The officer orders the wagons to go into the river, thus making it harder for the Apaches to fight on horseback. Mrs. O'Feeney's baby falls from the wagon as it reaches the river, and Heinze rescues the child. Some warriors capture the wagon carrying the children, driving it away.

As the fight escalates, Jeff rescues a wounded Boone, before he is struck in his shoulder by an arrow. Kathleen yanks it out and tends to his wound when the lieutenant orders him to return to the fort for help. Jeff is chased by three Apaches as Tyree rides up and takes Jeff's rifle. Tyree wheels his horse around and kills the three pursuers. After Jeff details the attack to his father, Sheridan gives Yorke an unofficial order to cross into Mexico to attack Natchez, adding that he will handpick members of any court-martial.

As the troopers move out, the wagons carrying the women return to the fort, but Yorke does not see Kathleen. Arriving at the Rio Grande, Yorke's column finds Tyree, who relays that the children are held in an old church while the Apaches drink and dance. Knowing this is a vengeance dance that will go on until dawn, Yorke asks Tyree if he can get into the church without being spotted. "With two men I pick, sir," Tyree replies, calling Jeff and Boone, who, despite their wounds, are ready. Yorke orders the trio to sneak into the church under cover of darkness, and ring the church bell at dawn to start the attack.

Ford opens this sequence by having Tyree ride to a bluff as the camera pans to show the wagon train approaching. Hiding behind a large rock, Tyree waits for Jeff and Boone at the end of the column, advising them he saw "heap big Injun signs." Jeff and Boone ride off to warn the officers just as the wagons are attacked. The wagons race to get away as mounted Apaches chase them. The driver of Kathleen's wagon is shot, falling between the running horses, when another trooper rides up and takes control of the wagon. The left rear wheel of the children's wagon snaps off as the wagon driver is shot. The horses drag the wagon away as Heinze, dismounting to offer cover, is killed. The remaining wagons take cover on a ridge, unhitching the horses and overturning the wagons as the Apaches attack. Jeff is ordered to go back to the fort for help and Kathleen watches him gallop off. Ford then cuts to Tyree, who gallops alongside Jeff and takes his pistol. Bringing his horse to a halt and forcing the animal to lie down as cover, Tyree kills the Apaches.

Yorke soon arrives to learn the children's wagon was captured and promises to bring them back. Riding through the night, the column comes across the remnants of a burned wagon, with the wide-brimmed straw hat belonging to Corporal Bell's wife lying against a wagon wheel. Discovering her body (it is never shown on camera), Captain St. Jacques says in French, "Mother of God! The barbarous savages." Ford inserts another shot of the hat lying near a wheel before featuring the column a few feet away, with Corporal Bell behind the colonel.

Yorke requests Bell to come up alongside, placing his hand on the man's shoulder. "Sorry, son," he says quietly. Bell requests permission to go ahead, but the colonel tells him to stay. Crying out that it is his wife, Bell asks Yorke, "If it was your wife, wouldn't you want to go to her?" Yorke replies, "Yes, I would! If I had a friend, he'd keep me here. Stay with me, boy."

Ford keeps the camera on the two men as the scene dissolves to the column riding through the night, eventually reaching the river where they meet up with Tyree. He reports the children's location in the church and assures the colonel he can get in the church with two men of his choosing. Acknowledging he's a good judge of horseflesh, Yorke asks how good he is at judging men. "I consider myself a good judge of the men I trust, sir," Tyree replies. Yorke agrees, telling him to call his volunteers—Jeff and Boone. "Get it done, boy," the colonel says.

The script details troopers removing canvas coverings from the wagons after Tyree gets Yorke's permission, then having the troop on the move near where the body of Corporal Bell's wife is discovered. As the column moves past the burial detail, the script notes the men's faces displaying the "horror, pity, anger—but, above all, grim determination for vengeance." McGuinness describes the Mexican village as a former Franciscan agriculture community, with irrigation canals, and the church standing on a small rise looking down at the village buildings.

Apaches are dancing, celebrating their victory, as Tyree sneaks up behind an Apache at the church and strangles him. Dragging the body into the church with the help of Jeff and Boone, Tyree warns the children to be quiet. (The church's interior consists of three "loose pews," a dirt floor, and a bare altar.) As dawn approaches, Jeff pulls the rope attached to the church bell to signal Yorke's attack, but the rope breaks. Tyree gets Margaret Mary to climb up to the belfry and push a pole against the bell to make it ring.

The Apaches are stunned by the sound as Yorke orders the troop to charge. Some Apaches on horseback race to the church and batter down the doors, entering the building. Tyree and Jeff fight for their lives, while Boone ushers the children behind the altar. (The PCA would never approve of children so close to killing, let alone it happening inside a church.) Quincannon's group rides in, killing the Apaches and rescuing the children. Margaret Mary jumps from the belfry into Quincannon's arms and he exits with her and another child under his arms. Running past the altar, Quincannon stops and genuflects before exiting the church, and other children follow his example.

As Yorke and his men race through the village, the script includes a shot of a water tower toppling, causing the pony herd to stampede. Corporal Bell is seen "riding frantically" as he strikes braves with his saber in a "cold, efficient rage." Shot from his saddle, Bell dies while his horse "rears, then stands quietly by the body of its fallen master." Yorke, wounded by an arrow, falls from his saddle as Jeff rides up and kills the Apache. His father asks him to "yank this blasted stick out of my shoulder." Jeff does so, then his father breaks the arrow in two, handing it to Jeff. "Some people in the East value these trifles as souvenirs," he says, as the bugler sounds "Recall."

Once again, Ford eliminated some of the script's dialogue and action while adding a few of his own choices. Gone was the cavalry removing the canvas coverings, Tyree killing the Apache guarding the church, and Apaches storming into the church. Instead, after Yorke gives Tyree approval, Ford cuts to a close-up of Natchez singing, then shows other Apaches singing, drinking, and dancing, with the church in the background. He returns to shots of Yorke leading the cavalry across the Rio Grande and desert terrain, before cutting back to Tyree, Jeff, and Boone using the pony herd as cover to reach the church.

Opening the door, Margaret Mary hits Boone on the head with her school bell. Observing that the children are safe, Tyree takes Margaret Mary with him to the belfry to look at the street. As dawn breaks, Tyree sees the Apaches approaching the church and pushes a sleeping Boone off a pew ("Let's go Alamo!"). Margaret Mary rings the church bell, as Yorke orders the cavalry to charge. Tyree and Boone begin shooting from the church while Yorke and his men ride up the village street, scattering the Apaches. Riding into the church, Yorke tells Tyree to load up the children. Wagons filled with troopers arrive on the church steps where the men form a defensive line, as the children are placed in the wagons. Quincannon rushes into the church to get Margaret Mary, and as they pass the altar, both genuflect before exiting. (Ford eliminated other children following Quincannon and Margaret Mary's action, as it would have diminished the humor of the moment.) Yorke's column makes one more run through the village when he is hit with an arrow, falling to the ground. (Ford does not show Jeff or any soldier killing the Apache who shot the arrow.) Troopers gather around as Yorke tells his son to pull out the arrow. Completing the task, Jeff helps his father to his horse.

The final two scenes in the script begin with the return of the children to the fort. Many children yell excitedly, while others cry, as their mothers, "forgetting military etiquette," rush to the wagons and "respond just as childishly." Following this reunion, the script features a military review with Sheridan in attendance. Quincannon, watching both the mounts of Yorke and the general, is too interested in the parade when Tyree suddenly grabs Sheridan's horse and gallops off, leaving the marshal behind. Kathleen comments that Tyree is "presumptuous enough" to eventually become a general, while Sheridan admires his judgment of good horseflesh. Quincannon asks the marshal if he'll ever catch Tyree. "Not as long as he picks those kinds of horses," the lawman replies.

With the conclusion of the review, Sheridan, Yorke, and Kathleen walk back to his tent, where Yorke reveals he has been summoned to Washington. Expecting to be court-martialed, Sheridan tells him both he and General Sherman threatened to resign if they tried to prosecute Yorke. Instead, he offers the colonel a military post at the Court of St. James with a rank of brigadier-general. Yorke comments that Queen Victoria "reigns over a very proper and formal court," and thinks she wouldn't approve of a military attaché that was "in a sense—unmarried." Kathleen, "smiling winningly," wonders aloud what the court is like in person.

As Sheridan excuses himself, Kathleen asks Quincannon to have her things brought to the colonel's tent. Yorke says he doubts he'd find happiness in England, or anywhere else, but where he is—with his wife and son. Calling him a "big, stern, impossible darling," Kathleen promises to make up for the lost years. "The country is coming back together again. It should never have been apart. Neither should we. Come back, Kathleen. Come back, Mavourneen," he says. Entering his tent, they embrace as

Yorke lets the tent flap down. The script ends with the tinkle of the music box playing "Mavourneen," rising "in triumphant volume."

Ford made substantial changes to both scenes, starting with a close-up of a worried Kathleen. He cuts to a reverse angle (over Kathleen's back) as the cavalry column enters the fort, led by Captains St. Jacques and Prescott. Not seeing her husband in the lead, she begins to walk down the line of wounded soldiers being pulled by a travois. Finding Jeff behind the one with his father, Yorke looks at her. "Our boy did well," he says weakly. Taking his hand, Kathleen slowly walks alongside.

Ford then cuts to the military review, with Tyree, Jeff, Boone, Corporal Bell, and Navajo scout, Son of Many Mules, standing in line next to Quincannon as Captain Prescott reads a proclamation commending their bravery. The marshal spots Tyree, yelling "Hey! Soldier boy!" Yorke jumps up to announce Tyree has a seven-day furlough, and the trooper jumps on Sheridan's horse and gallops away. As the parade begins, the cavalry column marches past the reviewing stand while the military band plays "Dixie." Yorke and Kathleen are surprised at the music, and look at Sheridan, who points at himself. As the review passes the camera, the film fades out.

* * *

With the script completed, Steve Goodman of Republic Pictures sent two copies to Joseph Breen at the Producers Code Administration on May 8, 1950. Four days later, Breen replied that the script "seems to conform with the requirements of the Production Code," but noted there were a "few details which will need correction." He went on to stress "the greatest possible care in selection and photographing the dresses and costume of your women." Breen repeated the warning of the Production Code, which explicitly stated that any intimate parts of the body—specifically, a woman's breasts—had to be fully covered at all times, or the PCA would withhold approval of the picture.[21]

Like Ford's previous cavalry films, Breen asked that they contact Mel Morse at the American Humane Association regarding "all scenes in which animals are used." He also requested that copies of all the lyrics used in the film be sent for approval. When it came to Tyree's backstory, Breen suggested the reason why the marshal wants to arrest him be changed. "We could not approve the rather tacit condonation of the crime of manslaughter, which is present in the story, nor could we approve the indication that the criminal will escape the process of the law," Breen stated. He suggested the marshal's line be changed to, "Fellow I'm looking for is from Texas. Wanted for questioning in connection with a killing." (Ford agreed to use that line in the scene.) Breen also noted that it was the PCA's "considered opinion that it behooves the industry to see to it that Indians in motion pictures are fairly presented."[22]

The PCA felt it would be better to omit Yorke's line to the Mexican lieutenant about the Apaches: "[they] are a scourge to your country and mine—thieves and murderers." (Ford kept part of the line: "Natchez's band is a scourge to your country and mine.") Breen also cautioned that "care will be needed in photographing the fight scenes, to avoid offensive brutality and gruesomeness." Another objection by Breen had to do with the Apaches riding their horses into the old church with Tyree and Jeff firing at them near the altar and killing some Indians. He wrote that this sequence "should be carefully revised in such a manner as to eliminate the actual invasion of, and fighting in, the church proper." Breen suggested that Tyree and Jeff "would be in the vestibule and would be shown firing upon the Indians before they actually ride their horses through the doorway." (In the film, all the Apaches killed only approach the exterior of the church doors.) In a letter dated June 7, 1950, Breen noted that the script (and all revisions) "conform with the regulations of the Production Code," thus giving Ford the green light for production.[23]

On May 7, Republic's legal department found a 1926 novel by Edwin L. Sabin using the same title, *Rio Bravo*, as McGuinness's script. Ford refused to meet the author's demand of $5,000 to use his title. The studio changed the film's title to *Rio Grande Command* on August 22, 1950, and four weeks later it was revised for the final time to *Rio Grande*.[24]

* * *

Casting the film was once again a family affair, as many members of Ford's stock company were summoned for various roles. Ford biographer Scott Eyman relates how Yates told the director he could have anyone for the lead but John Wayne. It seems Yates and the actor had had a fight, *possibly* over Wayne wanting to star and direct a film about the Alamo.[25] Eyman notes that Ford told Wayne to apologize to the studio head so he could use him in this film, and in *The Quiet Man*.[26] Wayne also agreed to waive his percentage deal for *Rio Grande* and *The Quiet Man*, just taking a salary of $100,000. Maureen O'Hara, who was granted a loan-out by 20th Century-Fox, was paid $50,000 for her role as Kathleen. (It has been speculated that Ford cast Wayne and O'Hara in this film as a warm-up for their roles in *The Quiet Man*.)

Victor McLaglen was assigned the role of Quincannon, while Ben Johnson and Harry Carey Jr. were cast as Tyree and Boone, respectively. J. Carrol Naish, bearing an uncanny resemblance, would play General Sheridan, while Chill Wills was set for Dr. Wilkins. Alberto Morin, an officer in the OSS during World War II, was cast as the Mexican lieutenant. Other members of Ford's stock company in the cast included Jack Pennick (*Sergeant*), Don Summers (*Corporal Bell*), Peter Ortiz (*Captain St. Jacques*), stuntmen Chuck Hayward (Captain), Cliff Lyons (*Lieutenant*), Fred Kennedy (*Heinze*), and Frank McGrath (*Derice, the Bugler*). Karolyn Grimes, who played Zuzu in Frank Capra's *It's a Wonderful Life*, was cast as Margaret Mary. Wayne's son and Ford's godson, Patrick, made his film debut as one of the boys in the wagon. Shug Fisher, a member of the Sons of the Pioneers, played the confused bugler who blows "Reveille" during the fort attack. (Fisher, who had a lengthy career as a character actor, would appear in six more films for Ford.)

For Patrick Wayne, being the godson of the director had its benefits. Besides making his film debut and earning ten dollars a day to portray one of the children in the fort, Patrick stated that working on this film was very special for him. Since his other three siblings had no interest in appearing in the film, it gave him more time to spend with his father on the set, and he didn't have to worry about being "in the barrel" with his godfather.

Stan Jones, cast as one of the sergeants, first came in contact with Ford on *3 Godfathers* in Death Valley. Jones violated the unspoken commandment on a Ford set: telling the director he was wrong. Ford was filming the scene of the three outlaws escaping the posse across the desert;

having run out of water, Wayne's character uses a machete to whack off the top of a barrelhead cactus and squeezes water from the pulp into a canteen. Jones, the park ranger assigned to the film's production, spoke out during a take, stating that no one could get water from a barrelhead cactus. Everyone on the set went deathly quiet, expecting Ford's wrath to erupt. Asking Jones what made him such an authority on cactus, the ranger explained that this type of cactus could never hold water. Ford said little else, going on to film another scene before calling it a day.

The following morning, Ford returned to the cactus scene, and this time, as Wayne squeezed the cactus pulp, water dripped out. Ford called Jones over to show him he was wrong, and the park ranger simply chuckled. What Jones did not know was that Ford had had a crew member soak the barrelhead cactus in a large bucket of water overnight.[27]

During his time as a park ranger, Jones composed several Western-style songs. In 1949, his career as a park ranger came to an end when his song, "Ghost Riders in the Sky," was released and became a major hit.[28] Shortly before Harry Carey Jr. was to start filming *Wagon Master*, George O'Brien invited him to his house to meet a friend. It was Stan Jones, who sang "Ghost Riders in the Sky" for him. O'Brien and Carey then took Jones over to Ford's office at RKO-Pathé Studios. Before walking into the office, Carey cautioned Jones not to mention the cactus incident in Death Valley. After introductions, Jones sang "Ghost Riders in the Sky" and "Rollin' Dust" for Ford, who never mentioned anything about the cactus. The director was enamored with the songs, asking Jones if he could write two or three more songs for his upcoming movie. Jones replied that he could finish three songs by the following evening, and suggested Ford consider the singing group Sons of the Pioneers before he scored the movie. As Jones walked out of the office, Ford told him not to write anything about cactus. "You don't know a goddamn thing about cactus!" he said.[29] (Jones wrote three songs for *Rio Grande*: "My Gal Is Purple," "Footsore Cavalry," and "Yellow Stripes."[30])

The Sons of the Pioneers was a popular country-western singing group formed in 1934, and one of the four original singers was a young man called Leonard Slye, later known as Roy Rogers. As a major star at Republic Pictures, Rogers managed to persuade Herbert Yates to sign the singing group to a studio contract, and they appeared in several of his films. Ken Curtis, who took over as lead singer with Tommy Dorsey's band after Frank Sinatra left, joined the group in 1949. After listening to the group, Ford decided to have them record songs for *Wagon Master*. This is where Curtis first met Ford's daughter, Barbara, and, by the time *Rio Grande* began production, the couple was engaged.[31]

Stan Jones found himself in trouble with Ford when he accidentally told someone Ken and Barbara were engaged. John and Mary Ford had wanted to keep the engagement quiet until they could make an official announcement. Harry Carey Jr. said word got back to Ford that Jones had spilled the beans. You might say Jones was "in the barrel" with Ford, but in a different way. For the entire film, Ford never talked to Jones. If he needed Jones for something, he would walk up to the man and then call Carey over.

> Uncle Jack would yell for me. He'd either give me directions to tell Stan, or have me ask a question. He refused to address Stan by his name. So, I'd either relay the directions or ask a question, and Stan would give me his reply. Uncle Jack would ask what did he say, and I'd have to repeat Stan's answer. You have to understand that all of this happened with the three of us standing no more than a foot apart from each other![32]

(This could be the reason why Jones does not have a speaking part in the film.)

There are conflicting stories about who actually wanted the Sons of the Pioneers to appear in *Rio Grande*. It was believed Herbert Yates insisted the group be cast, as he'd never seen a Western that he felt couldn't be improved by adding singing cowboys. (Michael Wayne, the actor's son, once claimed Ford never wanted to use the group.) However, in an interview with his grandson, Dan, the director stated that the reason he chose to use the group was because his daughter was involved with the lead singer, and "he wanted to give him some exposure."

At the ripe age of fifteen, Claude Jarman Jr. had racked up quite a résumé. Plucked from obscurity to play the lead juvenile role of Jody in Clarence Brown's *The Yearling* (1946), Claude was given a special Oscar (a smaller version of the original) for his performance, which was hailed by critics and the film industry.[33] His interview with Ford consisted of the director sitting at his desk smoking a pipe, eyeing the young man behind his dark glasses, saying nothing for what Claude later described as an "eternity." When Ford did speak, he asked the young man how his school grades were, and if he could ride a horse. Replying he had ridden horses in two previous films, the ten-minute interview was over. There was no reading from the script, no improvisations. Nothing.[34]

Bert Glennon, who had worked with Ford on seven films,[35] was hired as cinematographer, while Archie Stout, the cinematographer of *Fort Apache*, would handle second unit photography. (Ford had wanted to shoot in Technicolor, but Yates flatly refused, citing its high cost.) Wingate Smith again handled duties as assistant director, and Ford's daughter, Barbara, worked as an assistant editor to Jack Murray.[36] Philip Kieffer returned as technical advisor, as did D. R. O. Hatswell as wardrobe consultant. For the cavalry uniforms, Western Costume pulled much of the same wardrobe that had been used on Ford's two previous cavalry films. Fat Jones Stables would again supply the primary horses and wagons, while the company rented an additional one hundred horses from local Moab ranches.

* * *

When it came to choosing a location, the obvious choice of Monument Valley was quickly quashed by Herbert Yates. The estimated costs to transport, house, and feed a cast and crew in Monument Valley was more than the studio head was willing to spend. Ford's second choice was Moab, Utah, where he had filmed *Wagon Master*. Yates readily approved Moab, since it was a cheaper location, with several motels, better roads, and a local airport to transport cast and crew with a direct flight from Los Angeles.[37]

Moab sits in a valley along the eastern bank of the Colorado River in what is known as the Colorado Plateau. The name "Moab" comes from the Bible, referring to a small kingdom in central Transjordan; however, some historians speculate its origins may have come from the Paiute word *moapa*, meaning mosquito. (For many centuries, the area had been populated by Navajo, Hopi, Ute, and Paiute tribes.) With the creation of the Old Spanish Trail (Santa Fe to Los Angeles) in 1830, Moab became a favored river crossing. Mormon settlers established a stone fort in June 1855, which they abandoned by September due to conflicts with Indian tribes. By 1878, under the direction of Brigham Young, another Mormon settlement was founded and turned Moab into a thriving farming community. In the 1950s, uranium turned the area into a booming mining district before its decline in the early 1980s. Today, Moab is a popular tourist destination, with two nearby national parks (Arches and Canyonlands).

When it came to finding a location for the military fort, Ford picked White's Ranch, located along the Colorado River fourteen miles from Moab. The ranch had enough acreage to allow Ford room to shoot numerous scenes without ever having to make a major move. The ranch's open field would be used for the Roman-riding sequence, White's residence served as the exterior of the sutler's store and fort schoolhouse, while the scenes of laundresses' row would use the nearby riverbank. At the main entrance to the ranch, a wooden stockade, complete with bastion and gate, was built. (This set remained standing for many years, and was used in a portion of Ford's 1964 film, *Cheyenne Autumn*.) George White, who began ranching in Moab in 1926, was like Harry Goulding and became a much-welcome source of information for Ford. During a location scout for *Wagon Master*, White introduced the director to Professor Valley, which Ford made ample use of in that film. Professor Valley, about twenty miles from White's Ranch, would once again furnish Ford with an impressive location.[38]

In later years, when asked to recall their first memory about the Moab location, both Claude Jarman Jr. and Harry Carey Jr. immediately stated, "The heat!" During the company's stay in Moab, daytime temperatures hovered between 100 to 105 degrees, although Claude noted that it was a "comfortable dry heat" compared to the humid conditions he had experienced when filming *The Yearling* in Florida.[39]

* * *

When a film company comes to a small town it is big news, and Moab was no different. The *Times-Independent*, the town's weekly paper, detailed the various comings and goings of Ford's new production team. According to the May 4, 1950, edition, it was believed Ford would arrive in Moab by June 1 or 2 with his production company to begin filming. (They were off by thirteen days.) The following week the newspaper announced 150 local people would be employed, including 100 men as cavalrymen, 20 women ("not over 40"), and 10 or 12 children to work as extras. (The additional 20 locals would fill positions of wranglers, carpenters, and drivers.) "All of the housing accommodations available at local auto courts and hotels will be used by the company," the paper noted. The Arches ballroom, with a large kitchen erected next to the building, served as the dining room for evening meals.[40] Ford described the ballroom as a "big communal dining room" where everyone on the film ate together.

Unit manager Lee Lukather, construction foreman Whitey Gibbs, and transportation captain George Coleman arrived in Moab on Thursday, May 11, while Ford flew in from Reno, Nevada, on Sunday.[41] The men spent the next three days selecting various locations before heading back to Hollywood. Before he left, Ford expressed his appreciation to the people in Moab for their "very helpful and cooperative attitude."[42]

By May 25, construction material was arriving at White's Ranch not only for the fort set, but for several corrals and sheds to house horses and other equipment. Unlike the laborious trek to get a cast and crew to Monument Valley, the Moab newspaper announced that a United Airlines DC-6 plane would fly everyone concerned from Los Angeles directly to the local airport. To prepare for the company's arrival, the airport runways had been "gravel-surfaced," and given a sealcoating of oil. Despite the company scooping up all the available motel rooms, Anderson Company, who had provided housing for Ford's company in Monument Valley, built a tent camp on a vacant lot opposite Bowen's Court on Main Street to handle the overflow of production personnel.

On Thursday, May 31, a DC-3 airliner landed at the local airport and deposited fifteen crew members to begin setting up the necessary support equipment, such as costumes, saddles, tack, props, and feed for the horses. The *Times-Independent* reported that the river road between

Moab and White's Ranch would be widened and graded with a coat of oil to keep dust down.[43] Although he wasn't filming in Monument Valley, Ford did not forget the Navajo people. He had Harry Goulding and Lee Bradley bring sixty Navajos, including two of his favorites, John Stanley and Many Mules.

* * *

As things were progressing in Moab, John Ford summoned Harry Carey Jr. and Ben Johnson to his office at Republic Pictures where they learned there would be a Roman-riding sequence. (According to Ford, they would "grab two teams of horses and do your stuff.") Since neither man knew how to Roman-ride, they would have to learn quickly, as filming began in a month. Johnson knew it would take at least two weeks for the wranglers to break in a team, and a week later they went out to Fat Jones Stables to see how the horses were shaping up.

Kenny Lee, one of the wranglers at the stable, had a pair of quarter horses working nicely, while the other team, two thoroughbreds, were, in Carey's words, "idiotic." To have a successful Roman-riding team, both horses must work in synchronization with each other, something the thoroughbreds did not understand. It took Kenny Lee another week to smooth out that team, which Johnson would ride.[44] The third week, Johnson and Carey started training under Lee's instruction. The trick for the rider was to sit on the back of the left horse, with feet on an angle at the side behind the withers (the ridge between the shoulder bones) as they start out at a gallop. Once the horses are running, the rider places their right hand on the other horse's withers and pushes themselves up, placing one foot on each animal's back.

After a few times in the riding ring, both Johnson and Carey felt their legs collapse under them, and Johnson suggested they go to a whirlpool bath used by stuntmen to help relax the leg muscles. The following morning Ford came out to see how they were progressing, telling both of the actors they looked good. One of the problems Johnson and Carey faced was that by riding in a ring, they were always in a semi-crouched position. Another wrangler, Hank Potts, saw this and made both riders take the horses out to a dirt road next to the stables that was about five hundred yards in length. Potts knew the straightaway would allow both actors to stand up straight. Johnson's first try found him standing up and in total control of the mounts. Carey had more difficulty, freezing twice in his attempt to stand. The third time worked like a charm, partially because Potts threatened to throw a rock at his head if he didn't stand up.[45]

A few days later, Claude Jarman Jr. and his father came to the stables for his lesson. It had been planned he'd start out walking the horse team while standing on their backs. Much to the surprise of everyone, the young actor asked if he could try it down the same straightaway. Mounting his horses, Claude let the team go and within seconds was standing on the horses at a full gallop on his first time out. Johnson quipped that the reason it was so easy for Claude was "his feet are so goddamned big they just wrapped around the horse's back!"[46] (In the film's sequence, all three are wearing flat-soled shoes, not boots.)

* * *

Two DC-6 charter flights delivered cast and crew to Moab on June 14, with filming commencing the following day, Thursday. The production schedule had set aside the first two days (which overlapped into an additional day) for the scenes of Yorke and the cavalry making their way through the desert, Tyree meeting up with Jeff and Boone, and the Apaches attacking the wagons in the narrow canyon and stealing the children.[47] (All of these scenes were filmed around Ida Gulch and the Stearns Mesa vicinity.[48])

As the cavalry and wagons are attacked, Ford included four different shots of the Apaches shooting down at the wagons, and one of mounted Apaches on a ridge before they suddenly spur their mounts down the hill. All of these individual shots were *not* filmed in Moab. They originally appeared in *Fort Apache* and were inserted into this scene. Since Argosy still owned the rights to *Fort Apache*, they could use the film clips without having to pay a usage fee. It was common practice for studios to cannibalize shots from their other productions. Warner Bros. filmed *The Sea Hawk* (1940) in black-and-white in order to incorporate various battle scenes from another Warner Bros. production, *Captain Blood* (1935). The studio was notorious for lifting footage from their Westerns (i.e., establishing shots of a bustling town or saloon or an Indian attack) to be used in their television shows, such as *Lawman*, *Cheyenne*, or *Maverick*.

During the attack, Ford filmed several wagons furiously galloping to escape the Apaches. The driver (Post Park) of the wagon carrying Kathleen is shot, rises from the wagon seat, and falls between the horses. (Park actually landed between the horses, resting on the wagon's tongue.) Ford then cut to another angle as the body (a dummy) falls beneath the wagon and lies on the ground. Cutting back to the running wagon, minus its driver, another cavalry officer (Cliff Lyons) makes a transfer from his horse to the wagon and takes over the lines. Watching the film on DVD, one can clearly see the hands of a stuntman behind the seat "blind driving" the wagon during the fall by Park and Lyons' transfer.

On Sunday, June 18, the company moved to White's Ranch to film the opening scenes of Yorke and the cavalry returning to the fort. The rest of the day was spent filming various shots of the wagons with the women and children leaving the fort. Monday, the 19th, not only was spent shooting the new recruits' arrival and Yorke addressing them, but also the Roman-riding sequences with Tyree, Boone, and Jeff, as well as the marshal looking for Tyree. Ford had wanted Johnson, Jarman, and Carey to be able to do their own Roman riding so the camera could show it was really them and not stunt doubles. (The only time a double, Kenny Lee, was used is when Carey's character does a "crupper," vaulting from behind a horse and into the saddle.) Many years later, Claude Jarman Jr. was at an event when some people asked if he really did his own Roman riding in the film. Despite his insistence, the group did not believe him. Claude called over Patrick Wayne and asked him to verify that he did indeed do his own Roman riding. "No," Patrick replied mischievously.[49]

Harry Carey Jr. confessed he had no idea what his role was about, as he only had a few lines in the script. "I had no idea, but Uncle Jack sure did. The first morning he has me put a piece of straw in my mouth that would be present throughout the film. He also invented the bit of Vic [Victor McLaglen] asking me to put my hat back on and my reply, 'Not at all, Doc.' Then when it came to me responding to my name [at roll call] he told me to say 'Yes, sir,' and then 'Yeah?' When Vic tells me to say 'Yo,' it became my standard line in the film. The same with Ben, having him say 'Get 'er done, Reb' several times to Claude. I knew Uncle Jack would take care of me and give my character more attention," the actor recalled.[50]

Tuesday, June 20, was spent filming Kathleen's arrival at the fort and walking with Yorke to his tent. Once these scenes were completed, Ford then covered Yorke leading his troop out after the Apaches' escape from the fort. The parade review, including Tyree's escape on General Sheridan's horse, started out the day on Wednesday, June 21. (Some of the dialogue scenes on the reviewing stand would be filmed later at Republic Pictures.) Moving to the fort gate, Ford then shot the wounded Yorke's return.

Thursday and Friday were spent covering numerous scenes of the Apache attack on the fort, which included Natchez and his men escaping, Tyree and Boone protecting Kathleen and her fainting, terrified horses escaping the fire from the picket line, and the Navajo scout identifying the dead Apaches. Saturday, June 24, rounded out the company's first week in Moab with filming Margaret Mary running to Quincannon during the attack, Yorke's reaction to the attack, and riding to Jeff's tent where he orders him to take Kathleen back to his tent. The last shot of the day was Sheridan riding into the fort and asking for a cup of coffee. (Stuntman Frank McGrath doubled J. Carrol Naish riding in for the wide shot.)

Sunday's work included Yorke's return after chasing the Apaches and walking Kathleen back to her tent after they kissed. Monday and Tuesday, June 26 and 27, were spent along the riverbank filming Kathleen taking Quincannon's clothes, as well as the marshal arresting Tyree. By Friday, June 30, the company had moved to the Colorado River near Professor Valley to film the scene of Yorke and the Mexican lieutenant meeting in the river on horseback. Once this was completed, Ford turned to the scene of Yorke walking alone on the banks of the river as we hear the song "My Gal Is Purple."

Saturday to Monday, July 1 to 3, found the company in Professor Valley filming the script's rescue sequence. This included the approach to the church by Tyree, Jeff, and Boone, the Apaches dancing, the cavalry attacking, the rescue of the children, and Yorke wounded by an arrow.

The *Times-Independent* marveled at the construction of the village and church set, noting "Its erection in the course of a few days was a striking illustration of the ingenuity of the technicians engaged in motion picture work."[51]

Rio Grande was the first of four films stuntman Terry Wilson would make with Ford before getting his big break as Bill Hawks in the television series, *Wagon Train*.[52] Wilson came directly to the Moab location from working on another film in Colorado. The stuntman who doubled Wayne taking the hit by the arrow was supposed to fall backwards off the horse. The stunt, according to Wilson, "didn't work too good," and Ford asked stunt coordinator Cliff Lyons if Wilson could do a better job. When Lyons confirmed he could, Ford told Wilson, "Now, I want you to go ahead and do it, and do it good!" Wilson performed the stunt as planned, and, more importantly, to Ford's approval.[53]

* * *

During that week, studio head Herbert Yates and his soon-to-be brother-in-law, Rudy Ralston, showed up on location. Yates was oblivious to another unspoken commandment on a Ford film: A studio executive was not needed, or wanted, on the set. According to Harry Carey Jr., Yates was allowed only one visit, and Ralston was forbidden to get anywhere near the set.

Their first night in Moab was one Ford made certain they would not forget. Alberto Morin, the actor playing the Mexican lieutenant, had met Ford during their time in the OSS and was a highly decorated officer who spoke seven languages. This night in Moab, Ford had Morin dress up as a waiter to serve Yates and his brother-in-law. As the unsuspecting duo arrived, Morin, speaking in a broken French accent, rushed over to them, making a big fuss. He escorted them to the main table where Ford and select others sat, the whole time carrying on the most unbelievable gobbledygook conversation. "I don't think Yates understood a word Alberto was saying. I sure didn't!" Carey recalled.[54] As the evening meal progressed, Morin went on to spill their glasses of water, break several dishes, and dump soup over the two men. No one else at the table was in on Ford's joke, and anyone who did know was not about to reveal it to Yates and his brother-in-law. The two men left Moab two days later.[55]

* * *

Ford wanted to convey his appreciation to the residents of Moab by staging a benefit show for the town's Lions Club Christmas Cheer Fund for "all children and all needy families in Moab." (Ford arranged a similar show when he was in town filming *Wagon Master*.) Over three evenings (June 26 to 28) the show was presented at Moab's high school auditorium, with tickets for adults costing one dollar, and fifty cents for children. "The people of Moab and the surrounding area had the privilege . . . of being entertained by some of the most famous stars in Hollywood," commented the *Times-Independent*. "The show, given under the personal direction of John Ford, the famous producer-director, was a tremendous hit."

> The auditorium was filled to its utmost capacity all three nights. . . . The show was a collection of skits; musical numbers, both humorous and serious; two or three dramatic acts; and a "ya-ba-chi" dance by 12 Navajo Indians. Chill Wills, the noted comedian, was master of ceremonies, and kept the show going at a rapid pace and the audience convulsed with laughter.
>
> Outstanding among the numbers were a collection of songs by the Sons of the Pioneers and Stan Jones, the songwriter. Maureen O'Hara, beautiful in a gorgeous white gown, sang three solos that brought down the house. John Wayne and Victor McLaglen, in the role of prize fight promoters, put on a fight skit, with Fred Kennedy and Steve Pendleton, stunt men, as the gladiators. This number was tumultuously received.
>
> A group of cavalrymen from the *Rio Bravo* cast, including John Wayne, Victor McLaglen, Ben Johnson, Harry (Dobe) Carey, Jr., Claude Jarman, Jr., Peter Ortiz, Jack Pennick, Don Summers, and several others, sang an original song written especially for the show. They made up in volume what might have been considered lacking in musical quality. At the last performance Mr. Ford, the director, could not restrain himself

> any longer, and appearing from behind the scenes he drenched the songbirds with a pailful of water.
>
> A highlight of the show was the concluding act, "The Purple Heart," with Grant Withers and J. Carrol Naish in the part of an aged Civil War veteran, [which] will long be remembered.[56]

(The three-night event raised $890, the equivalent of $11,109.86 in 2023 dollars.)

If that wasn't enough entertainment for the local residents, the weekly newspaper noted that "Moab will receive nationwide publicity Friday evening" when the Sons of the Pioneers would give a live performance to be recorded for Rex Allen's weekly radio show on the CBS radio network.[57] The *Times-Independent* went on to state that several cast members and Stan Jones would make an appearance, and the public was invited to attend the free event at the high school. The newspaper added that this was the first time the Sons of the Pioneers would do a program away from a radio studio, and the show would "publicize Moab and southeastern Utah in a degree never before accomplished."[58]

During the recording of the show, Rex Allen interviewed John Wayne, Maureen O'Hara, Victor McLaglen, and others. "A packed auditorium greeted the entertainers, who put on a two-hour show," commented the newspaper. (Only a half-hour of the event was recorded for Allen's show, which aired on CBS radio network on Friday, July 14, at 8:00 p.m.)

That same edition published an editorial titled, "An Appreciation to Mr. Ford and Company."

> Moab is again the host to Director John Ford and his company of Republic Productions personnel, who are making another motion picture in this vicinity. Moab is happy to have these good people back, and the community is doing everything possible to make their stay pleasant and profitable . . . That the spirit of the people of Moab is appreciated by Mr. Ford and company was again illustrated this week, when the famous director and his personnel presented a benefit show three nights, giving all the proceeds to the Moab Lions Club Christmas

> Fund. The cast, including some of the most famous names in moving pictures, worked hard for 10 days rehearsing for the show, and the entertainment they gave would have been a stellar attraction in any large city. It was truly a splendid gesture on the part of this company, and *The Times-Independent*, speaking on behalf of the people of Moab, wants to express profound appreciation and gratitude.[59]

* * *

Maureen O'Hara claimed in her autobiography that two stuntmen died while filming scenes of the cavalry crossing the river. She asserted they drowned in the heavy river and no one on the crew saw them fall because the mud was so thick, adding that it was never mentioned publicly. (During the summer months, when this movie was filmed in Moab, the Colorado River is *not* thick with mud, as numerous tourists enjoy various water sports on the river.) There is absolutely no independent proof this incident ever happened. There was no mention in any industry trade paper, the Moab newspaper, or any files of either Republic Pictures or Argosy Productions. Not one stuntman, past or present, has ever mentioned such an incident, as they often share stories about various accidents on film sets. When this author asked Harry Carey Jr. if O'Hara's claim was true, he said the *only* stuntman who was hurt on the set was Chuck Hayward, and *no one* died during filming.[60] (Some film historians contend that other comments made by O'Hara in her book are not accurate and debate her veracity.)

While the stage show allowed some good times and laughs, filming was not without a number of hazards. During the filming at White's Ranch of the Apaches attacking the fort set, second-unit cinematographer Archie Stout set up his camera behind a tent. One of the riders accidentally ran over Stout, knocking him unconscious.[61] (The set medic revived and treated him for a few bumps and bruises.)

Like his father had done early in his career, Patrick Ford performed some stunt work on the film as one of the cavalrymen. At one point during filming, Patrick was thrown from a galloping horse when the saddle cinch broke loose, leaving him with three broken ribs. Dan Ford recalled his father had several injuries when he was doing stunt work; luckily, "most of them were pretty minor."[62]

For stuntman Chuck Hayward, it was another story. During the third day of filming the Apaches ambushing the wagons, Hayward was set to do a "drag" stunt. According to stuntman Terry Wilson, the horse "laid down on top of him" and broke his eardrum and knocked him unconscious. (Footage of the fall is in the film.) "He [Ford] ran up to Chuck when he came to and said, 'What kind of a drag was that?' " Wilson recalled. Ford's comment was to get "Chuck mad so he'd forget about the hurt and all."[63] Hayward, kicked in the head by the horse, suffered a skull fracture. Because of his injury, he could not do any riding, let alone any additional stunts in the film. Hayward recalled Ford stepped in to keep him on the payroll.

> They took me to Colorado to the hospital and then back to Moab and put me in the hospital there. I got two checks for disability, so I know the studio took me off salary. He [Ford] went to the phone and called the studio and ate them up. He said, "You don't take any actor off the picture. I need him." Well, he put me in a lieutenant's uniform every day and rehearsed me for a scene. I'm still on the picture and we come back to Republic [Pictures], I still hadn't done my scene until we wrapped. But he got me the money while I was healing up.[64]

Rio Grande was the beginning of Chuck Roberson working with Ford, and he would become Wayne's stunt double for nearly thirty years. When he was not working as a cavalryman, an officer in Sheridan's group, or playing an Apache, Roberson and other stuntmen were drilled every day by Jack Pennick so they looked like a real cavalry unit. Every morning after breakfast, the stuntmen would line up to get their uniforms "dusted down" by the wardrobe department, even though they still had the previous day's dirt on them. Roberson recalled the uniforms were not washed during the entire production for a realistic look, and by the end of the film, their uniforms could "just about stand up in the corner all by themselves."[65] Ford gave Roberson the nickname of "Bad Chuck" after he snuck a lady into his room one night. Despite Roberson's repeated pleas to be quiet, the lady could not help but vocalize her feelings. The following morning, Ford was inspecting Roberson in his wardrobe, adjusting his hat several times, then his bandana. Before walking away, he suggested Roberson pick a quiet girl next time, adding "You kept the whole camp awake." Roberson had no idea how, but somehow Ford *knew*.[66]

Roberson's first attempt at a horse fall was an even bigger blunder. Upon Fred Kennedy's recommendation, Ford chose him to be one of the Apaches that chases Jeff Yorke and is killed by Tyree. At that time, horse falls were done at a canter, and the director would alter the camera speed to make it appear faster on screen. Waiting for his cue, Roberson, who had never performed a horse fall, thought the fall would look better at a full gallop. Given his cue, Roberson spurred the horse and came toward the camera at a full gallop. Unfortunately, Roberson and the horse did not fall on their predetermined mark, but fifteen feet beyond, knocking down "a row of folding chairs like a cannonball."[67] Fred Kennedy did the stunt at a canter and everyone, especially Ford, was pleased. Smarting from his failed attempt, Roberson was determined to find the right horse and train it to do a fall at a full gallop. One year later, Roberson had obtained his horse, Cocaine, and together the duo would perform numerous horse falls at a gallop for the next twenty years.

* * *

With a few days remaining on location, Ben Johnson had "a big spat" with Ford at dinner. An unspoken commandment was no shop talk during lunch or dinner, especially at Ford's table. One evening, as Johnson and Carey sat next to each other, Johnson commented that they did a lot of shooting, but didn't kill many Indians. Within a few seconds, Ford, at the head of table, asked, "What did you say?" Johnson tried to diffuse the moment by telling him he was "talking to Dobe." Harry Carey Jr. knew his friend had broken the no-shop-talk rule.

> Uncle Jack repeated his question, and Ben tried to pacify him by saying he was talking to me. Then Uncle Jack erupted, "Hey, stupid! I asked a question. What did you say?" The whole room went silent, and at our table everyone wished they were someplace else. Ben got up and walked

> over to Uncle Jack and whispered in his ear before walking out of the dining tent. He told Uncle Jack to take this film and shove it up his ass. Of course, Uncle Jack realized he was wrong and asked me to bring Ben back. He let his damn Irish temper get loose. Instead of *him* going after Ben and apologize, he sent me. Uncle Jack could never admit he was wrong. Ben honestly thought he'd be fired, but he refused to go back to the dining tent. The next day Uncle Jack acted like nothing had happened.[68]

Years later Johnson admitted he "shouldn't have done it." While he finished the picture, and Ford never displayed any anger toward him, Johnson would not work for Ford for thirteen years. Harry Carey Jr. claimed the real reason for Johnson's banishment was due to his agent's "take it or leave it" demand to Ford for a higher salary for the leading man role in *The Sun Shines Bright* (1953).[69] Ford's Irish wrath exploded and an unknowing Johnson was on the outs. (However, a preproduction note for *The Searchers* reveals that Ford had considered Johnson for one of the Texas Rangers.) In later years, Johnson would wonder how so many people could idolize Ford when he could be "so damned obnoxious sometimes."

* * *

July 7 marked the last day of location filming, and the company returned to Los Angeles to complete interior scenes at Republic Pictures. Ford began on July 10 with Quincannon stopping Jeff and Heinze from fighting, before moving on to complete the entire fight sequence. The rest of the week was spent filming various scenes that included the dinner between Yorke and Kathleen and being serenaded by the regimental singers, Tyree's escape, Kathleen and Jeff meeting and his refusing to leave the army, the formal dinner with General Sheridan, and Jeff and Yorke's first meeting.

It was after this week's work (including Saturdays) that John Wayne went on strike. His contract called for him to receive a percentage from the box office revenue for *Sands of Iwo Jima* (1949), but Yates was refusing to pay him. Wayne did not show up and no celluloid ran through the camera. The same thing happened the next day, causing Yates to walk on the stage and instruct Ford to shoot scenes not requiring Wayne. Ford refused, adding that filming would resume when Yates paid his employee. The studio head got the message, and Wayne returned after receiving a check from Yates.[70]

Rio Grande completed filming at 3:48 p.m. on Thursday, July 21.[71] The last day consisted of filming various scenes against a rear-screen projection, including Tyree warning Jeff and Boone about Apache signs, and close-ups of Yorke speaking to the Mexican lieutenant, among others. The production was listed as two days behind its thirty-day schedule, mainly due to Wayne's walkout.

* * *

Passing over Richard Hageman, Ford chose composer Victor Young to score the film. The prolific composer holds the record for twenty-two Oscar nominations for Best Original Score, twice earning four nominations in the same year (1940 and 1941). (He posthumously won an Oscar in 1956 for *Around the World in Eighty Days*.[72]) Young would also score Ford's *The Quiet Man* (1952) and *The Sun Shines Bright* (1953).

Young's score opens with a flourish of horns and a drumbeat as the credits show the cavalry riding through the desert, before a slower melody takes over (featuring horns and strings), to create a forlorn emotion. This is one of many motifs Young created for the film for a specific character or location. In the case of this melody, it is always presented in various scenes around the fort. (I refer to it as the "Returning to Fort" theme.) As the credits end, the score slowly fades to hear the bugler blowing the "Guard Mounting" call. Horns and drums once again come to the forefront as the color guard rides past the camera, with the composer switching to a lighthearted theme to reflect the schoolchildren as they run from the schoolhouse to greet the troopers. As the color guard rides through the open gate, the horn section and a repetitive drumbeat imply a militaristic tone as the cavalry returns. Young quickly segues back to the "Returning to Fort" theme with muted horns and strings, which enhance the shots of the soldiers' wives waiting along the fort road, looking longingly for their men.

For the reunion of Yorke and his son, Jeff, Young creates another motif that is used in scenes relating to the father-and-son relationship. (I refer to this as "Jeff's Theme.") Relying mainly on the prominent use of a violin, the theme is played slowly and softly, reflecting the melancholy emotions between the father and son. However, as Yorke measures his height against that of his son in the tent, Young gives the theme a lighter feel as it ends with a sharp, sliding note. Young will return to "Jeff's Theme" when Tyree calls Jeff and Boone for his mission, and after Jeff removes the arrow out of his father's chest and helps him up.

When it comes to Kathleen's first reaction to seeing Yorke, Young lets the string section bloom into a rich, sensitive theme, reflecting Kathleen's Irish background. The use of the strings and soft horns in this segment, like the "Returning to Fort" theme, creates an aching loneliness that mirrors the couple's reunion. For Kathleen's theme, the composer chose "I'll Take You Home Again, Kathleen," and makes good use of it throughout the film. Young's first use of her theme is not in an orchestral mode, but a music box version when she opens the device, with a soft, lilting style. Young continues to use her theme in several other scenes, such as when Yorke and Kathleen passionately kiss in his tent, Kathleen watching Jeff riding to bring help, and when Yorke rides off to rescue the captive children. Kathleen's theme is never more poignant than when she waits along the fort road with the other women, looking for Yorke, enhancing the emotion of the scene. This time Young uses muted strings, letting the somber sound of the horn section come to the forefront.

Tyree had his own motif, using a four-bar count from "Aha! San Antone." Young will repeat this, usually going to a higher key for the repeat. The first use of this theme is when Tyree, after escaping on Yorke's horse, tops a rise. Young starts with the use of horns and muted strings in the background; then, as the camera shows the wagons moving through open land, Young mixes the score with strings before returning to Tyree's theme (played in lower keys) as Jeff and Boone show up. When Jeff is chased by the Apaches, Tyree's theme comes up, with the string section supporting the horns as he gallops toward Jeff. Young then uses a repetitive short count of sharp horn notes in a lower key as Tyree races past the Apaches before returning to Tyree's motif.

The score for the action scenes (Apaches attacking the fort and the wagons, as well as the final rescue) is played under sounds of gunfire, galloping horses, and yells. Young resorts to a typical Indian-type theme, using drums and lower notes from horns, as the string section plays in a staccato fashion. Young's score in these sections is vibrant, adding to the tension and excitement of the scenes. As the film ends with the military review, Young launches into a vigorous rendition of "Dixie" as the cavalry rides past the camera.

* * *

Herbert Yates and Ford had several disagreements over the budget, which Yates tried to hack away at in the weeks before filming began. Yates finally relented and approved a $1.2 million budget. By the completion of production, the budget tallied up at $1,287,185. Despite the $87,185 overage, Yates was indubitably happy, as the worldwide box office receipts for *Rio Grande* had reaped $2,945,782 by August 22, 1953. (In 2023 dollars the amount would be $36,772,160.04.)[73] When it came time for a cast and crew screening, the ever-penny-pinching Herbert Yates announced that no family members could attend, until Ford and Wayne protested loudly, forcing Yates to renounce his directive.

Republic held a premiere in San Antonio, Texas, at the Majestic Theatre, with Wayne and O'Hara attending. (During their time in the city, they visited soldiers in a military hospital.) Republic also held "simultaneous premieres" in thirty-two other cities, including Los Angeles, New York City, Philadelphia, Atlanta, and Dallas.[74]

"Possessing all the grandeur, excitement, and dramatic qualities that seem synonymous with the name of John Ford, *Rio Grande* is an impressive western that holds one completely absorbed from beginning to end," commented the *Hollywood Reporter*.[75] "This is an epic bit of Americana that will enthuse adults and youngsters . . . Ford's direction is of his customary top-notch quality, keeping the action well to the fore, while getting full value out of the drama elements . . . Wayne gives a splendid performance as the colonel, with sensitive restraint and understanding." *Variety* stated that the film was "delivered in the John Ford manner to attract a strong play at the box office . . . the Ford treatment insures entertainment and the marquee worthy of the cast names . . . it features big, brawling mass action clashes, mixed together with a substantial portion of good, honest sentiment, ingredients that, when as well done as in this, practically always meet a good reception in the general market . . . the eight songs that are woven in the background as well [are] neatly vocaled by the Sons of the Pioneers."[76]

The *New York Times* noted that Ford's "romance with the United States Cavalry, a basic strategy which has paid off several times previously, show few signs of wear and tear in *Rio Grande* . . . the horsemanship was never better, the Indians more dastardly, and the cavalry never answered a bugle call more quickly . . . Despite Sheridan's pensive aside, 'I wonder what history will say about this,' Mr. Ford needn't worry. Chances are his public will eat it up."[77] *Cue* wrote, "It's a thoroughly good job this *Rio Grande*, with a top flight cast . . . As Western or drama, *Rio Grande* goes to the head of the class."[78]

The exhibitor publication *Motion Picture Daily* reported, "A historical outdoor action drama of ambitious dimensions has been fashioned by John Ford . . . His imaginative touch is in evidence frequently and he has directed with nimbleness and drive. Cast-wise the picture has been packaged for strong box office appeal."[79] According to the *Los Angeles Times*, the film "triumphs in scenery, song, action, and various embellishments . . . Savingly Ford always brings to his pictures colorful characters and incidents. Notably is Victor McLaglen restored to a good role as Sgt. Quincannon . . . Jarman does an especially good portrayal . . . Dale Evans contributed words and music and the 'San Antone' number, credited to her, is particularly good."[80]

Rio Grande reached the Ides Theatre in Moab on January 9, 1951, playing for three days, with two nightly showings.[81]

* * *

It has been said the military can be a very demanding mistress. Entering military life, one takes an oath that demands complete allegiance, forcing an enlistee to make many sacrifices during their time of service. Obviously, danger and death are two of the greatest sacrifices that come to mind, but another sacrifice, rarely spoken of, is the separation from family and loved ones. There is no medal for this sacrifice for either those who serve or those who wait, both struggling to carry on while hiding behind a mask of stoutheartedness. The demands of duty can become too much for some families, causing a rupture, such as in the case of Kirby Yorke and his wife, Kathleen.

The four years of the Civil War in America generated a large chasm between North and South, brother against brother, family fighting family. It is a division that still leads to arguments and protests 160 years later. Literally split apart over choosing a side to support and fight for, some family's dissension wouldn't heal for generations—if at all.[82] Kathleen Yorke, with her son in her arms, watched as her husband's Union cavalry burned down her home, barns, and crops during the Shenandoah campaign of 1864.[83] She has remained unforgiving, not only of her husband's actions, but the entire "Yankee army." When the war ended, Yorke found his marriage emotionally scarred, leaving him to bury himself in the far-flung military posts of the West. He has entombed his emotions relating to his family life, giving his attention to his mistress, the US Army.

Unlike Colonel Thursday, Yorke is not a martinet. His leadership skill is without question; he demands that his men, like himself, honor their oath to serve. A soldier's word is more important than anything else to Yorke, who believes it is the measure of a man. He treats his troopers with fairness and respect, which they do in return. He understands his orders and obeys them, even if he personally disagrees. As Sheridan reminds him, soldiers "do not make policy, they merely carry it out." Yorke and the general want to do more, yet their hands are tied by the politicians.

Yorke is stern when he addresses the new recruits for the first time. His words, hardly welcoming, are designed to put the fear of God in the men. He reminds them, as he does his son in a later conversation, that life in the cavalry is not a romantic or heroic adventure. When he first speaks to his son, there is little evidence in Yorke of a man who cares about his son, demanding more from Jeff, especially after his failure at West Point. He reminds his son that while he has chosen his way of life, he hopes he has "the guts to endure it."

Maintaining a brusque mien, we do occasionally see glimpses of Yorke's fatherly concern. When Jeff falls off the horses while Roman-riding, Yorke's first reaction is to go to him, but he quickly stops himself. As much as he might want to rush to Jeff's aid, he cannot show favoritism to his son over the other men he commands. Walking into the fight between Jeff and Heinze, he can do nothing to aid his son, even though it is obvious that Jeff is outweighed and outmuscled by Heinze. Jeff's refusal to state the reasons behind his fight earns him the respect of his father. This is obvious the following morning as Yorke walks past the window of the hospital, attempting to be none too obvious, and sees that his son is battered and bruised but smiling. Yorke grins when his son takes the dose of castor oil, feeling proud, but his smile fades quickly as he realizes how much he has missed out on, seeing his son grow up. The sacrifice of duty weighs heavily on him.

His fatherly concern is again shown when Tyree calls Jeff as one of his volunteers. Yorke's position doesn't allow him to give any words of encouragement to Jeff. All he can do is worry and hope. Wounded by an arrow, Yorke calls on his son to pull it out, then says, "Son, help me to my horse." It is the first time he addresses Jeff as his son in front of the other troopers.

Kathleen Yorke is bitter over a war that arrived on her doorstep, and toward the army, her husband's mistress, that caused a separation. As stated in the script, Kathleen views soldiers as "repugnant." The war and the destruction it brought to her personally is still a fresh wound. Quincannon's appearance ignites the memories and unleashes her anger by verbally slapping him with the word "arsonist." Although she has an immense dislike for the Union Army, Kathleen is not upset that Jeff chose to go to West Point, since it was part of her family's tradition for many years prior to the Civil War. Kathleen's class distinction is evident when she desires to buy Jeff's release, as she will not let her son be something as philistine as a regular soldier.

Her anger toward her husband has not diminished since his burning of Bridesdale. If anything, her animus has only grown since their separation. Yorke's refusal to sign Jeff's papers only exacerbates things, along with his comment, "special privilege for special born." Yet, when she finds his music box and hears the tune, she cannot help but be whisked away to happier times with Yorke. It is at this moment that Kathleen's rigid countenance begins to hint at cracking. When she and Yorke are serenaded by the regimental singers, the feelings she had bottled up gradually bloom. Returning from chasing the Apaches that attacked the fort, Yorke finds Kathleen in his darkened tent. Without words, he grabs her and firmly kisses her, displaying his love. As if boyishly ashamed of his action, he quickly lets her go and apologizes. Kathleen, who willingly went along with his kiss, is taken aback and a bit confused. As they walk back to her tent, she is still pushing her plan to have Jeff released from the army, even allowing that if Yorke did grant her request, she would come back to him. Kathleen is frustrated not only by Yorke declining to sign the release papers, but also by his reminding her that their son must honor his oath.

At the dinner for General Sheridan, Kathleen offers a toast to her only rival, the United States Cavalry. Yorke drains his glass, turning it over on the table (signifying the toast cannot be topped) as Kathleen smiles and finishes her drink. The scene that cements their reconciliation happens when Kathleen, like the other wives at the fort, waits as the men ride in from their mission. For her, the anticipation turns to worry, then to dread, as Yorke is not leading the column. Jeff walks behind his father on a travois when it stops next to Kathleen. Yorke, weak from his wound, mentions *their* son did well. Kathleen says nothing, only taking Yorke's hand, walking alongside. Neither needs to say anything more, as her action speaks volumes. Attending the military review, Yorke and Kathleen are surprised when the military band plays "Dixie." When Sheridan indicates it was his request, it not only indicates the reuniting of a nation, but the renewal of Yorke and Kathleen's love for each other.

Jeff Yorke faces the difficulty all sons face with their fathers. How does a son measure up? Can he make his father proud of his achievements? Will years of separation and the pain they have both experienced ever be healed? These are hardships many children face growing up, doubly so in a family with a long history in the military. Failing at West Point, without a father to guide him in his early years, Jeff is more than ashamed. He must prove not only to himself, but to his father, that he is worthy of respect.

Enlisting as a regular recruit, it is by happenstance that Jeff is assigned to his father's post. Their first meeting is chilly at best, with Jeff informing his father he did not come to the post as his son, but as Trooper Jefferson Yorke. When Heinze insults him, Jeff stands up not for his father, but for himself. Outmatched in the fight, Jeff will not give up. Yet when Heinze refuses to tell Yorke the reason for the fight, Jeff respects the soldier and apologizes. Jeff is now considered one of the troopers.

Jeff is somewhat embarrassed by his mother's arrival, especially when he learns of her desire to buy his release. Jeff demonstrates he is more of an adult by refusing to take an easy way out, stating that he will take responsibility and do it himself. Trying to understand a father he has barely known, he asks his mother what kind of a man he is. When she tells him he is very lonely, Jeff reflects on the image of his father being a great soldier, something he has likely clung to growing up. Now he must attempt to balance this with the reality of his father. He finally proves himself worthy of his father's respect when he helps Tyree and Boone rescue the children. Yorke's only concession of praise for Jeff is not given to him, but to Kathleen, when he says, "Our boy did well." That is enough for all—the reunited father, mother, and son.

* * *

The basic plot of *Rio Grande* is another typical cavalry-versus-Indians plot that any studio could have produced at the time. Under another director's leadership, the lead roles of Yorke and Kathleen could have been played by numerous actors, although it's likely they would have lacked the strong presence and chemistry John Wayne and Maureen O'Hara brought to the roles.

As a dedicated officer, husband, and father hiding his pain and loneliness, Wayne offers a gradational performance. He presents a man, much like his previous character of Captain Brittles, who is stern, when necessary, yet respected by the men he commands. Despite his gruff approach toward his son, the softer, fatherly side is visible in many scenes. Wayne demonstrates emotions ranging from a father's pride and concern to guilt for the years he was absent from Jeff's life.

When it comes to Kathleen, Wayne's first reaction is surprise. Wayne exposes his character's deeply buried emotions slowly, notably in the dinner scene where they look at each other with no spoken dialogue. Their emotions are expressed solely in the eyes of Wayne and O'Hara, as their chemistry is overwhelmingly palpable, hinting at their characters' constrained passion. (Interestingly, not one film reviewer mentioned anything about their on-screen chemistry in this scene.)

None of this chemistry would have been possible if it hadn't been for casting Maureen O'Hara as Kathleen. The charisma between the two, which literally ignites on the screen, was based on their fond, longtime friendship. (Wayne often referred to O'Hara as "a great guy.") O'Hara portrays Kathleen as a resolute woman whose family heritage was certainly patrician, but that doesn't mean she is above doing hard work, whether rebuilding Bridesdale, doing laundry for the soldiers, or helping to push over a wagon as a fortification against attacking Apaches. O'Hara brings a harshness to her performance as Kathleen, born out of the hardships of the war. She cannot forgive her husband, or the Yankee army, for the damages to her family plantation.

Yet for all her sternness, we are shown Kathleen's softer side in several scenes, if only for a few moments. Opening the music box in Yorke's tent and listening to its melody takes her back to a happier time before the war. (As she listens, Ford has her close-up go slightly out of focus for a moment, suggesting that she's recalling better memories.) O'Hara displays Kathleen's emotional conflict in subtle ways, such as when she arrives at the fort. Seeing Yorke for the first time in years, she does a subtle double take, slowly revealing her suppressed emotions by lightly biting her lower lip for a brief second. Kathleen catches herself and averts her gaze, wiping the dust from her jacket to regain her composure. It is a beautifully played moment by O'Hara, one of several she delivers in the film.

During the regimental singers' serenade, O'Hara displays an adroit range of emotions. At first, Kathleen is surprised at the choice of song; then, as the singers continue, her emotional remembrance as to what the song means to her and Yorke begins to take hold. Her head slowly drifts toward Yorke as she is lost in her thoughts, but she quickly looks away when she sees him looking at her. The unspoken poignancy of this entire sequence, just as in their dinner table scene, is presented by Wayne and O'Hara with just facial reactions.

When the cavalry returns from their rescue mission, O'Hara has no spoken dialogue, simply expressing her feelings facially. Like the other women who wait, O'Hara conveys apprehension when she notices Yorke is not leading the column. Offering an ever-so-brief reaction of relief as the children's wagon passes by, her concern quickly returns as she walks past the wounded men, only to see her son behind the travois carrying Yorke. Looking at Jeff, and then at her husband, Kathleen's expression is one of acceptance and relief. In this moment, O'Hara's facial expression reveals all of Kathleen's emotion.

Claude Jarman Jr. delivers a strong performance as a son who struggles to understand his father and gain his acceptance. In the hands of another director and actor, this role could have been easily overplayed when showing emotions in several scenes, but Jarman demonstrates Jeff's conflict with well-played reactions, such as his momentary hesitance at Roman-riding when he sees his father watching, or the fear after pulling the arrow from his father's body. Jarman imbues Jeff with the qualities of a likable young man yearning for his father's approval, which quickly garners the audience's sympathy.

Victor McLaglen's Quincannon in this film is the comedic relief, never failing to provide the right balance of humor without overplaying the moment. Ben Johnson's performance shows why he quickly became a popular actor, as his Tyree is played with Johnson's natural easy manner. Harry Carey Jr. said that his character of Boone was basically like his role of Sandy in *Wagon Master*—something of a smart aleck, without being obnoxious. (It has been speculated that Ford suggested Carey's character be called Sandy by Tyree and Jeff, even though his character is named Daniel Boone in the film.)

While *Rio Grande* was shot quickly by Ford—in just thirty-two days—his deft artistry and touches are still evident.[84] One particular haunting, yet tremendously powerful, moment happens when Yorke arrives after the children have been kidnapped, saying they came as soon as they could. Ford cuts to a reaction shot of several women standing among the rocks, looking at Yorke in silence as the wind ruffles their aprons and skirts.[85]

While Ford came up with the idea of Boone always having a piece of straw in his mouth, he used this trait for a piece of physical comedy at the end of the film. As Boone and the others are standing at attention while the commendation for their bravery is being read, Quincannon notices the straw in Boone's mouth. He leans over and yanks it out of his mouth. Throughout the film, the audience has become accustomed to seeing Boone with the straw in his mouth. Thus, Quincannon's reaction, which is not expected, adds a touch of humor to the scene. Another piece of business Ford came up with takes place when Tyree calls Boone and Jeff as his volunteers. As the two step forward, Jeff suddenly rubs his nose in a childlike manner.

Despite the carping of some film historians and academics, the songs by the Sons of the Pioneers do not hinder the storyline. As Ford biographer Scott Eyman has noted, the director manages to use the singers as "a sort of musical Greek chorus, Cavalry style." The singing group does enhance a scene's emotion, such as their rendition of "I'll Take You Home Again, Kathleen" or "My Gal Is Purple" as we see Yorke walking alone on the riverbank. The film's inclusion of songs is also a precursor to a specific theme song enhancing a film's narrative, such as in *High Noon* or Ford's *The Searchers*.

In the case of "Aha! San Antone," Harry Carey Jr. said it was a spontaneous idea by Ford to include it in the film, and another way to give future son-in-law Ken Curtis some extra screen time. "Ken and Shug Fisher knew the song and taught it to us right on the set before filming. You can kinda tell we hesitate with the words in one chorus for a minute, but Ken just carried on and we jumped in," he recalled.[86]

Ford's boisterous comedy is not as prominent in *Rio Grande* as compared to *Fort Apache*'s horse-riding sequence or Quincannon's brawl in *She Wore a Yellow Ribbon*. What might be considered the most raucous moment is when Dr. Wilkins breaks the stick over Quincannon's hand. Whether this moment brings a hearty laugh, an embarrassed chuckle, or stony silence is dependent on the viewer's sense of humor. Most of the film's humor is more restrained in comparison to the other two films. A perfect example is when Kathleen puts her hands through the holes in the seat of Quincannon's long johns. His reluctance to let her have them sets up the laugh, while the facial reactions of Kathleen and Quincannon build the humor and allow Wilkins to deliver the punch line: "As a doctor, I would diagnose those as saddle sores."

Ford added two humorous touches during the climactic rescue at the church in the Mexican village. In the first, Jeff is loading the Winchesters as Tyree and Boone shoot at the Apaches. At one point, Jeff accidentally fires a shot from the rifle he's loading, barely missing Boone's behind. Boone, expressing his surprise, physically moves the rifle barrel away from his posterior as Jeff apologizes. The other moment, which Ford developed during the script writing, is Quincannon exiting the church with Margaret Mary, where they suddenly turn and both genuflect before running out.

One of the glaring misfires in this film compared to *Fort Apache* and *She Wore a Yellow Ribbon* is the stereotyping of the Apaches as villains. Unlike Cochise or Pony That Walks, the Apaches in *Rio Grande* have zero character development, which would have allowed for sympathy or understanding as to why they are raiding and killing. Like other Westerns of the time, the Indians in *Rio Grande* simply serve as the villains the cavalry must fight and defeat. It has been speculated that James Kevin McGuinness had more of a pro-military attitude toward Indian culture in general, lacking the thoughtful touches Frank Nugent displayed in the previous films. One is left to hypothesize why the director ignored the chance to develop stronger character backgrounds for the Apaches. It's possible Ford might have felt he needed to incorporate more action (Cavalry vs. Apaches) to make *Rio Grande* a box office success, in order to ultimately obtain approval to make *The Quiet Man*.

Over the years there has been a group of cinema academics who claim *Rio Grande* was Ford's response to America's early involvement in the Korean War. There is nothing in any of Ford's papers that comes anywhere near supporting this assertion, just personal reasoning by a few without any supporting facts.[87] Because of James Kevin McGuinness's conservative views, there is a theory held by some that his dialogue of Sheridan giving Yorke his unofficial order is a reflection of the writer's personal views. ("Hit the Apache and burn him out. I'm tired of hit and run. I'm sick of diplomatic hide and seek.") However, that dialogue is also found in Bellah's short story, written in 1947. (*Rio Grande*'s script was completed in early May of 1950.) One certainly could make a theoretical argument that Yorke's chasing the Apaches across an international border was analogous to General MacArthur's crossing the 38th Parallel after the retreating North Korean military. However, there is no definite proof Ford viewed this film as a parable about the Korean conflict, and without it, this theory is nothing but conjecture.

* * *

Rio Grande marked the end of John Ford's cavalry trilogy.

Ford never intended the three films to be considered as a triad, but it did allow the director to reflect the honor of the military, and the country's relentless endurance during any difficult period, just as it had done in the recent world war.

Despite Ford's later dismissive attitude toward the trilogy, it is very obvious he loved making the films. They show a passion for the material, letting Ford display his mastery of storytelling that, nearly eight decades later, still enthralls audiences.

RIO GRANDE

Argosy Pictures–Republic Pictures. *Released:* November 15, 1950. *In production:* June 16, 1950, to July 21, 1950, thirty-two days. *Producer:* Merian C. Cooper. *Director:* John Ford. *Screenplay:* James Kevin McGuinness, based on the short story "Mission with No Record" by James Warner Bellah. *Cinematographer:* Bert Glennon. *Second Unit Cinematographer:* Archie Stout. *Editor:* Jack Murray. *Assistant Editor:* Barbara Ford. *Art Director:* Dudley Holmes. *Set Decorator:* John McCarthy, Charles Thompson. *Musical Score:* Victor Young. *Musical Director:* Sidney Cutner, Leo Shuken. *Sound:* Earl Crain Sr., Howard Wilson. *Assistant Director:* Wingate Smith. *Second Unit Director:* Cliff Lyons. *Production Manager:* Lowell Farrell. *Wardrobe:* Adele Palmer. *Wardrobe Researcher:* D. R. O. Hatswell. *Makeup Supervision:* Bob Marks. *Hairstylist:* Peggy Gray. *Special Effects:* Howard Lydecker, Theodore Lydecker. *Script Supervisor:* Meta

Stern. *Military Technical Advisor:* Major Philip Kieffer, US Army (Ret'd). *Set Accordionist:* Danny Borzage. *Running Time:* 104 minutes. *Budget:* $1,287,185.00. *Domestic Rental Gross:* $2,945,782.00. *Working Titles: Rio Bravo, Rio Grande Command.* Rereleased in 1956.

Filmed at Republic Pictures, White's Ranch, Moab, Utah. Mexican Hat, Utah.

Cast

John Wayne (*Lt. Col. Kirby Yorke*), Maureen O'Hara (*Kathleen Yorke*), Ben Johnson (*Trooper Travis Tyree*), Claude Jarman Jr. (*Trooper Jefferson "Jeff" Yorke*), Harry Carey Jr. (*Trooper Daniel "Sandy" Boone*), Victor McLaglen (*Sgt. Quincannon*), Chill Wills (*Dr. Wilkins*), Karolyn Grimes (*Margaret Mary*), J. Carrol Naish (*Lt. General Philip Sheridan*), Peter Ortiz (*Captain St. Jacques*), Steve Pendleton (*Captain Prescott*), Alberto Morin (*Mexican Army Lieutenant*), Frank McGrath (*Cpl. Derice, Bugler*), Don Summers (*Cpl. Bell*), Grant Withers (*US Marshal*), Stan Jones (*Sergeant),* Fred Kennedy (*Trooper Heinze*), Cliff Lyons (*Trooper Cliff*), Jack Pennick (*Sgt. Major*), Frank Baker (*Sgt. Major*), Patrick Wayne (*Young Boy*), Ken Curtis, Hugh Farr, Shug Fisher, Karl Farr, Lloyd Perryman, Tommy Doss (*Regimental Singers*), Lee Bradley (*Sergeant*), Son of Many Mules (*Navajo Scout*), Many Mules, John Stanley, Barlow Simpson (*Apache Indians*).

Stunts

Frank McGrath, Fred Kennedy, Terry Wilson, John Hudkins, Cliff Lyons, Bob Rose, Everett Creach, Chuck Hayward, Chuck Roberson, Norm Taylor, Jerry Brown, Barlow Simpson.

Taps

Can't you ever end a sentence with anything but a question mark?

—John Ford

Surprisingly, Herbert Yates stuck to his promise and, in June of 1951, John Ford began filming his dream project, *The Quiet Man*, in Ireland. However, the quintessential skinflint studio head continually harassed Ford on location with telegrams ranging from the concern of overrunning the $1.4 million budget to complaining that the Irish scenery was *too green*!

Once the company had returned to Hollywood, Yates did not let up. Argosy's contract with Republic called for each film to run no longer than 111 minutes, and Yates was adamant on sticking to the running time. (Ford's final cut of *The Quiet Man* came in at 129 minutes.) The studio arranged a screening of the film for a small group of guests, along with Ford and Yates. As the film unspooled, it cast its spell and enamored the audience. Just as the fight between John Wayne and Victor McLaglen was about to be unleashed, the screen went blank. The lights in the screening room came up, leaving all in attendance puzzled.

Ford turned to Yates and told him that he had decided to cut out the fight to keep it under the studio head's dictate of 111 minutes. Yates got the message, and the film was released at the full 129 minutes.

The Quiet Man proved to be a major hit when released in 1952. (It grossed over $5 million within three years of its release.) It was not only Republic's biggest box office hit, but their *only* movie to ever receive a

Best Picture Oscar nomination. (The film garnered seven Oscar nominations, including Ford winning his fourth, and last, Best Director Oscar.)[1]

* * *

In the summer of 1952, Argosy's treasurer, Lee Van Hoozer, sent Herbert Yates a letter in regard to the studio's bookkeeping tallies on *Rio Grande*. While the film had brought in $735,131.38 in foreign earnings, Republic's accounting books claimed Argosy's percentage of the film (50 percent of net earnings) only amounted to $82,425.90. (Van Hoozer estimated the company should have collected closer to $250,000.) Seven months later Argosy hired Price Waterhouse to perform an expensive audit of Republic Pictures' accounting books. Not only were the foreign earnings for *Rio Grande* under examination, but also those of *The Quiet Man*. Republic was claiming the latter film only earned a net profit of $1.29 million, which meant Argosy's cut was around $600,000. As in other cases of Hollywood's creative bookkeeping, Argosy was forced to file a lawsuit against Republic, which wound its way through the courts until December of 1956, when both Ford and Cooper received a total payment of $194,670.[2]

Ford made *The Sun Shines Bright* in 1953, a remake of *Judge Priest*, as his final film under the Republic deal, but the recent events had left a sour taste in his mouth. Ford's relationship with Merian Cooper was never really the same, as Ford felt Cooper should have been paying more attention to the fine print of Argosy's deal with Yates. Ford's friendship with Wayne also suffered for a time, as he blamed the actor for getting him involved with a Poverty Row studio, and did not speak to him for several months. This was nothing new for Wayne; after he'd starred in *The Big Trail* (1930) at Fox, Ford had refused to talk to him for nearly three years. (Until the day he died, Wayne could never figure out why Ford just stopped talking to him during the early 1930s.)

* * *

Despite the strong box office earnings for *Rio Grande* and *The Quiet Man*, Argosy Productions was struggling to stay above the water line. Ford and Cooper had trimmed down expenses to the bare minimum, as well as deferring their salaries, but it did little to alleviate the company's debt. Aside from Republic's shenanigans with bookkeeping, another problem for Argosy was that many countries were holding back funds (i.e., foreign box office revenue) that would have lightened, if not paid off, Argosy's debt.[3] As Ford biographer Scott Eyman noted, the company had paid down their debt to nearly $209,000 by October of 1950, and within three years the earnings from *The Quiet Man* would have come to the company's rescue.[4]

Unfortunately, neither time nor the debt's accumulating interest was on Argosy's side. Ford and Cooper finally threw in the towel and dissolved the company in 1956.[5] A deal was negotiated with RKO granting them ownership of Argosy's five films in exchange for remunerating the company's debt.[6] The dream of owning their own product was over for Ford and Cooper.

* * *

In May of 1952, Merian C. Cooper took a break from Argosy and joined Cinerama Productions. With audiences staying home to be entertained by the new medium of television, Hollywood studios had to devise ways to divorce viewers from their television sets and get them back into theaters by promising something that could never be experienced on TV. Cinerama was a wide-screen process projected onto three deeply curved screens using three synchronized projectors, giving an audience member the feeling the movie screen was wrapped around them.[7] *This Is Cinerama* (1952), narrated by Lowell Thomas, was a major hit for the company, which produced more films that were equally popular. MGM produced two dramatic films using this process, *The Wonderful World of the Brothers Grimm* (1962) and *How the West Was Won* (1963). The latter film had three directors, including John Ford handling the Civil War sequence.[8] (At an early point in preproduction, Ford was scheduled to direct the entire Western epic.) Cinerama proved to be a costly investment, between the three cameras needed to capture an image, and modifying theaters to accommodate the three screens and projectors to show a film. Like 3D films, it was a short-lived concept.

C. V. Whitney was a wealthy investor in Cinerama and a great fan of Ford's cavalry trilogy. In 1954, he formed C. V. Whitney Pictures and brought along Merian Cooper. The new company purchased the film rights of two novels, *The Valiant Virginians* by James Warner Bellah and Alan Le May's *The Searchers*. Whitney and Cooper envisioned the Bellah novel as an epic-in-size production, and wanted Ford to direct both projects. Cooper suggested it was wiser for the new company to produce *The Searchers* first, as the budget was more reasonable compared to what would be required for Bellah's book.

* * *

The Searchers (1956) was the right project for Ford at the right time. MGM's *Mogambo* (1953), a remake of the studio's 1932 *Red Dust*, was Ford's last box office hit. *Long Gray Line* (1955) did not perform well; then the behind-the-scenes disaster on *Mister Roberts* (1955) left Hollywood wondering if Ford had lost his touch.[9] (While *Mister Roberts* was a box office success, Ford shared co-directing duties and credit with Mervyn LeRoy.) *The Searchers* proved that Ford had not lost his touch, making what many feel is his greatest film. (Ironically, the film did not garner a single Oscar nomination, although it was a solid box office attraction.) After the release of the film, C. V. Whitney pulled out of the moviemaking business, and plans for making *The Valiant Virginians* disappeared. Ending his career on a high note with *The Searchers*, Merian C. Cooper retired with his wife, actress Dorothy Jordan, to Coronado, across the bay from San Diego. He died on April 21, 1973, at the age of seventy-nine.

* * *

The growth of television was pulling audiences away from the movie theaters, resulting in lower studio earnings. Along with the Paramount Decree, now firmly enforced, studios began to cut back on the number of films they produced as a way of economizing. By 1968, the PCA was replaced by a new ratings system to guide audiences regarding a film's content. (Studios no longer had to submit a script prior to production for approval, only the final cut of a film.) Studio moguls were either ousted from their positions or died, often replaced by men of lesser talent. Many studios in the next two decades would become subsidiaries of bigger corporations, while agents peddled not just a script, but an entire package that included a star, script, and possibly a director. More stars formed their own companies, where they served a dual role as performer and producer. The days of the star or director under a long-term studio contract were gone, replaced by multipicture, nonexclusive deals. For John Ford, a man who had worked so well in the studio system, this change was an unwelcome guest.[10]

* * *

Age, as it does with everyone, was catching up to Ford, who was fifty-six years old when he finished *Rio Grande*. As time went on, Ford's enthusiasm, which generally started off strong at the beginning of a project, began to fade as the production wore on. Between 1950 and 1965, John Ford directed twenty movies that ranged from a masterpiece (*The Searchers*), to classic (*The Man Who Shot Liberty Valance*), to underrated (*The Last Hurrah*), and misguided (*What Price Glory*).

The deaths of friends, stock company members, and close associates hung in the air as the years went on, as well as the demise of the Hollywood studio system.[11] The days of dealing with a Zanuck, who lived and breathed movies, were gone. For a man who was fast approaching seventy, Ford was finding it more difficult to attract the interest of a new generation of studio executives, some who had no knowledge of John Ford. When he did reach the stage of finalizing a contract, it was no longer a simple deal between the studio, actor, and director. One only has to look at *The Horse Soldiers* as an example of how complicated things became regarding contract negotiations. It involved six corporations, six agents, and each group's lawyers to haggle out a 250-page contract over the span of six months. No wonder Ford once said that they should make the film in Lourdes, as it was "going to take a miracle to pull it off."[12]

Of the last ten films Ford directed, only three—*The Horse Soldiers*, *The Man Who Shot Liberty Valance*, and *How the West Was Won*—were box office successes.[13] (The latter one cannot really be considered a Ford film in its entirety, since he only directed the Civil War sequence.) Three box office hits out of ten is not a good track record for any director, let alone a director of Ford's stature. When his partner Merian C. Cooper retired after *The Searchers*, Ford considered the idea, but he just couldn't do it. Directing was his life, and without it he was lost. Yet as time went on, getting a film into production was becoming a major ordeal. Ford was used to going from one film to another at Fox, or planning his own productions at RKO, and the sudden lull between jobs began to take its toll. Anyone who spends a number of years in the film industry will admit to having the constant fear of never working again. It is an anxiety that is always there, and for many, this concern only increased with the demise of the studio system and the shift toward a freelance market.[14]

In 1962, Ford visited producer Samuel Bronson in Spain who was producing some big-budget films (*El Cid*, *55 Days at Peking*, *The Fall of the Roman Empire*). Ford discussed two potential projects: an Arthur Conan Doyle story (*The White Company*) and *The Wandering Jew*.[15] Bronson turned him down.

Samuel Goldwyn Jr. approached Ford in 1966 about directing *April Morning*, a story of the Revolutionary War based on Howard Fast's novel. Try as he might, the younger Goldwyn could not get the project into production. In the late 1960s, it was mentioned that Ford and Japanese director Akira Kurosawa would co-direct 20th Century-Fox's epic story of the attack on Pearl Harbor, *Tora! Tora! Tora!* The film would be told from the perspectives of both Japan and the United States, with a generous budget of nearly $25 million. Given Ford's association with the navy, not to mention the mutual admiration he and Kurosawa had for each other, it sounded like a surefire hit. While Ford may have expressed interest, he dropped out because his health would not allow him to tackle such an intensive production. (Kurosawa, who remained with the project, was replaced a few days into filming.)

By 1966, Ford still believed he would direct a few more projects, and kept trying to interest others. He maintained an office for a couple of years, going there several times a week, but there were no offers from any studios—even if the executives knew who he was. At first, he would tell interviewers that he had a few projects in the works. Two years later, his reply to the question of when he'd make another movie was a biting, "They won't let me do another picture."

John Ford had become a Lion in Winter.

Besides having plenty of time to read, Ford spent his days watching television, mostly in bed. He watched old Westerns and their TV counterparts, as well as the game show *Jeopardy!* He developed a fondness for some television shows, including Jack Webb's police drama, *Adam-12* (1968–1975), about two LAPD patrol officers. Ford visited the set one day in mid-1971, posing for a photograph with the two stars, Martin Milner and Kent McCord, story editor Stephen Cannell, assistant director Dennis Donnelly, and associate producer Tom Williams.[16]

Ford and his work were now being noticed by a new generation of filmmakers, fans, and historians. He was feted with awards and retrospectives, and inundated with interview requests from younger filmmakers or historians. Peter Bogdanovich would drive him crazy with unending questions, and at one point Ford bellowed, "Jesus Christ, Bogdanovich! Can't you ever end a sentence with anything but a question mark?" (Despite his gruffness, Ford took a liking to the young man, who would soon become a director in his own right.)

In 1971, Bogdanovich directed a documentary, *Directed by John Ford*, even getting Ford to sit for an on-camera interview at the point named after him in Monument Valley. Ford's reply to Bogdanovich's questions is pure gold, giving short answers ("I wouldn't know"), or a noncommittal reply ("Yeah, uh-huh"). He was playing the prickly John Ford character he had carefully crafted for over fifty years to the hilt. When the San Francisco International Film Festival presented Bogdanovich's documentary, festival director Claude Jarman Jr. invited his former *Rio Grande* director to attend. Ford wasn't interested. Jarman then asked if Ford wanted to say anything about the film which he could relay to the audience. "Tell them it wasn't directed by John Ford," he replied.[17]

The American West of John Ford was a one-hour special for CBS that aired in early December of 1971. The special, conceived by the director's grandson, Dan Ford, mixed film clips with James Stewart, Henry Fonda, and John Wayne sharing memories. Making what would be his last visit to Monument Valley, Ford is shown directing Chuck Roberson (doubling Wayne) performing a horse fall. In another sequence, the camera catches Wayne and Ford looking out over Monument Valley, and it is the standout moment of this special. In his narration, Wayne mentions that he came back to reminisce and had the feeling Ford came back to say good-bye to his beloved valley. We see two old friends caught in mid-conversation, sharing a memory about Ward Bond complaining how his horse had dumped him in the river, with Wayne riding up behind him during a scene in *The Searchers*. As much as Bond complained about falling off the horse, Ford kept repeating that it looked great. Wayne chuckles as he admits he rode his horse right behind Bond's backside. As they look out over the land, Wayne points out the *Stagecoach* location where Ford had the coach ride past and the rise where the Indians waited.

"The memories come back," Ford said.

* * *

Hollywood staged one last hurrah for the director.

The American Film Institute bestowed their first Lifetime Achievement award to Ford, honoring the filmmaker's work which "stood the test of time."[18] At the March 31, 1973, event, all of Hollywood turned out to honor Ford, many knowing he was seriously ill with inoperable cancer. President Richard Nixon presented him the Medal of Freedom, and announced he was promoting Ford to the rank of full admiral. The moment he accepted the award was probably the only time Ford let down some of his facade, admitting he was overcome with gratitude—"about all I can say before I break down."

As the months went by, friends and co-workers made the trip to Palm Desert for one last good-bye. (The Fords had sold their Bel Air residence in late 1972, moving to Palm Desert.) Peter Bogdanovich and Howard Hawks visited, with Ford asking Hawks whether the young director had asked him "all those damned questions." Wayne made his last visit on August 30, keeping up a strong front for his mentor.

John Ford died the following day, August 31, 1973, at 6:35 p.m.

Tributes flowed in from around the world. His funeral mass at the Blessed Sacrament Church in Hollywood was a major event. Everyone in Hollywood attended: John Wayne, James Stewart, Henry Fonda, Charlton Heston, Frank Capra, William Wyler, cinematographers William Clothier and Winton Hoch, George Cukor, and Iron Eyes Cody (in full Indian dress). Members of the Masquers Club filled two church pews. Stock company members Harry Carey Jr. and his mother Olive Carey were there, along with Anna Lee, Wingate Smith, Danny Borzage, George O'Brien, Chuck Roberson, Terry Wilson, Chuck Hayward, Hank Worden, and Frank Butler, among others.

At the end of the funeral mass, the organist played "Battle Hymn of the Republic" as his coffin, draped with the tattered American flag he had had since the Battle of Midway, was wheeled out. John Wayne walked down the aisle with his wife, Pilar, on one side and Mary Ford on the other. His face was tight with grief as tears streamed down his cheeks. This author, who was sixteen at the time, attended with his father and sat with other members of the Masquers Club. As I watched Ford's casket roll past me, listening to the organ music, I fought to hold back the tears. Try as I might, I couldn't do it when I saw John Wayne crying, and the floodgates opened. As the people in my aisle exited, I found myself walking alongside director William Wyler and Charlton Heston. Sobbing, I looked at the two men, and they nodded, understanding my grief.

* * *

During an interview for his biography on his grandfather, Dan Ford caught John Wayne in a reflective moment, recalling his two great friends, John Ford and Ward Bond. "Those were great days. You can't look back. You're not supposed to, but it's pretty hard not to when it was guys like Ward and Jack. You don't meet them every day."[19]

* * *

Little has changed in Monument Valley since John Ford first exposed a frame of celluloid over eighty-four years ago. East and West Mitten, Merrick Butte, Three Sisters, and Totem Pole have shown little effects of erosion.

Thanks to John Ford's films, the area is a popular tourist destination, not just for people of the United States, but from all over the world. To many visitors, Monument Valley embodies the American West and all it represents. There is an area where a plateau stands out alone, offering an amazing view of the valley. It is known as John Ford Point.[20]

From the visitors' center, and the recently built View Hotel, one can look at the East and West Mittens and the same dirt road the stagecoach and cavalry used in *Stagecoach*. Goulding's Lodge now provides numerous rooms and cabins for visitors, while the building that was the sutler's store in *She Wore a Yellow Ribbon* has been rebuilt as a restaurant. Goulding's original two-story trading post is a museum, with one room dedicated to the movies filmed in the area. The inside of the potato cellar building—the outside of which served as the exterior of Captain Brittles' quarters in *She Wore a Yellow Ribbon*—now features a re-creation of Brittles' living quarters, along with photographs from the film.

During the years Ford worked in the valley, he and cast members would sign the guest book at Goulding's Lodge. "Harry, you and I both owe these monuments a lot" Wayne inscribed during one visit. One of Ford's comments reads: "To Harry, Mike, Again I am sorry to say 'Adios' to you and your hospitality—My thanks to Old Fats who gave us such wonderful weather, and your crew, who took such good care of us."

Monument Valley remains timeless. The land is captivating, hypnotic, and stunning. Standing at John Ford Point, or any part of the valley, a magical feeling overtakes you. You are in a land so unique, it is easy to lose any sense of time. Listening to the wind as it blows across the sand, and taking in the boundless views, you can understand why John Ford loved this location so much.

Director John Milius was correct when he stated that Ford was having a love affair with the land when he filmed in Monument Valley.[21]

* * *

Critics say there were many layers to John Ford and his films. To understand both, you need to understand the Irish. So much of what made John Ford and his movies is rooted in his ancestral homeland and traditions.

Known for telling tales, or laying on the blarney, is an inherent trait of the Irish. They can take a true story, twist it this way and that, each time enhancing and adding another layer to the tale. Before you know it, the truth has been buried deep below the sod. Even if you realize you've been fibbed to, there is no harm. Blarney never deliberately hurts anyone.

Ford often laid on the blarney, not just to interviewers, but in his films. The gunfight in *My Darling Clementine* is not at all close to the true event, but Ford's version has its own romantic and heroic feel, facts be damned. (Ford claimed his version of the gunfight was exactly the way Wyatt Earp related it to him.) Like Carlton Young says in *The Man Who Shot Liberty Valance*, "When the legend becomes fact, print the legend."

Applying blarney allows the storyteller to hide his true self. Ford carefully crafted an image of a gruff, bite-your-head-off director. As much as John Wayne perfected his cinema persona, Ford did the same, creating the John Ford image many actors and interviewers came to fear. His rough exterior gave him the advantage when asserting control over his films, preventing anyone from interfering or questioning his vision. It also kept actors on edge—waiting and dreading the moment of being "in the barrel." His needling style was a deliberate tactic to get a certain performance out of his actors.

Stuntman Chuck Hayward observed that Ford had a "very sharp psychology" and used it differently on each person. Hayward said the director "could really get to them [an actor]" to bring out a performance. Ford's attitude also kept many producers at bay, who quickly learned to leave him alone. Even though they butted heads over a production, Darryl F. Zanuck was a producer Ford admired, and, to a different extent, the same was true of Merian C. Cooper. The rough outer shell hid Ford's sensitive and sentimental side. It would not do for anyone to see his softer side (even though many co-workers knew about it), as it would affect his carefully honed personality. This brusque characteristic of Ford dated back to his childhood, shielding him from the taunts of others who might have discovered his love of reading or his Irish sentimental side.

Another connection between John Ford and the Irish is the appreciation of family and community. A family may have its differences, with even brothers coming to blows, but an outsider quickly finds out a family cannot be divided by others. It is ironic that the loving family life we often see in Ford's films was not always a reflection of his own. While he had a strong and protective relationship with his daughter, Barbara, the one with his son, Patrick, was a different story. Some have said that Ford was a distant father figure to his son, often expecting more from him than he did from others. It can be a curse with many father–son relationships, especially if a father is very successful or famous. It is a shadow that is often hard to shake.

In his films, the father and mother figures are strong, kind, and loving, providing a good dose of discipline when needed. Even substitute father figures like Nathan Brittles or Ethan Edwards can be hard (in Ethan's case, very hard), yet still allow a tender side to be seen, however briefly. The family, whether it be a blood family, friends, or the military, gives each person a sense of importance and feeling needed. Ford also celebrates the feeling of family and community by portraying gatherings, such as a dinner scene in *How Green Was My Valley*, or in the dances found in *The Grapes of Wrath*, *My Darling Clementine*, *Fort Apache*, *Wagon Master*, or, briefly, *The Searchers*.

The other aspect of the Irish, which integrates with family and community, is death, talking to the dead, and the funeral ceremony. Death in a Ford film is often shown from a short or far distance, but rarely up close. Four notable exceptions would be Victor McLaglen in *The Informer*, Edna May Oliver in *Drums Along the Mohawk*, John Carradine in *Stagecoach*, and Victor Mature in *My Darling Clementine*.[22] In certain cases, we learn of the death afterward, such as James Earp in *My Darling Clementine* or Lucy in *The Searchers*.

While not an exclusive characteristic of the Irish, the act of speaking to the dead often appears in the cinema of John Ford. Speaking at the grave to a deceased relative is a common Irish attribute, one that Ford often used to help a character express their emotions, which would not be as powerful if spoken to a living person. Three of the most well-known graveside scenes found in Ford films are Abe Lincoln at Ann Rutledge's grave in *Young Mr. Lincoln*, Wyatt Earp at his younger brother's grave in *My Darling Clementine*, and Brittles at his wife's grave in *She Wore a Yellow Ribbon*.

Funerals play an important part in Ford's films. In some cases, the funeral has yet to take place or the burial has already occurred. Ford uses the funeral to display a variety of emotions, such as honoring a comrade in the Confederate officer's burial in *She Wore a Yellow Ribbon*; the prostitute's funeral procession that forces others to examine their prejudices in *The Sun Shines Bright*; the burial that is interrupted in order to seek vengeance in *The Searchers*; the gathering of old friends in *The Man Who Shot Liberty Valance*; or a Native American ceremony for a tribal leader in *Cheyenne Autumn*.

At least thirteen of John Ford's films are considered classics that still stand the test of time. No other director has won as many Oscars or New York Film Critics Circle awards as John Ford.[23] They are both records that have yet to be surpassed.

His films, including the cavalry trilogy, speak to all of us. The cavalry films honor the courage and duty to serve no matter the elements or the adversaries. Viewers who served in later generations understand what the soldiers in a Ford film are experiencing. For children and young adults, they see heroism, characters to inspire them to face their own day-to-day experiences with courage and honesty.

John Ford *did* have a love affair with the Monument Valley, and his films continue to share that love with thousands, encouraging many to make a pilgrimage to visit and connect with the land.

Somewhere in Monument Valley, off in the distance, a visitor might still hear a distant bugler blowing "Taps."

Acknowledgments

There are many who lend a hand, however large or small, in helping an author through the maze of writing a book. I wish to shine the spotlight on the folks who have been most helpful to me on this project.

The late Harry Carey Jr. spent hours talking about Ford and his films with me over the years, the greatest film history lessons one could ever ask for. He was also a family friend who always held the door open for a visit.

Dan Ford, the grandson of John Ford, was very generous in granting me access to his grandfather's papers, answering questions and supporting this project.

Joe Musso was more than generous in sharing his photos and information on the trilogy. Joe, you're a "top soldier" in my book.

A wonderful gift is the support and encouragement you get from fellow authors and film historians, and I have been blessed with some of the best. Scott Eyman didn't just offer suggestions and encouragement, but also his friendship, which I deeply appreciate. Leonard Maltin was like the US Cavalry coming to my aid whenever I needed help. Tom Weaver provided answers, sometimes at the drop of a hat, while Ed Hulse generously shared his knowledge about horse stunts and his conversations with Yakima Canutt. Alan K. Rode was always in my corner when I had doubts that this book would ever see the light of day. Steven Bingen was equally helpful and supportive as I made my way toward seeing this book published.

A grateful thank-you to everyone who granted my requests to view various materials: Isabel Planton of the Lilly Library at Indiana University; Megan Jacobson of the L. Tom Perry Special Collections at

Brigham Young University; Louise Hilton of the Special Collections at the Margaret Herrick Library of the Academy of Motion Picture Arts and Sciences; Emily Wittenberg of the Louis B. Mayer Library at the American Film Institute; and Tara Beresh of the Moab Museum.

A big thank-you to Melissa Hayes, for her sharp eye in editing, and to Janice Braunstein at TwoDot Books, for bringing this book to fruition.

Then there are the friends who have been "my cavalry": Jim Beaver, James Benesh, June Bracken, Jamie Capps, Carla Dean, Major Remy Garner of the US Army, George Gold, Steve Gustafson, Mike Hawks, Lolita Jerigan, Lisa Kelly, Terry Lamfers, Jenny Lerew, George Loomis, the late Michael Lubrano, Denise McAllister, Roger McGrath, Lydia Milars, Jeff Morey, Major Thomas Oblak of the US Army (Ret'd), Carrie Renfro, Dan and Patti Richmond, Celeste Rush, the late John Schultheiss, Terry Shulman, David C. Smith, Phil Spangenberger, Steve Tanner, Nate Thomas, Mitch Trimboli, and Beth Werling.

My daughter, Kim, has put up with my endless talk of John Ford over the years, yet is always interested in what I have to say. I am a very lucky fellow to have her in my life.

Last, but in no way least, the words "Thank you" are never enough when it comes to my wife, Linda. From trekking around Monument Valley and Moab, to endless (and I mean *endless*) viewings of Ford's cavalry trilogy, she has remained a constant companion and supporter. Thanks, soldier.

Notes

Preface

1. The word "cavalry" was anglicized from the French word *cavalerie*.

2. Gerald Peary, ed., *John Ford Interviews* (Jackson: University Press of Mississippi, 2001), 159.

3. Ford also said at this event that he was "a silent picture man." George J. Mitchell, "Ford on Ford," *Films in Review* (June–July 1964), 326.

4. Peary, ed., *John Ford Interviews*, 121.

5. After completing *Rio Grande*, Ford did not direct another Western for five years, until tackling *The Searchers* (1956).

6. Those films, in chronological order, are: *They Were Expendable* (1945), *Fort Apache* (1948), *She Wore a Yellow Ribbon* (1949), *Rio Grande* (1950), *When Willie Comes Marching Home* (1950), *What Price Glory* (1952), *The Long Gray Line* (1955), *Mister Roberts* (1955; shared directing credit with Mervyn LeRoy), *The Wings of Eagles* (1957), *The Horse Soldiers* (1959), *Sergeant Rutledge* (1960), and *Cheyenne Autumn* (1964). Ford also directed two military documentaries: *This is Korea!* (1951) and *Chesty: A Tribute to a Legend* (1976; about US Marine, General Lewis "Chesty" B. Puller). One could also consider Ford's Civil War segment of *How the West Was Won* (1963) as a military film.

The Director and the Adventurer

1. *Directed by John Ford* (documentary), American Film Institute, 1971.

2. The story has several versions of when and where this happened, as well as how many pages. Harry Carey Jr. told this author this incident took place at Fox Studios, and it was three pages. Cinematographer Joseph LaShelle told Peter Bogdanovich that it happened at Fox, but the producer sent his assistant to talk to Ford. In this version, Ford tore out eight pages that hadn't been filmed, and, according to LaShelle, were never filmed. Stuntman Chuck Hayward stated it happened at Republic Pictures, and it was studio head Herbert Yates who complained. Hayward said Ford tore three pages from the script.

3. Dan Ford, *Pappy: The Life of John Ford* (Englewood Cliffs, NJ: Prentice-Hall, Inc., 1979), 256–57.

4. Larry Blake to the author, March 1979.

5. Ben Johnson to Dan Ford, John Ford Collection, Lilly Library, Indiana University.

6. Ford was nominated five times for Best Director. In order: *The Informer* (1935), *Stagecoach* (1939), *The Grapes of Wrath* (1940), *How Green Was My Valley* (1941), and *The Quiet Man* (1952). His two short subjects were *The Battle of Midway* (1942) and *December 7th* (1943).

7. Ford knew about the Black and Tans firsthand. Ireland was full of political disturbance and violence between 1916 and 1921, as the country strove for independence. In 1921, Ford sailed to Ireland to visit relatives and get a glimpse of the Irish war for independence. Sinn Féin, a political party desiring independence, also supported the Irish Republican Army (IRA), a paramilitary organization that launched a guerrilla war against the British military. Their attempts during the Easter Rising of 1916 resulted in more than 260 civilians killed by British troops, not to mention several IRA members who were executed. By the time of Ford's arrival, the warfare between the IRA and the British was at its height. (Ford's father, John, had been a willing financial supporter of Sinn Féin.) Ford's arrival in his parents' native land put him on the radar of the British army. Not only was he well-known as a film director, but he was also the cousin of Martin Feeney, an IRA leader who had a bounty on his head. Giving the British the slip, Ford did manage to meet his cousin, who was in hiding, and supplied him with food and money. Throughout his visit, Ford was watched by the "Black and Tan Fraternity," often stopped for questioning, and at one point they roughed him up before being told to get on a boat for London and to never come back.

The Black and Tans were a group of constables that became part of the Royal Irish Constabulary to suppress the IRA in their quest for freedom. The term "Black and Tans" came from their uniform, which consisted of dark green (looking almost black) and khaki. They were notorious for their brutality (including murder, arson, and looting), attacking civilians and their property in retaliation for the IRA's arson and looting. With these merciless actions, it only deepened the resolve of the Irish public to be free of British rule. Ford, *Pappy*, 22–24.

8. Scott Eyman, *Print the Legend: The Life and Times of John Ford* (New York: Simon & Schuster, 1999), 117–18.

9. Harry Carey Jr. to Dan Ford, John Ford Collection, Lilly Library.

10. Peter Bogdanovich, *John Ford* (Berkeley: University of California Press, 1978), 15.

11. Terry Wilson to Dan Ford, John Ford Collection, Lilly Library.

12. Harry Carey Jr. to the author, June 19, 1996.

13. Ford's father, John, owned a bar in the city. Five of the eleven Ford children died in infancy.

14. Eyman, *Print the Legend*, 40.

15. Ford claimed he appeared as a Klansman in D. W. Griffith's *Birth of a Nation* (1915), saying he had to keep lifting the hood to see where his horse was going, until he fell off and was knocked unconscious. Ford was never a good rider. According to Ben Johnson, he "looked like a sack of walnuts on a horse." Ben Johnson to Dan Ford, John Ford Collection, Lilly Library.

16. Frank S. Nugent, "Hollywood's Favorite Rebel," *The Saturday Evening Post* (July 23, 1949).

17. Ford's first directing credit, a two-reeler, *The Tornado*, was released on March 3, 1917, followed by *The Scrapper*, released on June 9, 1917. Ford's first film with Harry Carey was *The Soul Herder*, released August 7, 1917. *Directed by John Ford* (documentary), American Film Institute, 1971.

18. Ford's second Oscar for Best Short Subject was *December 7th*, released in 1943.

19. Mark Cotta Vaz, *Living Dangerously: The Adventures of Merian C. Cooper* (New York: Villard Books, 2005), 14.

20. Ibid., 39–42.

21. Ibid., 69–71.

22. In the stampede sequence, the elephants destroy a small village. Cooper and Schoedsack built a miniature set and had baby elephants run through it.

23. Pan Am declared bankruptcy and ceased all operations in December 1991. Western Airlines was bought out by Delta Airlines in 1987.

24. The film would go on to earn over $2 million in its initial run, when ticket prices were an average of ten to fifteen cents. Cotta Vaz, *Living Dangerously*, 236–37.

25. David O. Selznick moved to MGM to set up shop. (Louis B. Mayer was his father-in-law.) He would leave the studio in a couple of years to become an independent producer.

The Gower Street lot in Hollywood (between Santa Monica Boulevard and Melrose Avenue) was originally Film Booking Offices of America, registered as FBO Pictures Corp., which produced low-budget films for smaller markets. In 1928, FBO merged with RCA and the Keith-Albee-Orpheum company (a large movie-theater circuit) to create RKO Pictures. In this merger RKO inherited the FBO studios on Gower Street and the Pathé Studios in Culver City. The latter had been built by producer Thomas H. Ince in 1918, and after his death in 1924, William DeMille (Cecil's brother) used the studio lot for various productions. (Joseph Kennedy maintained ownership of the lot under the name Pathé, until he sold it to RKO in 1930.) After the merger, the Culver City lot was known as RKO-Pathé, or RKO Culver. (The property on Gower Street was called RKO Gower.) The studio had several stages, and a twenty-eight-acre backlot for sets. David O. Selznick maintained his offices on the lot beginning in 1935, and many in the industry simply referred to it as the "Selznick lot," even though he never owned the property. Both lots remained in RKO's control until 1957, when the properties were sold to Lucille Ball and Desi Arnaz. They were renamed Desilu Gower and Desilu Culver respectively. Ball and Arnaz also purchased the Motion Picture Center studios on Cahuenga Boulevard, dubbing it Desilu Cahuenga. In 1967, the three lots were sold to Paramount (then owned by Gulf+Western company). Paramount kept the Gower Street lot (which it still owns), while selling the Culver City and Cahuenga Boulevard lots, which changed hands numerous times. The Cahuenga Boulevard property is now called Red Studios and is a rental lot for independent productions, such as the recent cable series *Bosch* and *Bosch: Legacy*. The Culver City location, dubbed Culver Studios, has recently undergone a major facelift, with new stages and other buildings.

26. Color film had been experimented with since the very beginning of cinema. Early versions, such as that used in Edison's *The Great Train Robbery* (1903), had individual frames tinted by hand. In the Edison film, gunshots were painted to look yellow, and red

when the bandits blow up the strongbox. Kinemacolor, developed in Britain, was popular for a brief period (1908–1914). Technicolor developed a two-strip version in 1917, producing *The Gulf Between* to spark the interest of motion picture producers and exhibitors.

A newer version of the two-strip process was developed a few years later, with *The Toll of the Sea* (1922) featuring the updated system. Throughout the 1920s, other films used the two-strip Technicolor process in certain sequences, such as *The Ten Commandments* (1923), *Phantom of the Opera* (1925), *Ben-Hur* (1925), and *King of Kings* (1927), while Douglas Fairbanks' *The Black Pirate* (1926) was filmed entirely in Technicolor.

By 1929, Technicolor was actively developing a full-color process with the hopes of turning out color films exclusively. However, the Great Depression forced studios to cut back on expenditures, and color films became more of a novelty than standard fare. Undaunted by the financial setbacks, technicians did create a three-strip Technicolor camera and a process that offered a full range of colors. Walt Disney signed a two-year exclusive deal that allowed him the use of the three-strip process for his animated shorts. His first one, *Flowers and Trees* (1932), won an Oscar for the Best Short Subject cartoon.

27. "Poverty Row" was an industry term dating back to the early 1920s. Originally, the area of Sunset Boulevard and Gower Street housed many independent production companies that produced films on a very low budget, in just two to four days. These films played the lower half of a double feature, or in second-run and third-run movie houses. Since so many of these companies made Westerns, the corner of Sunset and Gower was nicknamed "Gower Gulch" because of all the cowboys hanging around in hopes of landing a job.

28. Cotta Vaz, *Living Dangerously*, 274–75.

CHANGING WINDS AND INDEPENDENCE

1. Studios had taken a financial hit during the war with the loss of their foreign markets, especially Europe and Asia. Industry trade papers estimated overseas income amounted to between 40 to 50 percent of Hollywood's total revenues in the late 1930s. (Canadian box office receipts were counted as domestic earnings.)

2. The major Hollywood studios produced two types of films: "A" and "B" productions. An "A" film would feature a studio's top star, like MGM's Clark Gable, 20th Century-Fox's Tyrone Power, or Warner's Bette Davis in a drama, a large-scale biography, or a musical with budgets ranging from approximately $200,000 to over $500,000, and a two-hour running time. "B" films tended to feature second-tier stars, lower budgets (under $100,000 to $250,000), or was a "series," such as MGM's *Andy Hardy*, Columbia's *Blondie*, or Fox's *Charlie Chan*. "B" films were referred to in the industry as "programmers," as the storylines were fairly routine or interchangeable and they had lower production values, with a running time of sixty to eighty-five minutes.

3. The benefits for American productions filming in actual locations was primarily cost, but also presented a more realistic look. For the Italians, using actual locations was a matter of necessity, since much of Rome was in ruins from the war. Building a set was an unthinkable expense, which forced filmmakers to use actual locations. *Naked City* and *Call Northside 777*, both released in 1948, were filmed on actual locations partially due to the subject matter and to lower production costs.

4. Many of these deals varied, usually requiring the services for no more than three pictures over a three- or four-year agreement.

5. Thomas Schatz, *The Genius of the System: Hollywood Filmmaking in the Studio Era* (New York: Pantheon Books, 1998), 297.

6. The "Hollywood Ten" were writers Dalton Trumbo, Albert Maltz, Herbert Biberman, Lester Cole, Alvah Bessie, Ring Lardner Jr., John Howard Lawson, Samuel Ornitz, Adrian Scott, and director Edward Dmytryk. Most of the writers (with the exception of Samuel Ornitz) continued to write scripts for movies and television shows, albeit under an assumed name, or uncredited. Edward Dmytryk, after his time in jail, did go back to the HUAC, giving them the names of people who were associated with the Communist Party in Hollywood. He continued to direct films (*The Caine Mutiny*, *Broken Lance*, *Raintree County*, and *The Young Lions*, to name a few) before teaching at the University of Southern California school of cinema. With the release of *Spartacus* (1960), Dalton Trumbo received his first screen credit since 1950.

7. While television was making inroads as an entertainment medium in the late 1940s, its full impact on studios and theatrical film exhibition would not be felt until the following decade.

8. Olivia de Havilland, who had a memorable role in *Gone with the Wind*, returned to Warner Bros. hoping to land more mature and challenging roles, but Jack Warner refused. Her contract was set to expire in 1943, but the actress learned the studio extended it by an additional six months due to her 1941 suspension. Instead of accepting the additional six months, de Havilland sued the studio. In November of 1943, the California Superior Court ruled in favor of the actress, which was quickly appealed by Warner Bros. A year later, the California Court of Appeals upheld the Superior Court's ruling, and the decision became known as the De Havilland Law. De Havilland's suit sought a judgment that she was no longer bound to her contract due to a clause in the California labor law which disallowed an employer from enforcing an employee's contract longer than seven years from the first date of performance. While she won the lawsuit, de Havilland found herself blacklisted for two years, before signing a two-picture deal with Paramount. Her first film under this contract, *To Each His Own* (1946), won her the Oscar for Best Actress. She won her second Oscar in 1949 for *The Heiress*, also made for Paramount.

9. Darryl F. Zanuck of 20th Century-Fox served as an army officer, albeit with comforts most regular officers lacked. Jack Warner was commissioned a major in the Army Signal Corps, but never left his studio in Burbank.

10. Prior to talks with Cooper, Ford had agreed to join a newly formed company, Renowned Artists, made up of other filmmakers. For unknown reasons, the company never got off the ground. *Los Angeles Examiner*, June 3, 1937.

11. Ford's agent, Harry Wurtzel, held discussions with Fox, RKO, and Universal for a multipicture agreement with the fledging Argosy in 1940, but the outbreak of war put an end to any future meetings.

12. Bill Donovan, David Bruce, William Vanderbilt, and Otto Doering Jr. were the other financial backers of Argosy. Donovan had been Ford's supervisor in the Office of Strategic Services (OSS) during World War II. Cooper also brought aboard Donald Dewar as the company's vice president to help with business transactions. Dewar, a

lawyer, had a strong association with the two banks (Security Pacific and Bankers Trust), which provided the bulk of Argosy's financing.

13. William Boyd played Hopalong Cassidy in sixty-six films starting in 1935. In a savvy business move, Boyd sold his home and used all of his available cash in the late 1940s to purchase the rights to the Hopalong Cassidy film library, as well as the character's likeness. In 1948, he made a deal with a local Los Angeles television station to show one of his films, and the public response was tremendous, making Hopalong Cassidy massively popular again. Aside from showing the sixty-six Cassidy films, Boyd also produced additional half-hour television shows. With Hopalong Cassidy's acclaim, Boyd carefully merchandised items, allowing only one hundred companies to manufacture items such as lunchboxes, six-gun holsters, toys, books, clothes, and comics. Boyd was serious about the quality of Hoppy merchandise that was chosen, turning down things he felt were inappropriate, including bubble gum. It was estimated that over 2,500 Hopalong Cassidy products were merchandised, earning more than $70 million.

14. Ford planned for John Wayne and Harry Carey to star in the film. Carey was the star of the 1919 version Ford directed for Universal. Eyman, *Print the Legend*, 308.

15. The Monogram deal entailed using 50 percent of a bank loan, with Monogram putting up 35 percent of their money, and Argosy funding 15 percent. Ibid., 319.

16. The contract specified that Argosy would receive 66.5 percent of the profits, while Ford and Cooper chose to defer a portion of their salaries. Aside from *The Quiet Man*, Argosy's lineup included *The Fugitive*, *The Family*, and *Uncle Mike Meets Murder*. The company also optioned the rights to *The African Queen*, *Mister Roberts*, *In a Lonely Place*, and *The Glass Menagerie* by Tennessee Williams. All of these options were either allowed to lapse or sold by the company. Ibid., 319–20.

17. Ibid., 326.

18. Of the twenty-six films in Ford's post–World War II career (1946–1964), twelve were Westerns.

Fort Apache

1. While various Apache tribes resided and fought in the adjacent New Mexico territory, the majority of battles with the US Cavalry took place in Arizona.

2. Ford found many short stories that he later adapted into movies. *Judge Priest* (and its 1953 remake, *The Sun Shines Bright*), *Stagecoach*, *Fort Apache*, *She Wore a Yellow Ribbon*, *Rio Grande*, and *The Quiet Man* were all based on short stories. Every studio had a story department during the studio system era (1920–1960), and the sole job of a group of staffers was to scour novels and magazine short stories for potential productions.

3. John Ford to Dan Ford, John Ford Collection, Lilly Library.

4. When it came to Indians, the opinion was often mixed between military officers and enlisted men. Many believed one of the root causes of the problems stemmed from the foolish, overbearing, greedy, and dishonest Indian agents, along with the mismanagement of the Bureau of Indian Affairs. Some Indian agents were known to soak beef in water to make it weigh more, so the monthly required amount per Indian (say, four pounds) was really only two pounds of actual meat. The agent would then sell the remaining meat to civilians, pocketing the profit. Selling liquor was a strict violation of agency policy, as

it led to enormous problems for many tribes, yet it was done. Promises of rations and clothing were either inadequate or nonexistent, which left tribal members distrustful and full of resentment. A bad Indian agent could enrage a tribe, leading to pain and suffering on both sides. Anger at the betrayal by white agents led many Indians to raid various ranches for cattle. The raids often claimed the lives of innocent white settlers, victims of the Indians' wrath. For those who found the settlers' remains, it only fanned the flames of hatred against all Indians, no matter what tribe was responsible. Such anger led to brutal retribution, which then led to Indian tribes seeking revenge, causing an endless swirling of violence.

Adding to the fractious relationship between whites and Indians was their clash of cultures, neither completely understanding the other. Indians were viewed by many Eastern-cultured whites as savages based on their actions, traditions, and beliefs, while the Indians did not understand the white person's desire to own land or their obsession with finding gold.

5. James Warner Bellah, "Massacre" (New York: Lion Books, 1950), 181.

6. Ronald L. Davis, *John Ford: Hollywood's Old Master* (Norman: University of Oklahoma Press, 1995), 204.

7. James Warner Bellah to Dan Ford, John Ford Collection, Lilly Library.

8. *Fort Apache* budget, John Ford Collection, Lilly Library.

9. *Daily Variety*, December 31, 1965.

10. Nugent would go on to write another ten screenplays for Ford (*3 Godfathers*, *She Wore a Yellow Ribbon*, *Wagon Master*, *The Quiet Man*, *Mister Roberts*, *The Searchers*, *The Rising of the Moon*, *The Last Hurrah*, *Two Rode Together*, and *Donovan's Reef*). Nugent also penned the scripts for *Angel Face* (1953) and *The Tall Men* (1955). Nugent was fifty-seven when he died in 1965.

11. Frank Wead was a former naval aviator. He competed and won several aviation contests representing the US Navy, as well as served in World War I. Paralyzed by a fall in 1926, he turned to writing during his convalescence, which led to a new career as a screenwriter in Hollywood. His scripts included *Ceiling Zero* (1936; originally written by Wead as a Broadway play), *Test Pilot* and *The Citadel* (both 1938; Wead received Oscar nominations for both films), *Dive Bomber* (1941), and Ford's *They Were Expendable* (1945). Wead was fifty-two when he died in 1947. Ford directed *The Wings of Eagles* (1957), based on Wead's life, with John Wayne playing Wead and Ward Bond as John Dodge, a thinly disguised version of Ford. *Fort Apache* budget file, John Ford Collection, Lilly Library.

12. Letter to Lindsay Anderson, dated May 3, 1953. Lindsay Anderson, *About John Ford* (London, UK: Plexus Publishing Limited, 1981), 242.

13. Ibid., 242–43.

14. Nugent was wrong to call the Apache the "best light cavalry that ever lived." While the Apache used horses when the need arose, they were not a horse culture tribe. Historians agree that the best light cavalry among Indian tribes were the Comanche. Argosy Pictures Production file, Biography Notes, Box 24, Folders 1 and 8, L. Tom Lee Special Collections Library, Harold B. Lee Library, Brigham Young University [hereafter, BYU], Provo, Utah.

15. *Fort Apache* biography file, John Ford Collection, Lilly Library.

16. Ibid.

17. Ford did use Goulding's Trading Post for the exterior of the stage stop, although the interior set was filmed at RKO-Pathé Studios. *Fort Apache* script, John Ford Collection, Lilly Library.

18. Fort Bowie was located in southeastern Arizona, near the town of Willcox. The fort was built after the Battle of Apache Pass in July 1862, between the US Army and Chiricahua Apache. Looking more like a temporary camp (tents instead of buildings), a more substantial version was erected in 1868, and remained an active military post until 1894, when it was abandoned. Today, all that remains are sections of the fort's adobe walls, the post cemetery, and ruins of a Butterfield Stage Station. Fort Bowie became a National Historic Landmark in 1960.

19. Ford seemed to like the name Quincannon, as the first time it was used was in *The Lost Patrol* (1934). He used the name again in the films *She Wore a Yellow Ribbon* and *Rio Grande*.

20. Nugent's biography of Collingwood details that he was in charge of a cavalry regiment at the Battle of Spotsylvania (1864), and is blamed by critics for not performing well, leading up to the Union's defeat. Relieved of command, Collingwood sat out the rest of the war on staff duty. It's a blot on his record, and Thursday, who knew Collingwood at West Point, has no respect for him. Collingwood's presence, and his subsequent downgrade in military rank, reminds Thursday that "it can—unless he can alter the circumstances—be the mirror of his own destiny." Both the script and the film have a scene at command headquarters where Collingwood comments to Thursday that he did what he did and rose to glory, while he wound up at Fort Apache. "Well, you've wound up here, too," Collingwood says with a touch of irony. Thursday refutes the statement, saying he will find something to restore his honor.

21. The term "digger Indians" was a generic description for various tribes (generally in California and Nevada) that dug for roots and such for food. Thursday using this term showed his contempt for the Apache, viewing them as the lowest of the lows. Roger McGrath to the author, October 14, 2020.

22. Fifty percent of the military enlistees during the Indian Wars were made up of native-born Americans, while the Irish (20 percent) and Germans (12 percent) made up the largest number of immigrants in the military from 1866 to 1874. Other international members included English, Canadian, Scot, French, Swiss, Italian, and, in smaller numbers, Mexican and South American. Some foreign enlistees previously served in various European armies, many holding an officer's commission. A handicap faced by several foreign enlistees was the fact that they could barely speak or understand English, leaving them to learn in the field.

23. Nugent incorrectly has Yorke stating the Winchester rifles held by the Indians were "7-shot repeaters." Winchester's 1873 rifles came in two styles: the traditional rifle (15 rounds) and the carbine (10 rounds). The Henry repeating rifle, made in 1860, held 16 rounds. The rifles in the box that Yorke opens were a mixture of 1873 and 1892 Winchesters. Studios generally used the 1892 versions in Westerns, as they were in greater supply. Filmmakers didn't concern themselves with the accuracy of guns from the

Western period, as their belief was "a Winchester was a Winchester." My thanks to Phil Spangenberger for this information.

24. Alcoholism was a serious problem for both officers and enlisted men. (The fort sutler was the main supplier of alcohol if no town was nearby.) Isolation, separation from family, mourning a deceased or lost love, resentment due to not advancing in rank, and just plain boredom turned many men to the bottle. By the 1880s, almost 41 out of 1,000 soldiers that were hospitalized were treated for alcoholism; however, the ratio was much smaller among the four regiments of Black troops. Punishment for drunkenness usually resulted in a fine of five dollars, time in the guardhouse, reduction of rank, and duty at the manure pile. A soldier found drunk while on campaign was forced to dismount and walk at the rear of the column.

25. The Apache learned to use the mirror to communicate from distances, just as did the military. Roger McGrath to the author, October 14, 2020.

26. *Buenas tardes, jefe* translates to "Good day, boss." In this case, *jefe* would mean the "leader" or "chief."

27. "Officer of the day" is a military term for the officer who has charge of the guard and prisoners on an assigned day at a military installation.

28. In 1873, the army chose to issue the Springfield carbine rifle, nicknamed the "Springfield Trapdoor" because of its breech-loading mechanism resembling a trapdoor. Compared to a Winchester repeating rifle, the Springfield had greater "knockdown" power, but was limited to a single shot. The soldier would open the latch, manually load a round, snap the "trapdoor" shut, cock the hammer back, and fire. Snapping open the latch, the expended casing would self-eject, allowing the soldier to place another round in the chamber. The military gave little consideration to issuing the Winchester repeater, mainly due to their belief that a rifle which held fifteen rounds would result in wasted ammunition during training purposes. Many of the Indians involved in the Battle of the Little Bighorn had repeating rifles, giving them an advantage in firepower. John Ford to Dan Ford, John Ford Collection, Lilly Library.

29. In many of Ford's films, the doctor is portrayed as a drunk or one who imbibes a great deal. Such examples can be found in *Stagecoach*, *My Darling Clementine*, and *The Man Who Shot Liberty Valance*.

30. The first film in which Ford used the "Grand March" dance was 1920's *The Prince of Avenue A*, featuring world heavyweight boxing champion James J. Corbett, better known as "Gentleman Jim." Traditionally, the "Grand March" was the first dance of any event. In the film it is accompanied by the song "All Praise to St. Patrick." Bogdanovich, *John Ford*, 86.

31. Traditionally, "Goodnight, Ladies" was played for the last dance.

32. Bogdanovich, *John Ford*, 87.

33. Nichols was a star reporter for the *New York Post* before turning to Hollywood. He wrote fifteen screenplays for Ford: *Men Without Women* (1930), *Born Reckless* (1930), *Seas Beneath* (1931), *Pilgrimage* (1933), *The Lost Patrol* (1934), *Judge Priest* (1934), *The Informer* (1935), *Steamboat Around the Bend* (1935), *Mary of Scotland* (1936), *Plough and the Stars* (1936), *The Hurricane* (1937), *Stagecoach* (1939), *The Long Voyage Home* (1940), *Battle of Midway* (1942; documentary), and *The Fugitive* (1946). Nichols also wrote the

screenplays for *Bringing Up Baby* (1938), *Gunga Din* (1939), *For Whom the Bell Tolls* (1943), and *The Big Sky* (1952).

34. Eyman, *Print the Legend*, 333.

35. John Wayne to Dan Ford, John Ford Collection, Lilly Library.

36. Alchesay (1853–1928) served as an Apache Indian scout, with a rank of sergeant, under General George Crook during the 1872–1873 Chiricahua uprising. A close friend of Geronimo, he tried unsuccessfully to get his friend to surrender peacefully. When the military pursued Geronimo into Mexico, he served Crook as an advisor. When the Apache Wars ended in 1886, Alchesay became a successful cattleman and farmer. Santana (1810–1876) was the leader of the Sierra Blanco Mescaleros. While hardly known to many whites, he remained a steadfast friend to them until his death. Geronimo (1829–1909) was never a chief or leader of the Chiricahua, but his raiding and battle tactics were so exceptional that many followed him. He surrendered to General Nelson Miles in 1886, and then was sent as a prisoner of war to Fort Pickens in Florida. In 1894, he was transferred to Fort Sill in Oklahoma, where he died in 1909. On his deathbed he reportedly stated that he never should have surrendered, and should have fought until he was the last one alive.

37. Nugent's biography of Collingwood includes the following: "Collingwood had the chance to make a hell-for-leather charge into almost certain destruction at Spotsylvania. Later Thursday orders him to a parallel charge at the climax of the picture. Collingwood goes to his death with a bitter smile: his fate has caught up with him." Argosy Pictures Production file, Biography Notes, Box 4, Folder 25, L. Tom Lee Special Collections Library, Harold B. Lee Library, BYU.

38. Ibid.

39. While Ford liked the look of cavalrymen carrying their sabers in the field, during the Indian Wars period, the cavalry did not carry them, as they were useless in combat against any Indian tribe. After the Civil War, sabers were regulated to formal dress and ceremonial events. In the field, soldiers relied on their pistols and rifles. Pitched battles or close contact fighting between Indians and the cavalry were generally avoided, as Indian tribes could not risk the loss of warriors. Most tribes fought when they held the advantage over their opponent, their favored gambit being to strike quickly without any warning. A quick attack was followed by an equally quick withdrawal that usually kept casualties to a minimum. Unlike many movie plots, it was a rare occurrence for a tribe to attack a fort, given the firepower a fort contained. However, a small group of warriors could taunt soldiers into chasing them, as in the Fetterman Massacre in December 1866. Soldiers, protecting a group cutting wood, were harassed by ten Sioux warriors. Captain William Fetterman led his men after them, charging over the Lodge Trail Ridge despite strict orders not to cross the ridge. Behind the ridge they were met by a Sioux force of over one thousand warriors. There were no survivors among the eighty-one men. In *Fort Apache*, Cochise and some warriors do the same thing to Colonel Thursday and his men, leading them into an ambush in Blind Canyon.

40. A troop's departure was serenaded by the fort band, playing a variety of military and sentimental tunes. Passing the fort's commanding officer and mounted detachment carrying the national and US Army flags, the mounted officers would offer a crisp salute.

41. Roscoe "Fatty" Arbuckle was falsely charged with raping and the ultimate death of an actress during a Labor Day party at the St. Francis Hotel in San Francisco. An ambitious DA, Matthew Brady, had eyes on the governor's seat and used this case to bolster himself. The first two trials ended in a hung jury, while the third jury took six minutes to find the actor not guilty. Paramount Studios, where Arbuckle was under contract, dumped him and Will Hays banned him from appearing in films. He turned to directing and later made a comeback as an actor in 1932, appearing in several two-reel comedies before his death on June 28, 1933, at the age of forty-six.

William Desmond Taylor, a popular director, was found murdered in his apartment. Suspects ranged from actress Mary Miles Minter, who made several films with Taylor, and comedienne Mabel Normand. Newspapers quickly linked Minter to having a personal relationship with Taylor, as did Normand. The case remains unsolved; however, many believe the killer was Minter's mother, Charlotte Shelby.

Wallace Reid was a popular star in the early 1920s. Under contract to Paramount Studios, Reid suffered an injury while filming on location. He was given morphine to help with his pain while he continued to work. Sadly, Paramount had Reid grind out picture after picture, with the studio continuing to supply him with morphine for his pain. He died in 1923 at a sanitarium after his health collapsed from drug addiction. He was only thirty-one.

42. A "rump spring" refers to the condition of a chair, or area of a sofa, that has been "form-fitted" over time to a specific person's behind. In this case it is the chair that Dr. Wilkens donates to Philadelphia, and her father gets caught in. Breen allowed the term to be used.

43. Carl Spaatz graduated from West Point in 1914. Trained to fly planes, he assisted General John ("Black Jack") Pershing's Punitive Expedition against Pancho Villa. During World War I, he flew several missions before being assigned to train additional pilots. In World War II, he was promoted to major-general of the US Army's Air Force Combat Command. He was responsible for launching various bombing missions in Germany, mainly attacking V-1 rocket sites, and railroad and oil industries. When the US Air Force was formed in 1947, Spaatz was appointed its first chief of staff. He retired in 1948, and passed away in 1974.

44. The letter was sent from Argosy's offices at Enterprise Studio at 5255 Clinton Street in Hollywood. The studio was a very small independent rental facility with a few offices south of Melrose Avenue, between Bronson and Norton Avenues. Producers Studios (now Raleigh Studios) backed up to this location. Paramount (across the street on Melrose) and RKO Studios (at Gower Street and Melrose Avenue) were nearby. Argosy moved their offices to RKO Culver Studios at the beginning of preproduction of the film. *Fort Apache* Producers Code Administration file, Margaret Herrick Library, Beverly Hills, California.

45. The American Humane Association (AHA) became involved in Hollywood film productions after a horse broke its spine in a scene for *Jesse James* (1939) and was put down. That stunt involved a rider leaping a horse off a seventy-foot cliff.

46. In these scenes, Ford is very careful to reveal the dead men. We very briefly get a glimpse that one man's feet are black, while the other victim's arms and feet are black.

Throughout the two sequences, there are brief shots of the men, usually in a medium or full wide shot. Ford portrays the torture with these brief glimpses, along with the actors' reactions, and the smoke still smoldering from the burned wagon. *Fort Apache* Producers Code Administration file, Margaret Herrick Library.

47. The film was given the PCA approval seal, #12819, on December 17, 1947. At this time the film's title was *War Party*. Ibid.

48. Ford had some men wear kepi hats in the field for a varied look. The kepi was a cap with a flat circular top and a small visor, mainly reserved for formal dress occasions or around a military post. No soldier ever wore one on a campaign, since it offered little protection from the elements.

49. Joseph McBride, *Searching for John Ford: A Life* (New York: St. Martin's Press, 2001), 447.

50. Based on the success of *The Covered Wagon*, MGM signed McCoy in 1925 to star in outdoor action films. When his contract was not renewed in 1929, McCoy starred in various "B" Westerns produced at Universal and Columbia, before appearing with the Ringling Bros. and Barnum & Bailey Circus in 1935. He launched his own Wild West show in 1938, but it quickly folded, and he returned to films. McCoy teamed with Buck Jones and Raymond Hatton in a series of Westerns produced by Monogram Pictures. During World War II, McCoy served with the US Army Air Corps, retiring with the rank of colonel. In 1952, he hosted a children's Saturday-morning show on Los Angeles television, talking about the history of the West, and teaching Indian sign language. (The show won a local Emmy award as Best Children's Show.) He retired to a farm in Pennsylvania, but made three more appearances in films: *Around the World in 80 Days* (1956), *Run of the Arrow* (1957), and *Requiem for a Gunfighter* (1965). He died in 1978.

51. Kieffer worked as technical advisor for *Duel in the Sun* (1946), *The Half-Breed* (1952), and *Hondo* (1953). He also appeared in Ford's *The Sun Shines Bright* (1953), *The Long Gray Line* (1955), and *The Searchers* (1956). He died in 1962.

52. A completion bond was a contractual guarantee for financers, such as a bank, that the film will be completed by a specific date and at a specific cost. The bond also allowed for any cost overruns, as well as allowing the one who held the bond to take over the production under certain circumstances.

53. *Fort Apache* contract, Argosy Papers, Box 1, Folder 33, BYU.

54. The distribution fee was money paid to a distributor, in this case RKO, by the exhibitor (theater owner or chain). That money went to the distributor's cost/overhead for releasing that specific film. The fee is figured on a percentage of the rental fee, which is a percentage of the gross receipts of the box office of the specific film. Ibid.

55. Fonda would appear in six Ford films; his first three were made back to back (1939's *Young Mr. Lincoln* and *Drums Along the Mohawk*, and *The Grapes of Wrath* in 1940). The other titles were *My Darling Clementine* (1946), *The Fugitive* (1947), and *Mister Roberts* (1955). Wayne first worked with Ford in *Mother Machree* (1927), herding a flock of geese on the set. *Hangman's House* (1928) would mark the first of Wayne's seventeen films with Ford. Fonda and Wayne appeared together in *In Harm's Way* (1965). While they also starred in *How the West Was Won* and *The Longest Day* (both 1962), they did not appear together.

56. Larry Swindell, "Yes, John Ford Knew a Thing or Two About Art," *Philadelphia Enquirer*, September 16, 1973.

57. Harry Carey Jr. to the author, June 19, 1996.

58. Pennick served with the U.S. Marines in China in 1912 as a Peking Legation Guard, and then in Europe during World War I. Afterwards, he worked as a horse wrangler, which led to employment in motion pictures. His bulldog features soon opened the door to acting roles. During World War II, he was given the rank of chief petty officer while working in Ford's Field Photographic Unit. His last screen role was in Ford's Civil War segment of *How the West Was Won*, released in 1962. He died two years later, at age sixty-eight.

59. Victor McLaglen's first film with Ford was *The Fighting Heart* (1925), the first of twelve films between 1925 and 1952. Anna Lee, who always said working on a Ford film was special no matter how small the part, appeared in seven of his films, from *How Green Was My Valley* (1941) to Ford's last film, *7 Women* (1964). Ward Bond began working for Ford in 1930 (*Born Reckless*) and went on to appear in twenty films, including *Young Mr. Lincoln* (1939), *Drums Along the Mohawk* (1939), *The Long Voyage Home* (1940), *Wagon Master* (1950), *The Long Gray Line* (1955), and *The Searchers* (1956). Bond, who starred in the television series *Wagon Train* for four seasons, had Ford direct an episode, "The Colter Craven Story," during the fourth season. The episode aired as a tribute to Bond who had died a few weeks earlier.

Mae Marsh appeared in 202 films during a career that began in 1910 working for D. W. Griffith, including his two landmark epics, *Birth of a Nation* (1915) and *Intolerance* (1916). She first worked for Ford in *Drums Along the Mohawk* (1939). Marsh would go on to appear in seventeen more films for the director, with *Cheyenne Autumn* (1964) marking her final screen appearance. Mickey Simpson appeared in nine Ford films, including *My Darling Clementine* (1946), *She Wore a Yellow Ribbon* (1949), and *What Price Glory* (1952). Jane Crowley had small roles in thirteen of Ford's films, from *Young Mr. Lincoln* (1939) to *The Man Who Shot Liberty Valance* (1962). Harry Tenbrook shows up in twenty-seven films, from *The Blue Eagle* (1926) to *The Last Hurrah* (1958).

Fort Apache marked the last of three Ford films Pedro Armendáriz appeared in, the other two being *The Fugitive* (1946) and *3 Godfathers* (1948). Of Hank Worden's eight appearances in Ford films, his best-known role is Mose Harper in *The Searchers* (1956). He also played one of the villainous Clegg boys in *Wagon Master* (1950), and the Deacon in *The Horse Soldiers* (1959). Grant Withers first worked for Ford in 1927's *Upstream*, later appearing in *My Darling Clementine* (1946), *Rio Grande* (1950), and *The Sun Shines Bright* (1953). Francis Ford made his first appearance in his younger brother's film *The Village Blacksmith* (1922). He would go on to work in twenty-nine films, usually in a small role.

60. *Fort Apache* salary list, John Ford Collection, Libby Library.

61. Ford was unaware that Shirley was in the early stages of pregnancy with her first child when filming began. The actress wasn't concerned that her riding scenes could cause a miscarriage; she was more bothered by the tight corset she had to wear. Temple and Agar's child, Linda, was born on January 31, 1948.

62. After producing nine films in three years, including his blockbuster and Oscar-winning *Gone with the Wind* (1939), Selznick was at a crossroads. Exhausted

from overseeing his massive output, he decided to close Selznick International Pictures (partially for tax benefits) and began loaning out performers he had under contract to other studios, as well as packaging a movie (i.e., assembling cast and script) and then selling it to other studios. Selznick returned to producing pictures in 1944 with *Since You Went Away*.

63. Cliff Lyons gave up college to follow the rodeo circuit, which led to Hollywood, where he found work in low-budget Westerns, playing either a villain or a hero, starting in 1925. His voice wasn't a good fit with the birth of talking pictures, but he kept busy as a stuntman and eventually as a stunt coordinator. Lyons appeared in both versions of *Ben-Hur* (1925 and 1959), driving a chariot in the famous race. He appeared in seven of Ford's films in small roles, from *3 Godfathers* (1948) to *Two Rode Together* (1961). His nickname among stuntmen was "Mother," as he was always telling the stuntmen where to go and what to do. Chuck Hayward called Lyons the "toughest guy that ever lived." His last job was as stunt coordinator on John Wayne's *The Train Robbers* (1974). Lyons was seventy-two when he died in 1974.

William Steele was born in Texas and landed in Los Angeles around 1910, eventually finding work as a stuntman or the occasional heavy. He first worked for Ford in a 1917 Harry Carey Western, *The Soul Herder*. Between 1917 and 1921, Steele (who was originally billed by his birth name, William Gettinger) appeared in six Ford–Carey films. His last film with Ford was *The Searchers* (1956), playing the role of Nesby. He died in 1966 at the age of seventy-seven.

Fred Kennedy began doing stunt work in the late 1930s, and because of his excellent horsemanship found employment in numerous Westerns. Ford used Kennedy extensively in his cavalry trilogy, even giving him a featured role as Trooper Heinze in *Rio Grande*. During filming of *The Horse Soldiers* (1959), Fred broke his neck and died while performing a horse fall. He was forty-eight.

Post Park was considered one of Hollywood's top drivers of a stagecoach or wagon. He also worked on Ford's *Wagon Master* (1950), *Rio Grande* (1950), and *The Quiet Man* (1952). Park continued working right up to his death in 1955. John Hudkins began performing stunts in the late 1930s. He was the nephew of Ace Hudkins, who owned the Hudkins Stables in Hollywood. John worked in eight of Ford's films, including *The Searchers* (1956), *Wings of Eagles* (1957), *The Horse Soldiers* (1959), *The Man Who Shot Liberty Valance* (1962), and *Cheyenne Autumn* (1964). He was still doing stunt work into the mid-1990s before his death in 1997 at seventy-nine. Bryan "Slim" Hightower was a cowboy from Texas whose stunt career dates back to 1931. Between 1949 and 1964, Hightower worked in nine of Ford's films, including *Wagon Master* (1950), *The Searchers* (1956), and *Cheyenne Autumn* (1964). Hightower was seventy-three when he died in 1978.

Frank McGrath began his career as an actor and occasional stuntman in 1932. Because of his close resemblance to actor Warner Baxter, he served as his stand-in and stunt double. The two men became very close friends and McGrath was written into Baxter's contract. His first film with John Ford was *They Were Expendable* (1945) as Slim, one of the PT boat sailors. In 1957, he became a regular on the television series *Wagon Train* (1957–1962), appearing in all 272 episodes. He continued acting in supporting roles until his death in 1967.

Chuck Hayward began following the rodeo circuit when he was sixteen, eventually finding work in Hollywood as a wrangler. He became fast friends with John Wayne when they worked together at Republic Pictures, with Hayward often performing stunts for the star. He went on to work in twelve Ford films, occasionally appearing in a small role. Hayward retired from stunt work in 1981, but continued acting until 1989. Hayward passed away in 1998 at the age of seventy-eight.

Chuck Roberson was born in Texas and grew up on cattle ranches. By the age of thirteen, he'd left home to find work as a cowboy or in the oilfields. Recently married at age twenty-one, he moved to Los Angeles where he joined the Culver City police department while moonlighting as a guard at MGM. In 1946, stuntman Fred Kennedy recommended him for a job doubling actor John Carroll at Republic Pictures, which began a forty-one-year career as a stuntman and occasional actor. For nearly thirty years Roberson was Wayne's stunt double. Ford dubbed Roberson "Bad Chuck" because of his raucous behavior, while Hayward was called "Good Chuck" because he was the opposite. Roberson, who published his autobiography *The Fall Guy* in 1980, was sixty-nine when he died in 1988.

Terry Wilson, a Southern California native, began his stunt career in 1947. His first film with Ford was *Rio Grande*. Like fellow stuntman Frank McGrath, Wilson joined the cast of *Wagon Train* at the insistence of star Ward Bond. He continued doing stunts and acting until he retired in 1981. He died in 1999 at the age of seventy-five.

64. Many claim the translation means "Valley of Rocks." However, in the Navajo language it translates to "rock(s)-within-white-streaks-around," or "the streaks that go around in the rocks." This refers to the various streaks found in many of the rock layers within the valley. At one point during the Mesozoic period, seventy-five million years ago, nearly 50 percent of the North American continent was covered by seas. There is geological evidence that Monument Valley was submerged at one point during this period.

65. It is believed the Navajo are descendants of the Athabascans, who originally migrated from the Asian mainland (likely present-day Mongolia and eastern Siberia), crossing the Bering Land Bridge into what is now Alaska and Canada, before some tribal members migrated south into what is the United States. The Bering Land Bridge was a massive area of land that covered 620,000 square miles, primarily made up of grassland plain, connecting present-day Siberia, Alaska, and Canada. As the last ice age came to an end, rising seas enveloped the land bridge, creating the separation we know today. Four Corners is the only location in the United States where four states meet: the southwestern corner of Colorado, the southeastern corner of Utah, the northeastern corner of Arizona, and the northwestern corner of New Mexico. The region belongs to four Native American nations: Navajo, Hopi, Ute, and Zuni.

66. Her name was Leone, but Harry had a hard time pronouncing it. Reportedly, he told her he could easily say and write Mike, and she readily agreed.

67. Bogdanovich, *John Ford*, 69–70.

68. Todd McCarthy, "John Ford and Monument Valley," *American Film* (May 1978), 10–16; Samuel Moon, *Tall Sheep: Harry Goulding Monument Valley Trader* (Norman: University of Oklahoma Press, 1992), 144–47.

69. Paramount's 1925 version of Zane Grey's novel, *The Vanishing American*, was the *first* movie to film in Monument Valley. A major reason a film company would choose Flagstaff was that its location along the Atchison, Topeka, and Santa Fe railroad route allowed easy transportation of personnel and equipment from Hollywood. Flagstaff also had enough hotel and motel rooms to house cast and crew.

70. John Wetherill and his family set up a trading post in 1910 in Kayenta, and remained there until his death in 1944. Not only did he operate a trading post, but he also guided visitors into remote regions via horseback, including author Zane Grey and former president Theodore Roosevelt. He also served as superintendent of the Navajo National Monument from 1909 to 1938.

71. The real Fort Apache was located east of the Tonto National Forest, near the east and north forks of the White River. It was an "open fort" (no stockade walls enclosing it) when it was set up in 1870, and originally named Camp Ord. The following year it was renamed Camp Apache, eventually becoming a permanent post in 1873. It was designated Fort Apache in 1879. Soldiers stationed at Fort Apache were heavily involved in military campaigns during the Apache Wars era, mainly against the Chiricahua tribes. With the end of the Apache Wars in 1886, Fort Apache remained an active military post until its closure in 1924. The area was then turned over to the Bureau of Indian Affairs, which managed the Theodore Roosevelt Indian School. Today, Fort Apache is part of the White Mountain Apache Reservation, and many of the original fort buildings are still standing in the historic district.

72. The majority of productions that used Corrigan's Ranch were Westerns, mainly "B" Westerns and television shows like *The Lone Ranger* and *Have Gun—Will Travel*. With the popularity of Westerns in the early 1950s, Corrigan opened his ranch, now dubbed Corriganville, to the public. Visitors could ride a stagecoach, see a stunt show, and meet Western stars from movies and television. In 1965, Corrigan sold his property to Bob Hope, who built a housing development on a portion of the land. In 1988, the city of Simi Valley purchased 190 acres of the property, and it is now called Corriganville Park. There are signs and photographs pointing out the various filming locations. Some historic photos and memorabilia from Corriganville can be viewed at the Santa Susana Depot.

73. The cost of building the exterior fort set was $53,411.69, while all interior sets were filmed at RKO-Pathé Studios in Culver City. *Fort Apache* budget file, John Ford Collection, Lilly Library.

74. George Turner, "Dust and Danger at Fort Apache," *American Cinematographer* (June 1996).

75. Clothier later served as cinematographer on Ford's *The Horse Soldiers* (1959), *The Man Who Shot Liberty Valance* (1962), *Donovan's Reef* (1963), and *Cheyenne Autumn* (1964).

76. Second units primarily handle stunt sequences not requiring principal actors, as well as establishing shots. They might even shoot scenes with actors if the production was on a tight schedule.

77. *Fort Apache* budget file, John Ford Collection, Lilly Library.

78. The terms "six-up" or "four-up" refer to the number of horses used to pull a wagon or stagecoach.

79. Western Costume came into existence in the early 1910s and was located on Broadway in downtown Los Angeles. In 1932 the company moved to a multistory building on Melrose Avenue, in front of Paramount Studios. After the sale of the property to Paramount Studios, Western Costume moved to the San Fernando Valley in 1989, where it still supplies wardrobe for film and television productions to this day. During the studio era, every studio had their own wardrobe department, yet would still turn to Western Costume for additional or special material.

80. *Fort Apache* budget file, John Ford Collection, Lilly Library.

81. Ibid.

82. Ibid.

83. The production manager, also known as unit production manager (UPM for short), managed the production by keeping track of costs, and generally keeping the project on schedule and within budget. The job of the first assistant director (1st AD) was to assist the director and keep the production on its daily schedule.

84. *Fort Apache* travel schedule, John Ford Collection, Lilly Library.

85. The listing of dates, locations, and scenes are based on the July 10, 1947, shooting schedule. *Fort Apache* shooting schedule, John Ford Collection, Lilly Library.

86. The San Juan River was used by Ford in many films, including *Fort Apache*, *She Wore a Yellow Ribbon*, and *The Searchers*.

87. A running shot refers to a moving shot which follows and keeps pace with a character, animal, or car. In this case it was the wagon. A camera car, usually a pickup truck, is outfitted to have one or two cameras and other necessary equipment for running shots.

88. In the opening credits of *Fort Apache*, there is a shot of the cavalry moving from right to left on camera, followed by another angle of them moving in the opposite direction (left to right). The next shot has the troopers moving in the original direction. Bogdanovich, *John Ford*, 70.

89. Ford shot other horse falls when the cavalry charges into the ambush, with no accidents for horse or rider. Workers' compensation insurance rates were much better in Arizona than in Utah, and this is why Ford chose to film any stunt work in Arizona. According to stuntman Terry Wilson, at the time, workers' compensation was 65 percent of your weekly salary. Since the accident happened in Arizona, Hudkins got a healthy workers' compensation pay of $235 a week ($2,980.65 a week in 2023 dollars) for over a year. The state of Arizona was worried that if a star like Wayne or Fonda were hurt, their weekly payout could bankrupt the state fund. Because of this, Arizona soon changed the workers' compensation law relating to the amount a person earned. Terry Wilson said the new law was called the Hudkins Law. Terry Wilson to Dan Ford, John Ford Collection, Lilly Library.

90. Ed Hulse to the author, November 12, 2020.

91. Any film that did not meet the AHA's guidelines was not given its seal of approval. Producers found that other countries (like Mexico and Spain) were more than willing to let them use the Running W stunt, with no repercussions. Unfortunately, the AHA had no power to enforce rules on films produced outside the United States. Ibid.

92. George Loomis to the author, November 15, 2020.

93. John Ford to Dan Ford, John Ford Collection, Lilly Library.

94. Some of the best-known falling horses during this time included Jerry Brown, Alamo, Mr. Dugan, and Mickey Boyle. Many stuntmen felt that Jerry Brown was the best falling horse in Hollywood. Both Chuck Roberson and Chuck Hayward also had falling horses, named Cocaine and Twinkle Toes respectively.

95. Chuck Hayward to Dan Ford, John Ford Collection, Lilly Library.

96. *Directed by John Ford* (documentary), American Film Institute, 1971.

97. Ibid.

98. Larry Blake to the author, March 20, 1979.

99. Ford, *Pappy*, 212.

100. Wayne, Bond, and Ford were inseparable friends.

101. Harry Carey Jr. to Dan Ford, John Ford Collection, Lilly Library.

102. Harry Carey Jr., *A Company of Heroes: My Life as an Actor in the John Ford Stock Company* (Metuchen, NJ: The Scarecrow Press, 1994), 190.

103. Shirley Temple, *Child Star: An Autobiography* (New York: McGraw-Hill, 1988).

104. Ronald L. Davis, *John Ford: Hollywood's Old Master* (Norman: University of Oklahoma Press, 1995), 210.

105. John Wayne to Dan Ford, John Ford Collection, Lilly Library.

106. *Fort Apache* shooting schedule, John Ford Collection, Lilly Library.

107. Davis, *John Ford: Hollywood's Old Master*, 161, 211.

108. Ben Johnson was born in Foraker, Oklahoma, on June 13, 1918. His father, Ben Sr., was a cattleman and a multiple winner of rodeo steer-roping contests. From an early age, Ben was riding horses, and in late 1940, found himself taking a carload of horses to Hollywood. Howard Hughes purchased several horses from the ranch where his father worked as foreman for his film *The Outlaw* (made in 1941, released in 1943). Ben, who was making $175 a week with Howard Hughes compared to his $30-per-month salary at the ranch, made the decision to stay in Hollywood, finding work as a wrangler and stuntman. After signing with Argosy, Ben worked steadily as an actor in films and television shows, mostly Westerns. He left the film industry for a year to compete on the rodeo circuit, winning the championship buckle for team roping in 1953. He often said that award meant more to him than anything else. In 1971, he won the Best Supporting Oscar for his performance in *The Last Picture Show*. He worked right up until his death on April 6, 1996, at the age of seventy-seven.

109. *Fort Apache* shooting schedule, John Ford Collection, Lilly Library.

110. *Fort Apache* budget, John Ford Collection, Lilly Library.

111. Argosy had held a title naming contest with its employees, the winner receiving $100. It appears that Ford came up with *Fort Apache*, but there is no record of whether he took the money. Clearing a title meant that Argosy/RKO would have had to contact another studio and get their permission to use the title in question. For instance, Warner Bros. had registered the title *Boots and Saddles*, and if Argosy had wanted to use it, they would have had to pay a fee to Warner Bros. Since Argosy had already registered *Fort Apache* as a title, and it tested highly in the survey, it was an easy decision to change the title.

112. Scott Eyman, *Hank & Jim: The Fifty-Year Friendship of Henry Fonda and James Stewart* (New York: Simon & Schuster, 2017), 79–80.

113. Harry Carey Jr. to Dan Ford, John Ford Collection, Lilly Library.

114. Wingate Smith to Dan Ford, John Ford Collection, Lilly Library.

115. John Wayne to Dan Ford, John Ford Collection, Lilly Library.

116. During the editing of *Arrowsmith* (1931), Ford went on a bender. He was a no-show for several days, finally forcing producer Samuel Goldwyn to proceed with editing the film without Ford's input. Ford had been loaned out to Goldwyn by Fox, and they were furious at his behavior. Fox fired him in 1931, but trade papers claimed the reason he was leaving was because of financial reasons due to the ongoing Great Depression. He made *Air Mail* (Universal) and *Flesh* (MGM), both in 1932. He returned to Fox on a per-picture basis, making *Pilgrimage* and the first of his three films with Will Rogers, *Doctor Bull* (both in 1933). Ford didn't go off the wagon while making a film until the flare-up with Henry Fonda on *Mister Roberts* in 1955.

117. Hageman was born in the Netherlands in 1881. He was a child prodigy, and by age six was a concert pianist, later studying in Amsterdam and Brussels. In 1906, he accompanied cabaret singer Yvette Guilbert on a national tour of the United States, and remained behind, becoming a US citizen in 1925. Hageman went on to serve as conductor for New York's Metropolitan Opera from 1908 to 1922. He was conducting summer concerts at the Hollywood Bowl in 1938, when he was given the chance to compose his first film, *If I Were a King* (1938). Along with three other composers (W. Franke Harling, John Leipold, and Leo Shuken), Hageman won the Oscar for Best Music for *Stagecoach*. Hageman would go on to earn five Oscar nominations for Best Musical Score between 1938 and 1941. He made an appearance in *3 Godfathers*, playing the saloon piano player. Hageman's last film with Ford was *Wagon Master* (1950). He died in 1966 at the age of eighty-three.

118. *New York Times*, June 25, 1948.

119. *The Hollywood Reporter*, March 10, 1948.

120. *Daily Variety*, March 10, 1948.

121. *Motion Picture Exhibitor*, March 31, 1948.

122. *Motion Picture Herald*, March 13, 1948.

123. The average movie ticket price in 1948 was around forty cents. *Fort Apache* budget and earnings file, John Ford Collection, Lilly Library.

124. Besides John Wayne and Ward Bond, the radio cast included Lou Merrill, Sharon Douglas, Paul McVey, Don Stanley, Eddie Field, Tony Barrett, and Pat McGeehan. *Screen Director's Playhouse* aired on the NBC radio network from January 9, 1949, to September 28, 1951. A half-hour television version of the show aired on NBC for the 1955–1956 season. (In July 1956, the show aired on the ABC network until its conclusion in September.) The television version differed from the radio show, choosing to focus on original stories or adapted short stories. John Ford directed an episode titled "Rookie of the Year," featuring John Wayne, Vera Miles, Ward Bond, and Patrick Wayne.

125. Commissioned officers (lieutenants and higher ranks) did not fraternize with soldiers, speaking to them only when absolutely necessary. Noncommissioned officers' (sergeants) personal contact with officers was limited to military-related issues. It was extremely rare for a captain or lieutenant to speak on a personal level with a noncommissioned officer, and it was generally done in private.

126. It was considered improper dress for a man to have his suspenders showing. Usually, a man wore a vest or coat over them in public.

127. Joseph Musso to the author, October 11, 2021.

128. Bogdanovich, *John Ford*, 86.

129. During the attack, Ford was hit by shrapnel, leaving a three-inch hole in his left arm. Despite the wound, he kept filming the attack, eventually heading to the infirmary for treatment.

130. Ford donated the Field Photo Farm property, located in the San Fernando Valley suburb of Reseda, to the Motion Picture and Television Relief Fund in 1969.

131. John Ford to Dan Ford, John Ford Collection, Lilly Library.

132. Ibid.

133. In the script, after the second whiskey bottle goes into the punch bowl, Mrs. O'Rourke asks her husband if everything is all right. "You'd best not drink the punch tonight, woman," he warns. This line was cut by Ford on the set.

134. The first time we see Philadelphia, Mrs. Collingwood, and Mrs. O'Rourke, they are standing in order from left to right. Ford cuts from the women's reaction to the troop moving out. Returning to the three ladies, they are now standing (in order, left to right) Mrs. O'Rourke, Mrs. Collingwood, and Philadelphia.

She Wore a Yellow Ribbon

1. Between 1916 to 1974, six versions have been produced based on Peter B. Kyne's novel. About three minutes of footage from Ford's 1919 version was recently unearthed in Europe with Dutch intertitles.

2. Both stories had been published in *The Saturday Evening Post*. Eyman, *Print the Legend*, 352.

3. Before becoming a horse culture, many tribes would stampede a herd of buffalo off a precipice of at least one hundred feet. While some buffalo were killed in the fall, others would be severely hurt and Indians would then kill them with arrows, butchering the carcasses for their needs. These areas are now referred to as "buffalo jumps," and many sites display bones and skulls of the animals, providing archaeologists with great information. Buffalo jumps can be found in areas of Alberta (Canada), Montana, Wyoming, South Dakota, Idaho, Texas, Oklahoma, Minnesota, Colorado, and New Mexico.

4. Letter dated July 15, 1948. Eyman, *Print the Legend*, 350–51.

5. *Billy the Kid* (1941) and *The Harvey Girls* (1946) were filmed in Technicolor, and some scenes from each were shot in Monument Valley.

6. Eyman, *Print the Legend*, 350–51.

7. Ford altered it to "Never apologize, Mister. It's a sign of weakness." Bellah would later repeat this line in his script for *A Thunder of Drums* (1961).

8. James Warner Bellah draft, *She Wore a Yellow Ribbon* file, John Ford Collection, Lilly Library.

9. "Lap dissolve" was an abbreviated industry term for "overlapping dissolve," a transition between two scenes. The first scene would gradually fade out as the second scene faded in, overlapping each other. In the silent era, all dissolves were done in the camera, with exposed footage being rewound a few feet before filming the following scene. With

the development of the optical printer, dissolves were done in post-production. Today, the term is simply called "dissolve."

10. James Warner Bellah draft, *She Wore a Yellow Ribbon* file, John Ford Collection, Lilly Library.

11. *She Wore a Yellow Ribbon* notes, John Ford Collection, Lilly Library.

12. James Warner Bellah draft, *She Wore a Yellow Ribbon* file, John Ford Collection, Lilly Library

13. In the film, it is called Sudro's Wells, and this is a stage stop.

14. Benjamin Tyler Henry was awarded a patent on October 16, 1860, for his design of a lever-action repeating rifle. The rifle, produced by Oliver Winchester's company, was manufactured to use a rimfire metallic .44 caliber cartridge holding sixteen rounds in a tube that was underneath and parallel to the rifle barrel. For those who could afford the price (roughly $40 in 1860), many Union soldiers paid for the rifle and ammunition out of their own pocket. Confederate soldiers dubbed the Henry rifle that "damned Yankee rifle that can be loaded on Sunday and fired all week." In 1866, Winchester revised the rifle, with a loading port on the side. A new version, designed in 1873, became very popular throughout the West, known as "the rifle that won the West." Many Henry rifles were used by the Sioux and Cheyenne warriors at the Battle of the Little Bighorn in 1876.

15. Second draft, September 11, 1948, Author's Collection.

16. Laurence Stallings was a US Marine Corps World War I veteran who was wounded in the leg during the Battle of Belleau Wood, leading to its amputation in 1922. Stallings was the entertainment editor at the *New York World*, when he and playwright Maxwell Anderson wrote the World War I play, *What Price Glory*. It became an immediate hit, being adapted into two film versions (1926 and 1952). His novel, *Plumes*, became the basis for MGM's *The Big Parade* (1925). Leaving his newspaper job, Stallings worked for many years as a scriptwriter at MGM. He also wrote the screenplays for Ford's *3 Godfathers* (1948) and *The Sun Shines Bright* (1953). Stallings died in 1968.

17. Ford, 227–28.

18. *She Wore a Yellow Ribbon* story notes, John Ford Collection, Lilly Library.

19. Rynders whipping the warrior, who is Red Shirt's brother, is never explained in the script. No doubt Ford felt the dialogue between Tyree and Quincannon was unnecessary. Rynders does not whip any warrior before being killed in the film.

20. The only possible reason Ford could have wanted the soldiers using a Winchester was because it fired fifteen rounds before reloading, compared to the single-shot Springfield carbine the cavalry actually carried. *She Wore a Yellow Ribbon* story notes, John Ford Collection, Lilly Library.

21. *She Wore a Yellow Ribbon* shooting script, John Ford Collection, Lilly Library.

22. The inclusion of the Pony Express is hardly accurate, as the business lasted only eighteen months (April 1860 to October 1861). From its inception, the entire enterprise was a financial onus. Nearly two hundred relay stations, men to man them, and a large herd of horses were needed. It cost a customer $5 an ounce to send a letter. The completion of the transcontinental telegraph on October 24, 1861, was the final blow to the Pony Express.

23. To stage this scene, Ford had the stagecoach race along an open stretch of the desert, obviously without a driver. To illustrate how fast the stagecoach is actually going, Ford relied on an old cinematic trick of placing bushes and clumps of chaparral between the stagecoach and the camera car. Placing a stable image (in this case the vegetation) between the moving stagecoach and the camera car gives the viewer the sense of speed. To film this runaway stunt, a stuntman or wrangler would be inside the coach out of camera range. The lines are fed through small slots (usually under the seat) where the driver can control the horses. This is called "blind driving."

24. James Warner Bellah to Dan Ford, John Ford Collection, Lilly Library.

25. Quincannon is referring to the Battle of Chapultepec in 1847 during the Mexican-American War (1846–1848). US Army forces won a significant victory over the Mexican army outside of Mexico City.

26. Two headstones in the cemetery have the names of B. DeVoto (Bernard DeVoto) and Douglas Southall Freeman, two authors of American history that Ford greatly admired. DeVoto authored *Across the Wide Missouri* and *The Course of an Empire*, while Freeman wrote definitive biographies of Robert E. Lee and George Washington. It is not uncommon in movies to have names of people, usually cast and crew members, on headstones in a cemetery set.

In the script, as Olivia walks away, Brittles tells his wife she reminds him of her. The dialogue then goes on with him saying he understands why two young lieutenants "are pawing the ground like two buck elks in the spring." He ends with saying good night to her and asking her to tell the children good night for him. As he gets ready to leave, the bugle call "To the Colors" is heard. Brittles straightens up and salutes. The script describes him as "a lonely silhouette—and a small figure against the night sky and the outlines of graves." *She Wore a Yellow Ribbon* shooting script, John Ford Collection, Lilly Library.

27. Ibid.

28. This is the entire narration for this sequence: "So here they are, the dog-faced soldiers. The regulars, the fifty-cent-a-day professionals riding the outposts of a nation. From Fort Reno to Fort Apache, from Fort Phil Kearny to Fort Sheridan. They were all the same."

[Shot featuring Quincannon]: "In every troop a Sergeant Quincannon—with his time running out against his hashmarks." [Shot featuring Tyree]: "A young Tyree. Only three stripes on his sleeve now, but a captain to the men he commanded under Jubal Early when Marse Robert was a living god." [Shot featuring Brittles]: "And at the head of the column, always a Captain Brittles with the wisdom of his trade drawn from long years with the service." [Shot featuring Cohill and Pennell]: "And down the line of file-closers, the lieutenants he trained to follow him. Flint Cohill with nine years of service, Ross Pennell with four." [Shot of the rest of column and wagon leaving]: "Allshard, Brown, Krumrein, Davis—call the roll for them all. Men in dirty shirt blue and only a cold page in the history books to mark their passing." [Shot looking out from fort to the column riding off]: "But wherever they rode, and whatever they fought for, that place became the United States." Ibid.

29. A "whip pan" is the rapid movement by the camera from one point to another; also called a swish pan.

30. Cheyenne Dog Soldiers were the warrior or military society of the Cheyenne Nation, known for their bravery and fierceness in battle. They would protect the entire tribe during hunts, moving their camps, or take a rear-guard action when fleeing enemies.

31. James Warner Bellah to Dan Ford, John Ford Collection, Lilly Library.

32. The use of flares to help light a night shot dates back to the silent era when they were used occasionally to light exterior night scenes.

33. Harry Carey Jr. recalled that "Fred Graham was the greatest fight man in the business. He knew how to give or take a punch and looked great on camera. Duke always said he'd rather throw a punch at Fred Graham than anyone else because he'd 'take it' so perfectly." Harry Carey Jr. to the author, June 1992.

34. As Mrs. Allshard walks Quincannon to the guardhouse she asks the men if they are ashamed, eight men picking on one. The sergeant corrects her: "Only seven, ma'am." In reality, there were a total of six men.

35. The complete narration for this montage: "Signal smokes. War drums. Feathered bonnets against the Western sky. New messiahs, young leaders are ready to hurl the finest light cavalry in the world against Fort Starke. In the Kiowa village, the beat of the drums echoes in the pulse-beat of the young braves. Fighters under a common banner, old quarrels forgotten, Comanche rides with Arapaho, Apache with Cheyenne. All chant of war. War to drive the white man forever from the red man's hunting ground. Only the old men stand silent. Even Pony That Walks has been howled down at the council fires."

36. *She Wore a Yellow Ribbon* story notes, John Ford Collection, Lilly Library.

37. *She Wore a Yellow Ribbon* Producers Code Administration file, Margaret Herrick Library.

38. Letter dated October 25, 1948. Ibid.

39. "Counting coup" was a term used by Indians on the Great Plains for a brave deed or counting victory over an enemy. Striking or touching an enemy while alive was considered the bravest act, usually done with a gun, bow, lance, a long stick (known as a coup stick), or even a bare hand. One's actions would have to be witnessed by at least one or two warriors for the honor to be counted. One who was honored was given an eagle feather, or in other tribes they would wear white weasel skins (Blackfoot) or wolf tails on the heels of moccasins (Crow).

40. *She Wore a Yellow Ribbon* Producers Code Administration file, Margaret Herrick Library.

41. Ibid.

42. Weekly salaries for the cast ranged from McLaglen getting $7,000 for four weeks (the highest-paid actor on the film after Wayne) to Mildred Natwick and Joanne Dru being paid $2,250 and $1,250 for six weeks and eight and a half weeks, respectively. John Agar made $466.67 for ten weeks, while Harry Carey Jr. earned $300 for five and a half weeks and Ben Johnson got $250 for seven weeks. Arthur Shields was paid $1,250 for almost five weeks, and George O'Brien received $1,875 for eight weeks. Chief John Big Tree was paid $500 for three weeks, and Noble Johnson earned $600 for four weeks. Jack Pennick took home $350 for four weeks, with an additional $250 for six weeks as Ford's assistant. Both Francis Ford and Paul Fix were paid a daily rate of $150, with Francis

Ford working four days and Fix only one day. *She Wore a Yellow Ribbon* budget, John Ford Collection, Lilly Library.

43. McLaglen won for Best Actor in *The Informer* (1935) and was nominated for Best Supporting Actor in *The Quiet Man* (1952), both directed by Ford.

44. Noble Johnson had a long and varied career. He was a light-skinned Black man who began appearing in films by 1915, usually playing villains or exotic characters. Johnson and his brother George founded the Lincoln Motion Picture Company in 1916, producing films that featured all-Black casts (referred to back then as "race films"). Johnson used his earnings from his acting roles to fund the company, which eventually folded in 1921. Johnson's acting career continued to flourish, appearing in such films as *The Thief of Bagdad* (1924), *The King of Kings* (1927), *Moby Dick* (1930), *The Mummy* (1932), *King Kong* (1933), *Lost Horizon* (1937), and *Juarez* (1939). He retired in 1950 and died in 1978.

Chief John Big Tree, born Isaac Johnny John in 1877, was a member of the Seneca Nation. His film career dates back to 1915, and he appeared in three other Ford films: *The Iron Horse* (1924), *Drums Along the Mohawk*, and *Stagecoach* (both 1939). He claimed for many years to be the model for the Indian Head / Buffalo nickel. Over the years, this claim has been questioned, as the sculptor, James Earle Fraser, often stated he used three different Native Americans as his inspiration, which may or may not have included Chief John Big Tree. Whatever the truth might be, he appeared on the March 1964 *Esquire* magazine cover to commemorate the Indian Head nickel. He died in 1967 at the age of ninety.

45. Paul Fix had worked with Wayne in several of his early "B" Westerns, even teaching him how to develop that swaggering walk Wayne became well-known for. Unknown to Ford, Fix would meet every night with Wayne and coach him for the following day's scenes on *Stagecoach*. Wayne never forgot his friend, casting him in many of his films. However, Ford, for whatever reason, only cast him in one more film, *What Price Glory* (1953). Fix is best known as Sheriff Micah Torrance in the series *The Rifleman*. He was the father-in-law of Harry Carey Jr.

Peter Ortiz led a very interesting life. Born in New York City in 1913, he was educated at the University of Grenoble in France and could speak ten languages, including Spanish, French, German, and Arabic. In 1932, at the age of nineteen, he joined the French Foreign Legion, advancing to sergeant two years later. Ortiz was twice awarded the French Croix de Guerre, France's highest military medal, before leaving the service in 1937. Two years later, he reenlisted with the rank of sergeant, and was wounded during the German invasion of France. Escaping in 1941, Ortiz returned to America where he joined the US Marine Corps in June 1942. Because of his experience, he was commissioned a second lieutenant, and promoted to captain that December. He conducted reconnaissance missions behind German lines in Tunisia for the OSS (Office of Strategic Services), which he joined in 1944. During a 1944 mission behind enemy lines in Europe he was caught by German soldiers and sent to a POW camp, where he escaped a year later. Ortiz, who retired from the US Marines in 1955 as a colonel, returned to Hollywood to work as a technical advisor. The movies *13 Rue Madeleine* (1947) and *Operation Secret* (1950) were based on his World War II exploits. It is possible Ford and Ortiz met each other during their time in the OSS, or at least knew of each other. Ortiz was the most highly decorated officer in the OSS, with twenty-four medals from the United States, England, and France. He died in 1988 at age seventy-seven. In 1994, the village of Montgirod, in southeastern France, renamed their town hall square in his honor, Place du Colonel Peter Ortiz.

46. Harry Carey Jr. to the author, June 19, 1996.

47. Joanne Dru to Dan Ford, John Ford Collection, Lilly Library.

48. *She Wore a Yellow Ribbon*'s budget was $305,480 less than *Fort Apache*'s. *She Wore a Yellow Ribbon* budget, John Ford Collection, Lilly Library.

49. Harry Goulding earned a total of $24,277 for auto and truck rental, rooms, and meals, while Anderson Company was paid $79,916. Ibid.

50. For his acting role, Kieffer was paid $175 a week for four weeks, while earning $1,600 for five weeks as a technical advisor. Ibid.

51. Chuck Hayward stated to Dan Ford that *She Wore a Yellow Ribbon* was his first time working for Ford; however, his name does not appear in the film's cast or stunt budget list.

52. John Ford to Dan Ford, John Ford Collection, Lilly Library.

53. Ibid.

54. The total amount for each set includes such materials as paint, plaster, lumber, and miscellaneous supplies, as well as salaries for carpenters, electricians, grips, painters, plasterers, and laborers. *She Wore a Yellow Ribbon* budget, John Ford Collection, Lilly Library.

55. Ibid.

56. Aside from Fat Jones Stables, Hudkins Brothers Stables was the other major supplier of horses to the film industry. Their original stables were located behind Warner Bros. Studio, where Forest Lawn–Hollywood Hills cemetery now stands. Roy Rogers bought a golden palomino from Hudkins for $2,500 in 1943, renaming the horse Trigger.

57. Ben Johnson married Carol Jones, daughter of Fat Jones. When Ben won the Rodeo World Championship for team roping in 1953, he rode Steel. Harry Carey Jr. to the author, June 19, 1996.

58. Charles "Buffalo" Jones, a former buffalo hunter, became an ardent protector of the animals he once hunted. He began a conservation program to protect the buffalo and increase the herd's population. Jones brought eighty-seven buffalo to what is known as the Kaibab Plateau, a heavily forested area located in Coconino County of Arizona. The area was named the Grand Canyon Game Preserve (on the north rim of the canyon) in 1906 by President Theodore Roosevelt, designated for the sole purpose of protecting and breeding game animals. In 1927, the state of Arizona purchased the remaining buffalo (ninety-eight) from Jones's original herd. Their descendants now make up the herd at House Rock Valley.

59. *She Wore a Yellow Ribbon* budget, John Ford Collection, Lilly Library.

60. Harry Carey Jr. to the author, June 19, 1996.

61. Ben Johnson to Dan Ford, John Ford Collection, Lilly Library.

62. A hogan was a Navajo dwelling that was originally dome-shaped, although through the years it has changed to a more hexagonal or octagonal shape. It was made of logs and stone, the outside covered with mud or sod depending on what was readily available. A circular opening was located on the roof to allow smoke to escape. The entrance always faced east toward the rising sun. Hogans can be found throughout the Navajo Nation.

63. Both Joanne Dru and Mildred Natwick stayed in rooms on the second floor of Goulding's Trading Post. Carey Jr., *A Company of Heroes*, 57–58.

64. Harry Carey Jr. to the author, June 19, 1996.

65. The listing of dates, locations, and scenes are based on *She Wore a Yellow Ribbon* shooting schedule, John Ford Collection, Lilly Library.

66. Ben Johnson to Dan Ford, John Ford Collection, Lilly Library.

67. Matte shots date back to the silent era. During that period, the painting was done on a glass plate and placed in front of the camera and actors. It was generally done for wide-angle shots. Today, all forms of matte shots are done with computers.

68. The location of the fort and parade grounds is close to where the exterior set of the Edwards cabin was built for *The Searchers* (1956).

69. *Directed by John Ford* (documentary), American Film Institute, 1971.

70. McBride, *Searching for John Ford*, 460.

71. Hoch opening the camera's aperture allowed all available light to be absorbed by the film stock. What they caught on film is one of cinema's most memorable moments.

72. Harry Carey Jr. to the author, June 19, 1996.

73. Ibid.

74. Chuck Hayward to Dan Ford, John Ford Collection, Lilly Library.

75. *She Wore a Yellow Ribbon* shooting script, John Ford Collection, Lilly Library.

76. John Ford to Dan Ford, John Ford Collection, Lilly Library.

77. Harry Carey Jr. to the author, June 19, 1996.

78. Carey Jr., *A Company of Heroes*, 65.

79. John Wayne to Dan Ford, John Ford Collection, Lilly Library.

80. John Ford to Dan Ford, John Ford Collection, Lilly Library.

81. *She Wore a Yellow Ribbon* budget, John Ford Collection, Lilly Library.

82. Jester Hairston was a noted Black choir director and actor. The grandson of slaves, Hairston became the first Black student at Tufts University, graduating in 1929. As part of the Hall Johnson Choir, Hairston appeared on Broadway in *The Green Pastures* (1930), later appearing in the 1936 film version. Hairston remained in Hollywood working as an actor and arranging and directing choirs for various films. He formed the Jester Hairston Choir in 1943, and in addition to his film work with music, he conducted choral groups in colleges, taking a multiracial Jester Hairston Chorale to perform in China in 1985. His film credits include *The Alamo* (1960), *To Kill a Mockingbird* (1962), and *Sullivan's Travels* (1941), and he was a regular on the *Amen* television series. He passed away at age ninety-eight in 2000.

83. John Ford to Dan Ford, John Ford Collection, Lilly Library.

84. *She Wore a Yellow Ribbon* production file, John Ford Collection, Lilly Library.

85. From 1836 to 1861, minstrel shows were a very popular form of entertainment, but as the nineteenth century went on, they faded in popularity, eventually replaced by vaudeville. Most performers in minstrel shows were white actors made up in blackface, although William Henry Lane and Thomas Dilward were two early Black performers who appeared in shows. Kathryn Kalinak, *How the West Was Sung: Music in the Westerns of John Ford* (Berkeley: University of California Press, 2007), 141–42.

86. Ibid., 223 *n.* 59.

87. Many films released sheet music with a song that was tied to a movie's release. This practice dates back to silent films in the late 1910s. If a film had a popular song attached to it, it helped to promote the film at the box office.

88. Kalinak, *How the West Was Sung*, 142.

89. *Daily Variety*, July 27, 1949.

90. *New York Times*, November 18, 1949.

91. *Hollywood Reporter*, July 27, 1949.

92. *Cue*, November 19, 1949.

93. *Los Angeles Times*, October 27, 1949.

94. Average ticket prices for a movie in 1949 ranged between forty to fifty cents. *She Wore a Yellow Ribbon* budget and earnings file, John Ford Collection, Lilly Library.

95. John Ford to Dan Ford, John Ford Collection, Lilly Library.

96. Others in the radio cast were George Yeast, Burton Yarborough, Wally Mayer, Bill Johnston, Sondra Rodgers, Eddie Marr, Norman Fields, and Dan Riss. *Lux Radio Theatre* began airing from New York City in 1934, performing adapted versions of Broadway plays. The show moved to Hollywood in mid-1936, with director Cecil B. DeMille serving as the show's host for many years, with the format switching to adapting various motion pictures. A television version, *Lux Video Theatre*, premiered on October 2, 1950, as a live thirty-minute series, produced in New York City. Like the radio version, the series moved to Hollywood with the beginning of the CBS 1953–1954 season, switching to NBC in 1954 as an hour-long series that ran until 1957.

97. Wayne thought the film should have concluded after the cavalry scatters the pony herd and Brittles rides off. He said that it was Merian Cooper's idea for Brittles to be brought back and given the appointment as chief of civilian scouts. John Wayne to Dan Ford, John Ford Collection, Lilly Library.

98. Peter Bogdanovich, *Who the Hell's in It: Portraits and Conversations* (New York: Knopf, 2004), 287–88.

99. In the script, the direction notes, "The right leg is rather stiff, and at first has only a few degrees of motion. Through the ensuing scene, this leg, through careful exercise, will be restored to full ninety-degree action, in the midst of intermittent GROANINGS and flexings." In the scene, Brittles extends his left leg, which was closer to camera.

100. John Wayne to Dan Ford, John Ford Collection, Lilly Library.

101. John Ford to Dan Ford, John Ford Collection, Lilly Library.

102. Ibid.

103. Harry Carey Jr. to the author, June 12, 1996.

104. Viewing the recent restoration of this film, the land and its subjects are just breathtaking. This restored print is available on the recent Blu-Ray DVD.

105. Hoch photographed five films with Ford: *3 Godfathers* (1948), *She Wore a Yellow Ribbon* (1949), *The Quiet Man* (1952), *Mister Roberts* (1955), and *The Searchers* (1956). He won three Oscars for Best Color Cinematography: *Joan of Arc* (1948), *She Wore a Yellow Ribbon* (1949), and *The Quiet Man* (1952).

106. Ironically, Ford would experience a forced retirement in fifteen years. While he had a few projects he wanted to make, the new breed of studio executives viewed him as an antique and ignored him.

INTERMISSION

1. The play premiered at the Plymouth Theatre on Broadway on September 3, 1924, running for 435 performances before closing on September 13, 1925. *What Price Glory* was produced twice by Fox Studios as a motion picture. The 1927 film, directed by Raoul Walsh, starred Victor McLaglen as Captain Flagg and Edmund Lowe as Sergeant Quirt. Ford directed the 1952 version starring James Cagney as Flagg and Dan Dailey as Quirt. While the original Broadway production had a question mark after the word "glory," both the films, as well as Ford's stage production, dropped the question mark in the title.

2. Harry Carey Jr. to the author, June 12, 1996.

3. Ibid.

4. The Masquers Club was located north of Hollywood Boulevard at 1740 Sycamore Avenue. It was originally the home of silent screen actor Antonio Moreno, who donated the property to the club. The Masquers membership roster boasted almost every star and character actor in Hollywood, who would stop by for lunch or dinner.

5. Murphy directed such films as *Girl Without a Room* (1933), *Pacific Blackout* (1941), *Mrs. Wiggs of the Cabbage Patch* (1942), *The Man in Half-Moon Street* (1945), and *Dick Turpin's Ride* (1951). He also helmed many episodes of numerous television series, including *Mr. and Mrs. North*, *Lassie*, *Broken Arrow*, and *The Many Loves of Dobie Gillis*. Murphy died in 1967 at the age of seventy-one.

6. Harry Carey Jr. to the author, June 12, 1996.

7. John McCabe to the author, February 18, 1996.

8. The play's program included a disclaimer: "The speech of men under arms is universally and consistently interlarded with profanity. . . . The audience is asked to bear with certain expletives which, under other circumstances, might be used for melodramatic effect, but herein are employed because the mood and truth of the play demand their employment." *What Price Glory* program, Author's Collection.

9. The theater is now called by its original name, The El Capitan.

10. Harry Carey Jr. to the author, June 12, 1996.

11. Larry Blake to the author, January 16, 1982.

12. It was said the idea of the restaurant was based on Clifton Cafeteria in downtown Los Angeles, which sported an interior featuring waterfalls, volcanic rocks, and tropical foliage. At one time the outside front architecture resembled something that would have been found in the jungle set of *King Kong*.

13. Bogdanovich, *John Ford*, 138.

14. The Boers were of Dutch, German, or Huguenot descent, and settled in the area of Cape of Good Hope around 1652, establishing a shipping station in affiliation with the Dutch East India Company. The term *boer* meant "farmer" in the Afrikaans language, which was developed from a mixture of Dutch, indigenous African, and other languages. The Boers settled in rich farmlands, using slaves to work their fields. When the British took control of the area in 1806, the Boers resisted the changes the British Empire was enforcing, such as abolishing slavery. About 12,000 to 14,000 Boers left the Cape Town area in what was called the Great Trek (from 1835 to the early 1840s), moving to the great plains beyond the Orange River. In this area they were free from British rule and able to set up their own form of government. Between 1899 and 1902, the Boer War was

fought by the Boers over the British Empire's growing influence over the South African region. Realizing the fight for independence was futile, the Boers signed a peace treaty with England on May 31, 1902.

15. Eyman, *Print the Legend*, 364.

16. Ibid., 369.

Rio Grande

1. Abe Haberman to the author, September 15, 1979.

2. Consolidated Film Industries remained a busy film processing lab in Hollywood for years, even after Yates sold the company, finally closing its doors permanently in 2008.

3. The six Poverty Row companies were: Mascot Pictures, Monogram Pictures, Liberty Pictures, Majestic Pictures, Chesterfield Pictures, and Invincible Pictures. (John Wayne appeared in several Mascot serials and films early in his career.) Monogram eventually split from Republic and produced "B" movies, including the profitable *Bowery Boys* films (originally titled *East Side Kids*). In 1953, Monogram Studios changed its name to Allied Artists, which closed its production doors in 1966, reverting to distributing foreign films. However, in 1972, the company restarted its production arm by producing *Cabaret* (1972), *Papillon* (1973), and *The Man Who Would Be King* (1975). Allied Artists ceased making films in 1979, after filing for bankruptcy.

4. Mack Sennett's studio was originally located in the Edendale (now Silver Lake) area of Los Angeles. In 1927, Sennett was gifted twenty acres in the San Fernando Valley by real estate developers. Sennett named the area "Studio City," which became the name of the suburb. (Studio City is about three miles west of Universal Studios.) The Great Depression caused Sennett to lose ownership of the studio in 1933. It was renamed Republic Pictures when Yates took over the property, and remained so until it was sold to the CBS television network in 1964, and renamed CBS Studio Center. The studio, which has been bought and sold a few times since, remains a busy complex. Over the years several television shows have filmed on the lot, including *Gunsmoke*, *The Wild Wild West*, *Gilligan's Island*, *The Rifleman*, *My Three Sons*, *Seinfeld*, *Remington Steele*, and *Hill Street Blues*.

5. John Wayne to Dan Ford, John Ford Collection, Lilly Library.

6. Ibid.

7. Bellah was referring to Colonel Ranald Mackenzie's 1873 raid into the Mexican state of Coahuila. Both President Grant and General Sheridan were frustrated by the Kickapoo tribes raiding in the South Texas area (Rio Grande River to San Antonio), then crossing the southern border to safety. The Mexican government flatly refused to allow the US military to enter their country in pursuit. Sheridan gave Mackenzie verbal orders to cross into Mexico and destroy the Kickapoos' base. In the early hours of May 18, 1873, the cavalry attacked the first of three villages, taking forty women and children as hostages and burning lodges and food. Two other villages belonging to Lipan and Mescalero Apaches were also destroyed. Mackenzie and his men returned to Fort Clark with the hostages. (Two soldiers were wounded, and one died.) The Mexican government objected to the attack, but dropped the matter to avoid an international incident. The Mackenzie raid put an end to the border raids in that area by Indian tribes.

8. McGuinness also worked with Ford on *Salute* (1929) and *Men Without Women* (1930) at Fox Studios. He also served as a producer (uncredited) on *They Were Expendable* (1945) at MGM.

9. *Rio Grande* production file, John Ford Collection, Lilly Library.

10. Some film historians mistakenly claim that Wayne's character of Kirby Yorke in *Rio Grande* is the same character he played in *Fort Apache*. Although both characters share the same name, there is no supporting evidence they are the same character, any more than Victor McLaglen's role as Quincannon is the same character in *She Wore a Yellow Ribbon*. In *Fort Apache*, the character's name is spelled Kirby York, while in *Rio Grande* his last name is spelled Yorke.

11. *Rio Grande* shooting script, John Ford Collection, Lilly Library.

12. *Uhlan* was a term for the Polish light cavalry unit formed in the early 1700s. Other countries, such as France, Spain, and Germany, adopted a light cavalry unit by the early 1800s. Most Uhlan regiments were armed with long lancers, sabers, and pistols. Uhlan regiments were used during the early weeks of World War I, although some units were turned into infantry rifle units on the Western Front. Other units remained mounted, stationed on the Eastern Front, where the archaic landscape was more useful for a cavalry unit.

13. McGuinness places Jeff and Heinze apologizing later in the script, when they are escorting the wagons with women and children.

14. *Rio Grande* shooting script, John Ford Collection, Lilly Library.

15. The song was written by Roy Rogers' wife, Dale Evans, circa 1946.

16. Virginia Military Institute (VMI) is a public military college in Lexington, Virginia. Founded in 1839, it was America's first state military college. Thomas "Stonewall" Jackson began teaching at the college in 1851 until the outbreak of the Civil War. VMI has many distinguished alumni, including General George C. Marshall, Rear Admiral (and noted polar explorer) Richard Byrd, Colonel Frank McCarthy (producer of the 1970 Academy Award–winning film *Patton*), and both the grandfather and father of World War II general George S. Patton Jr.

17. *Rio Bravo* is the Spanish name for "Rio Grande."

18. *Rio Grande* shooting script, John Ford Collection, Lilly Library.

19. The song, also known as "Bold Fenian Men," was a tribute to the Irish nationalists who staged the 1916 rebellion during Easter week in an attempt to gain independence from British rule. Ireland was declared a "free state" in 1921, but actual independence didn't happen until 1949. Northern Ireland remains part of the United Kingdom.

20. Adding an "O" in front of Feeney was no doubt paying homage to Ford's last name. In *Fort Apache*, the telegraph operator character is named Tom O'Feeney.

21. *Rio Grande* Producers Code Administration file, Margaret Herrick Library.

22. Ibid.

23. Ibid.

24. John Ford to Dan Ford, John Ford Collection, Lilly Library.

25. Wayne, who was one of Republic's biggest stars, had approached Yates about making a movie about the famous Texas battle. Yates kept stalling his approval, usually complaining about the proposed $1.2 million budget. Wayne and Yates ended up in a

shouting match at the actor's office on the lot shortly before his contract with the studio expired in January 1952. Wayne walked off the Republic lot and never returned. In 1955, with Walt Disney's *Davy Crockett* proving to be a massive hit, Yates produced a smaller-budget version called *The Last Command.*

26. Eyman, *Print the Legend*, 389.

27. Carey Jr., *A Company of Heroes*, 35–36.

28. The recording by Burl Ives made the song very popular, but it was Vaughn Monroe's rendition that turned it into a smash hit.

29. Jones wrote the following songs for *Wagon Master*: "Wagons West," "Rollin' Shadows in the Dust," "Song of the Wagon Master," and "Chuck-A-Walla-Swing." Carey Jr., *A Company of Heroes*, 94.

30. The last two Ford films Jones composed songs for were *The Searchers* (1956) and *The Horse Soldiers* (1959). In the latter movie, Jones played General Grant in the opening scene. He also wrote the title song for the television series *Cheyenne*, and two Disney films, *The Great Locomotive Chase* and *Westward Ho!, the Wagons* (both 1956). Jones also appeared in *Ten Who Dared* (1960) and in the television series *The Sheriff of Cochise* (1956–1958) and *The Adventures of Spin and Marty* (1955). He died in 1963 at the age of forty-nine.

31. Ken Curtis left the group in 1952, the same year he married Barbara Ford. He appeared in eleven John Ford films, including *The Searchers* (1956), but he's best known for his role as Festus Haggen (1964–1975) in the long-running television series *Gunsmoke*. Ken and Barbara divorced in 1964, and Ken passed away in 1991, at the age of seventy-four.

32. Harry Carey Jr. to the author, June 12, 1991.

33. The Academy of Motion Picture Arts and Sciences awarded a special Oscar, a smaller version of the actual award, to child actors who delivered strong performances. Other child actors who received this statuette include Shirley Temple (receiving the first award in 1934), Deanna Durbin (1938), Mickey Rooney (1938), Judy Garland (1939), Margaret O'Brien (1944), Peggy Ann Garner (1945), Ivan Jandl (1948), Bobby Driscoll (1949), Jon Whiteley (1954), Vincent Winter (1954), and Hayley Mills (1960). Both Temple and Jarman were given full-size Oscars in later years, as was Mills, whose original award had been stolen.

34. Claude Jarman Jr., *My Life and the Final Days of Hollywood* (Murrells Inlet, SC: Covenant Books, 2018), 96.

35. Glennon's other credits on Ford films include *The Hurricane* (1937), *Stagecoach* (1939), *Young Mr. Lincoln* (1939), *Drums Along the Mohawk* (1939), *Wagon Master* (1950), and *Sergeant Rutledge* (1960).

36. Barbara Ford began working as an assistant editor on *Red River* (1948), as well as on *She Wore a Yellow Ribbon* (1949), *The Quiet Man* (1952), and *The Sun Shines Bright* (1953). Director Peter Bogdanovich hired her as the lead editor on this 1985 film, *Mask.* She died in 1985 at the age of sixty-two. Jack Murray edited fifteen films for Ford, beginning with *The Prisoner of Shark Island* in 1936. His other credits with Ford, aside from the cavalry trilogy, include *The Fugitive* (1947), *3 Godfathers* (1948), *Wagon Master* (1950), *The Quiet Man* (1952), *The Sun Shines Bright* (1953), *Mister Roberts* (1955), *The Searchers*

(1956), *The Last Hurrah* (1958), *The Horse Soldiers* (1959), *Sergeant Rutledge* (1960), and *Two Rode Together* (1961).

37. Over the years, some film historians have mistakenly claimed that Ford filmed parts of *Rio Grande* in Monument Valley. While the terrain of Moab is similar to Ford's beloved valley, all the exterior locations for the film were shot in and around Moab, Utah.

38. George White helped to establish Moab's film commission office around 1949. White sold the ranch to his son, Tommy, in 1965. Colin Fryer bought the property in 1990, reopening it in 2002 as Red Cliffs Lodge.

39. Harry Carey Jr. to the author, June 12, 1996; Claude Jarman Jr. to the author, October 8, 2021.

40. The ballroom, located at the corner of Center and 100 East, was the same place they fed evening meals to the cast and crew on *Wagon Master*. *The Times-Independent*, May 11, 1950.

41. Ford and Wayne were in Reno to accept the city's first Chamber of Commerce "Golden Spur" Award for *She Wore a Yellow Ribbon*.

42. *The Times-Independent*, May 18, 1950.

43. *The Times-Independent*, June 1, 1950.

44. Carey Jr., *A Company of Heroes*, 110–12.

45. Ibid., 113–15.

46. Jarman Jr., *My Life and the Final Days of Hollywood*, 97.

47. *Rio Grande* shooting schedule, June 5, 1950, John Ford Collection, Lilly Library.

48. The big boulder Tyree hides behind while waiting to meet up with Jeff and Boone is still there, about nine hundred feet from State Route 128, with Stearns Mesa overlooking the location.

49. Claude Jarman Jr. to the author, October 8, 2021.

50. Harry Carey Jr. to the author, June 12, 1996.

51. *The Times-Independent*, June 29, 1950.

52. When Ward Bond signed on to star in the series, he insisted the producers cast Wilson and Frank McGrath as regulars in the show. Wilson and McGrath became very popular character actors after the series ended in 1965.

53. Terry Wilson to Dan Ford, John Ford collection, Lilly Library.

54. Harry Carey Jr. to the author, June 12, 1996.

55. Ibid.

56. *The Times-Independent*, June 29, 1950.

57. Arizona-born Rex Allen left school to compete in various rodeos. His big break came when he landed a regular singing job on the *National Barn Dance*, broadcast on WSL (Chicago). By 1949, he had his own radio show on CBS, and Republic Pictures signed him to a contract in 1950. Allen was one of the top ten Western stars, appearing in nineteen films from 1950 to 1954. Also an accomplished songwriter, he recorded many records over the years. His rich, pleasant voice guaranteed him a career as a voice artist for several commercials, as well as providing narration for nine Walt Disney films, including *The Incredible Journey* (1963) and *Charlie, the Lonesome Cougar* (1967). Allen died at the age of seventy-eight in 1999.

58. CBS president Frank Stanton, CBS vice president and Pacific Coast executive Howard S. Marthan, and Ivor Sharp, managing director of KSL (Salt Lake City radio station) arrived in Moab for the radio show. *The Times-Independent*, June 29, 1950.

59. Ibid.

60. Maureen O'Hara, *'Tis Herself: A Memoir* (New York: Simon & Schuster, 2004), 138; Harry Carey Jr. to the author, November 6, 2005.

61. Bette L. Stanton, *Where God Put the West—Movie Making in the Desert: A Moab–Monument Valley History* (Moab, UT: Four Corners Press, 1994), 46.

62. Untitled clipping in John Ford biography file, October 2, 1950, Margaret Herrick Library; Dan Ford to the author, February 13, 2022.

63. Terry Wilson to Dan Ford, John Ford Collection, Lilly Library.

64. Chuck Hayward to Dan Ford, John Ford Collection, Lilly Library.

65. Chuck Roberson, *The Fall Guy: 30 Years as The Duke's Double* (North Vancouver, British Columbia: Hancock House Publishers, Ltd., 1980), 66.

66. Ibid., 74.

67. Ibid., 70–71.

68. Harry Carey Jr. to the author, June 12, 1996.

69. Ibid.

70. Eyman, *Print the Legend*, 393–94.

71. *Rio Grande* daily production report, John Ford Collection, Lilly Library.

72. Young, born in Chicago in 1899, began playing the violin at the age of six. When he was ten, his grandfather sent him to Poland to study at the Warsaw Imperial Conservatory. By the age of sixteen he was a concert violinist with the Warsaw Philharmonic. Arriving back in the United States in 1920, Young made his way to Los Angeles and became concertmaster for Paramount-Publix Theatres during the silent era. By 1930 he had begun composing scores for motion pictures. Among his numerous credits are *Union Pacific* (1939), *Northwest Mounted Police* (1940), *For Whom the Bell Tolls* (1943), *Unconquered* (1947), *Sands of Iwo Jima* (1949), *The Greatest Show on Earth* (1952), *Shane* (1953), and *The Country Girl* (1954). Young was also a well-known songwriter, and scored Richard Boone's television series, *Medic* (1954–1956). He was fifty-six when he died in 1956.

73. *Rio Grande* statement of income and costs, John Ford Collection, Lilly Library.

74. The thirty-one cities were New York City, Philadelphia, Washington, DC, Albany, Buffalo, New Haven, Pittsburgh, Cleveland, Cincinnati, Detroit, Chicago, Indianapolis, Milwaukee, Minneapolis, Kansas City, Omaha, Des Moines, St. Louis, Atlanta, Charlotte, New Orleans, Tampa, Memphis, Dallas, Oklahoma City, Seattle, Denver, Salt Lake City, Portland, San Francisco, and Los Angeles. *Rio Grande* four-page promotional handout, *Rio Grande* production file, Margaret Herrick Library.

75. *Hollywood Reporter*, November 2, 1950.

76. *Variety*, November 8, 1950.

77. *New York Times*, November 20, 1950.

78. *Cue*, November 25, 1950.

79. *Motion Picture Daily*, November 2, 1950.

80. *Los Angeles Times*, November 3, 1950.

81. Moab's movie theater only screened films for one or two days. *The Times-Independent*, January 4, 1951.

82. Mary Todd Lincoln, the wife of President Abraham Lincoln, came from a family that owned slaves. Two half brothers fought and died for the Confederacy, while two brothers fought for the Rebel side.

Theodore Roosevelt's mother, Martha, grew up on a Georgia plantation where her father owned slaves. Martha never wavered in her sympathies for the Southern cause. Theodore's father was a solid Unionist, but could not join the war due to the strain it would cause in his marriage. Instead, he paid a $300 fee for another person to fight in his place. Two of Theodore's uncles, James and Irvine Bulloch, both joined the Confederacy. Irvine served in the navy, while James worked as a Confederate agent in Europe.

83. General Grant was concerned that the fertile Shenandoah Valley, with its numerous farms and grazing land, was still able to supply needed material to the Confederate Army. In August 1864, Grant created the Army of the Shenandoah with General Philip Sheridan in charge. Sheridan's mission was twofold: to defeat Confederate Jubal Early and his troops in the area, and to lay waste to the numerous farms in the valley, similar to General Sherman's March to the Sea in Georgia and the Carolinas. Sheridan defeated Early's Confederate force in the Battle of Cedar Creek on October 19, 1864.

84. *Fort Apache* spent forty-five days in production, while *She Wore a Yellow Ribbon* was completed in thirty-one days.

85. There is a continuity problem with this scene. As Yorke rides off to rescue the children, both Boone and Jeff are left behind with the wagons. However, when Yorke lets Tyree call his two volunteers, Boone and Jeff appear with no explanation.

86. Harry Carey Jr. to the author, June 19, 1996.

87. At the request of the U.S. Navy department, Ford did go to Korea in early 1951 to make a documentary, *This Is Korea!* At Ford's suggestion, it was distributed by Republic Pictures in August of 1951, but did little business at the box office. The fifty-minute documentary, filmed in color, was written by an uncredited James Warner Bellah, and had four narrators: Ward Bond, John Ireland, director Allan Dwan, and Irving Pichel, who provided the narration for *She Wore a Yellow Ribbon.*

Taps

1. *The Quiet Man* was nominated for Best Picture, Best Director, Best Supporting Actor (Victor McLaglen), Best Writing (Screenplay), Best Cinematography (color), Best Art Direction–Set Decoration (color), and Best Sound. It took home Oscars for Best Director and Best Cinematography.

2. In 2023 dollars the amount would be $2,197,380.57. McBride, *Searching for John Ford*, 530.

3. *Rio Grande*'s earnings in England totaled $231,970.49, but the country held on to $165,576.68. That left $66,393.81 in Republic's coffers, and Argosy would get 50 percent of those net earnings. Italy was less generous, hanging on to the entire $122,000 box office take. As mentioned previously, many Hollywood studios began making films in certain European countries like England, France, and Italy to gain access to those restricted funds. Eyman, Print the Legend, 372.

4. Ibid., 373.

5. *The Sun Shines Bright* was the last film Argosy produced.

6. RKO took ownership of *The Fugitive*, *Fort Apache*, *She Wore a Yellow Ribbon*, *Wagon Master*, and *Mighty Joe Young*.

7. Cinerama was a forerunner of French filmmaker Abel Gance's Polyvision, which used three cameras to photograph an image, which was then projected onto three adjoining screens. (Gance only used the process for the finale of his 1927 epic, *Napoleon*.) Another wide-screen process was CinemaScope, which used an anamorphic-lens system. It was a much more cost-effective process compared to Cinerama, as only a special lens was attached to a camera. Another process that was fashionable for a short time with audiences was 3D, although the cost and audiences having to wear special glasses were drawbacks.

8. *How the West Was Won* was originally released in England in late 1962, but released in the United States in early 1963. It proved to be a major box office success, and went on to earn eight Oscar nominations, including Best Picture. (It won three awards: Best Story and Screenplay, Best Editing, and Best Sound.)

9. The relationship between Ford and Henry Fonda took a serious hit during filming. Fonda, who originated the role on Broadway, objected to Ford's changes in the dialogue and various characters' performances. When he tried to explain his concerns to Ford, the director hit him. From that point on, their relationship was frosty, to say the least. Ford broke his own rule and began drinking during production. By the time the company had returned to Hollywood from the Hawaii and Midway locations, the studio (Warner Bros.) stated that Ford left the production due to emergency gall bladder surgery and was replaced by Mervyn LeRoy. LeRoy and Ford shared directing credit. The film was a box office success.

10. However, the changes for Ford were not limited to just the film industry, but also to his personal life. With increased population growth in Los Angeles, more open space was being devoured for housing and freeways. Ford's Odin Street home of thirty years, across from the Hollywood Bowl, became the victim of eminent domain by the city of Los Angeles in 1954. The city, needing more parking spaces to handle the crowds for the Hollywood Bowl, paid Ford $46,000 for his property. (The Fords moved to Bel Air, north of the UCLA campus.)

As time went on fewer members gathered at his Field Photo Farm, with Ford often allowing the Masquers Club to hold their yearly picnic on the property, as well as several AA groups. The property became a shell of itself, and after a 1969 fire destroyed the buildings, Ford donated the land to the Motion Picture and Television Relief Fund. The area is now a residential neighborhood, while the small chapel, named after Ford, was moved to the Motion Picture Home in Woodland Hills.

Ford's beloved yacht *Araner* was showing its age, and its upkeep was a significant drain on his wallet. No longer able to sail to Hawaii or even Catalina Island because of his declining health, Ford sold the *Araner* in 1969 for roughly $25,000. (Earlier, during the making of *Donovan's Reef* [1963], Ford had rented the *Araner* to the production company, and it appeared in several scenes.)

11. Francis Ford died in 1953 of cancer, at the age of seventy-two. Ward Bond's death left Ford shaken. Ford's "favorite shit" and perennial target for verbal abuse died of a massive heart attack in 1960, at the age of fifty-seven. In the years after Ford's death, Harry Carey Jr. became the torchbearer for Ford memories. A delightful storyteller and always friendly to any fan who wrote or spoke to him, Carey quickly became the go-to person for John Ford. His book, *Company of Heroes: My Life as an Actor in the John Ford Stock Company*, was released in 1994 to much acclaim, and remains in print. He was forever willing to talk about his beloved "Uncle Jack" and his experiences working with him. On December 27, 2011, at the age of ninety-one, Harry Carey Jr., the last member of John Ford's stock company, died.

Other stock company members who passed away include J. Farrell MacDonald (1952), Tom Tyler (1954), Duke R. Lee (1959), Grant Withers (1959), Russell Simpson (1959), Victor McLaglen (1959), Harry Tenbrook (1960), Mary Gordon (1963), Jack Pennick (1964), William Steele (1966), Jane Darwell (1967), Mae Marsh (1968), Sam Harris (1969), Arthur Shields (1970), Danny Borzage (1975), Willis Bouchey (1977), Frank Baker (1980), William Henry (1982), Ray Hyke (1982), Shug Fisher (1984), Steve Pendleton (1984), George O'Brien (1985), Mickey Simpson (1985), John Qualen (1987), John Carradine (1988), Peter Ortiz (1988), Mike Mazurki (1990), Ken Curtis (1991), Hank Worden (1992), Carleton Young (1994), Mildred Natwick (1994), Fred Libby (1997), O. Z. Whitehead (1998), Ruth Clifford (1998), and Anna Lee (2004).

12. The six corporations consisted of United Artists, the Mirisch Company, John Ford Productions, Mahin-Rackin Productions, Wayne's Batjac Productions, and William Holden Productions. Ford, *Pappy*, 279–80.

13. The ten films were: *The Last Hurrah* (1958), *Gideon of Scotland Yard* (1959), *The Horse Soldiers* (1959), *Sergeant Rutledge* (1960), *Two Rode Together* (1961), *The Man Who Shot Liberty Valance* (1962), *How the West Was Won* (1962), *Donovan's Reef* (1963), *Cheyenne Autumn* (1964), and *7 Women* (1966).

14. This was why so many experienced crew members quickly chose to do television series, as a full season of a television show in the mid-1950s shot thirty-nine episodes. By 1967, the number of TV episodes produced varied. *Gunsmoke* produced 25, *Ironside* had a total of 28, while *The Lucy Show* did 22, and *Gomer Pyle, USMC* made 30. By 1970, the number of episodes for a network television show was 24. Today, that number of episodes has remained steady (provided they are not canceled!) for a network TV series. A cable TV series, like *Bosch* or *Westworld*, produces 10 episodes.

15. *The Wandering Jew* had been a project circling Hollywood for decades. MGM had announced the project for Lon Chaney in the 1927–1928 period, but it was never produced. There have been five film versions and one television version of the story: 1904, produced by George Méliès; 1912, by Roma Films in Italy; 1923, starring Matheson Lang in a silent British version; 1933, British talking version with Conrad Veidt; 1948, Italian version; and a 1947 BBC television special. Eyman, *Print the Legend*, 487.

16. Martin Milner appeared in two Ford films, *The Long Gray Line* and *Mister Roberts* (both 1955). Ford also visited John Wayne and Howard Hawks in 1965 during the filming of *El Dorado* in Tucson, Arizona. He also visited Wayne on the sets of *The Green Berets* (1968), *Rio Lobo* (1971), and *The Cowboys* (1972).

17. Jarman Jr., *My Life and the Final Days of Hollywood*, 132.

18. Other recipients included James Cagney, Orson Welles, Bette Davis, Henry Fonda, William Wyler, Alfred Hitchcock, Frank Capra, Billy Wilder, Lillian Gish, Gene Kelly, Fred Astaire, John Huston, Barbara Stanwyck, Robert Wise, David Lean, James Stewart, and Julie Andrews, to name a few.

19. John Wayne to Dan Ford, John Ford Collection, Lilly Library.

20. The first time Ford photographed this area was in *The Searchers* when Ethan Edwards looks down on Scar's village near the climax of the film. He returned to the location for a brief scene in *Cheyenne Autumn* (1964), as Richard Widmark and his cavalry column ride out on the plateau.

21. *Turning of the Earth: The Making of The Searchers*, Warner Bros. Home Video, 2000.

22. While I have only mentioned four notable on-camera deaths in Ford films, there have been others, such as Frank McGlynn in *The Prisoner of Shark Island*, Donald Crisp in *How Green was My Valley*, Charley Grapewin in *The Grapes of Wrath*, Tim Holt in *My Darling Clementine*, Rudy Bowman in *She Wore a Yellow Ribbon*, and Maureen O'Hara in *The Long Grey Line.*

23. Ford won four New York Film Critics Circle Awards for *The Informer* (1935), *Stagecoach* (1939), *The Grapes of Wrath* and *The Long Voyage Home* (both 1940) and *How Green Was My Valley* (1941). He received a nomination for *The Fugitive* (1947).

Bibliography

Books

Anderson, Lindsay. *About John Ford*. London: Plexus, 1981.

Bellah, James Warner. *Massacre*. New York: Lion Books, 1950.

Bogdanovich, Peter. *John Ford*. Berkeley, CA: University of California Press, 1978.

Brownlow, Kevin. *The War, the West, and the Wilderness*. New York: Alfred A. Knopf, Inc., 1978.

Capps, Benjamin. *The Old West: The Indians*. Alexander, VA: Time-Life Books, Inc., 1973.

———. *The Old West: The Great Chiefs*. Alexander, VA: Time-Life Books, Inc., 1975.

Carey, Harry, Jr. *Company of Heroes: My Life as an Actor in the John Ford Stock Company*. Metuchen, NJ: Scarecrow Press, 1994.

Cowie, Peter. *John Ford and the American West*. New York: Harry N. Abrams, Inc., 2004.

Davis, Ronald. *John Ford: Hollywood's Old Master*. Norman: University of Oklahoma Press, 1995.

Enns, Chris, and Howard Kazanjian. *Cowboys, Creatures and Classics: The Story of Republic Pictures*. Guilford, CT: Lyons Press. 2018.

Eyman, Scott. *Print the Legend: The Life and Times of John Ford*. New York: Simon & Schuster, 1999.

———. *John Wayne: The Life and Legend*. New York: Simon & Schuster, 2014.

———. *Hank and Jim: The Fifty-Year Friendship of Henry Fonda and James* Stewart. New York: Simon & Schuster, 2017.

Fernett, Gene. *American Film Studios: An Historical Encyclopedia*. Jefferson, NC: McFarland & Company, 1988.

Ford, Dan. *Pappy: The Life of John Ford*. Englewood Cliffs, NJ: Prentice Hall, 1979.

Gaberscek, Carlo. *Il West di John Ford*. Italy: Arti Grafiche Friulane, 1994.

Gallagher, Tag. *John Ford: The Man and His Films*. Berkeley: University of California Press, 1986.

Hardy, Phil, ed. *The Encyclopedia of Western Movies*. London: Octopus Books, 1985.

Jarman, Claude, Jr. *My Life and the Final Days of Hollywood*. Murrells Inlet, SC: Covenant Books, 2018.

Kalinak, Kathryn. *How the West Was Sung: Music in the Westerns of John Ford*. Berkeley: University of California Press, 2007.

Katz, Ephraim. *The Film Encyclopedia*. New York: Harper Perennial, 1994.

Klinck, Richard E. *Land of Room Enough and Time Enough*. Salt Lake City, UT: Peregrine Smith Books, Inc., 1984.
Lamar, Howard R., ed. *The American West: The Reader's Encyclopedia*. New York: Thomas Y. Crowell Company, 1977.
Levy, Bill. *John Ford: A Bio-Bibliography*. Westport, CT: Greenwood Press, 1998.
Malham, Joseph. *John Ford: Poet in the Desert*. Chicago, IL: Lake Street Press, 2013.
McBride, Joseph. *Searching for John Ford*. New York: St. Martin's Press, 2001.
McBride, Joseph, and Michael Wilmington. *John Ford*. London: Secker and Warburg, 1975.
Moon, Samuel. *Tall Sheep: Harry Goulding Monument Valley Trader*. Norman: University of Oklahoma Press, 1992.
O'Hara, Maureen. *'Tis Herself: A Memoir*. New York: Simon & Schuster, 2004.
Peary, Gerald, ed. *John Ford Interviews*. Jackson: University Press of Mississippi, 2001.
Roberson, Chuck, with Bodie Thoene. *The Fall Guy: 30 Years as The Duke's Double*. North Vancouver, British Columbia: Hancock House Publishers, Ltd., 1980.
Roberts, Randy, and James S. Olson. *John Wayne: American*. New York: Free Press, 1995.
Sinclair, Andrew. *John Ford*. New York: Dial Press/James Wade, 1979.
Stanton, Bette L. *Where God Put the West: Movie Making in the Desert. A Moab–Monument Valley History*. Moab, UT: Four Corners Publications, 1994.
Stoehr, Kevin L., and Michael C. Connolly, eds. *John Ford in Focus*. Jefferson, NC: McFarland and Co., 2008.

Magazine Articles

Behlmer, Rudy. "Merian C. Cooper." *Films in Review*, January 1966.
Bogdanovich, Peter. "The Autumn of John Ford." *Esquire*, April 1964.
Le Gravenese, Richard. "An Idol of Mine." *The Hollywood Reporter*, May 29, 1998.
McCarthy, Todd. "John Ford and Monument Valley." *American Film*, May 1978.
Mitchell, George J. "Ford on Ford." *Films in Review*, June–July 1964.
Nugent, Frank S. "Hollywood's Favorite Rebel." *The Saturday Evening Post*, July 23, 1949.
Pryor, Thomas M. "Services Today for Frank Nugent, Caustic Critic as Well as Author of Pix." *Daily Variety*, December 31, 1965.
Turner, George. "Dust and Danger at Fort Apache." *American Cinematographer*, June 1996.

Newspaper Articles

"Actors Falling Off Horses Threaten to Bankrupt Arizona." *St. Louis Star and Times*, December 12, 1947.
"An Appreciation to Mr. Ford and Company." *The Times-Independent*, June 29, 1950.
"Arizona of 70 Years Ago Depicted in Stirring Film Play, Fort Apache." *Arizona Republic*, March 25, 1948.
"Arrangements Completed for Filming New Moving Picture." *The Times-Independent*, May 18, 1950.
"Coast-to-Coast Broadcast Originates at Moab." *The Times-Independent*, July 6, 1950.
"Erection of New Movie Set Started." *The Times-Independent*, June 1, 1950.

"Filming of John Ford's New Picture, 'Rio Bravo,' Starts at Location Near Moab Today." *The Times-Independent*, June 15, 1950.
"Filming of New Moving Picture at Moab Starts Next Week." *The Times-Independent*, June 8, 1950.
"Filming of 'Rio Bravo' Nearing Completion; More Pictures Scheduled for Moab This Year." *The Times-Independent*, June 29, 1950.
"Filming of 'Rio Bravo,' Saga of U.S. Cavalry, Proceeding on Schedule; Republic Owner Visits Moab Location." *The Times-Independent*, June 22, 1950.
"Ford to Arrive June 1 to Make New Picture." *The Times-Independent*, May 4, 1950.
"Get Big Welcome." *Chicago Tribune*, March 31, 1948.
Johnson, John. "No Pain, No Gain: Old-Time Stuntmen Gather Over Coffee to Trade Movie War Stories." *Los Angeles Times*, January 5, 1992.
"Picture Stars Put on Great Show at Moab." *The Times-Independent*, June 29, 1950.
"Picture Troupe Finishes Film." *The Times-Independent*, July 13, 1950.
"Picture Work Ends Friday." *The Times-Independent*, July 6, 1950.
"Preparations Start for Filming New Picture, 'Rio Bravo,' at Moab Starting June 12." *The Times-Independent*, May 11, 1950.
" 'Rio Bravo' Cast to Give Show at Moab." *The Times-Independent*, June 22, 1950.
" 'Rio Grande' Had Its Premiere at San Antonio." *The Times-Independent*, November 9, 1950.
" 'Rio Grande,' Locally Filmed Picture, Proves Big Success." *The Times-Independent*, November 23, 1950.
" 'Rio Grande' to Show at Ides Jan. 9-10-11." *The Times-Independent*, January 4, 1950.
"Sons of the Pioneers" Will Broadcast from Moab Over Columbia Network." *The Times-Independent*, June 29, 1950.
Swindell, Larry. "Yes, John Ford Knew a Thing or Two About Art." *Philadelphia Enquirer*, September 16, 1973.
"Work on Movie Starts at Once." *The Times-Independent*, May 25, 1950.

Documentaries

American Film Institute's First Annual Life Achievement Award (John Ford), American Film Institute, 1973.
The American West of John Ford, Group One-Timex-CBS Productions, 1971.
Directed by John Ford, American Film Institute, 1971.
Hollywood: Out West, video documentary, Thames Television/HBO Video, 1980.
John Ford's America, American Movie Classics, 1989.

Interviews

Larry Blake to the author, March 20, 1979, April 30, 1981, January 16, 1982.
Harry Carey Jr. to the author, June 19, 1996, November 6, 2005.
Abe Haberman to the author, September 1979.
Ed Hulse to the author, November 12, 2020.
Claude Jarman Jr. to the author, October 8, 2021.

George Loomis to the author, September 27, 2021, November 15, 2020.
John McCabe to the author, February 18, 1996.
Roger McGrath to the author, October 14, 2020.

Special Collections

Argosy Productions Collection, L. Thomas Perry Library, Brigham Young University, Provo, Utah.
John Ford Collection, Lilly Library, Indiana University, Bloomington, Indiana.
Production Code Association records, Margaret Herrick Library, Academy of Motion Picture Arts and Sciences, Beverly Hills, California.

Index

About the Author

Michael F. Blake, a two-time Emmy-winning makeup artist, spent sixty years in the film and television industry before his retirement in 2018. His credits include *Westworld*, *X-Men: First Class*, *Spider-Man 3*, *Independence Day*, *Tough Guys*, *Soapdish*, *Police Academy II*, *The Munsters' Revenge*, and *Happy Days*. As a child actor, Michael appeared in such television shows as *Adam-12*, *The Lucy Show*, *The Munsters*, *Bonanza*, *Kung Fu*, *The Red Skelton Show*, and *Marcus Welby, M.D.*

A respected film scholar, with a master's degree from UCLA, Michael's books on silent screen legend Lon Chaney are the definitive works on the actor. His trilogy served as the basis for the Turner Classic Movies documentary, *Lon Chaney: A Thousand Faces* (2000), in which he was a special consultant and on-camera interviewee. Michael's books, *Code of Honor: The Making of High Noon, Shane, and The Searchers*, and *Hollywood and the O.K. Corral* have been recognized as important works about the Western film genre.

The Cowboy President: The American West and the Making of Theodore Roosevelt was named by *True West* magazine as Best Political Biography for 2018, and won the Will Rogers Gold Medallion Award for Best Biography/Memoir. His latest book, *Go West, Mr. President: Theodore Roosevelt's 1903 Great Loop Tour*, offers an insightful look into a little-known aspect of the president's life.

Michael has provided audio commentary for several Lon Chaney films, as well as appeared in documentaries about John Ford, Irving Thalberg, and Max Factor. He has written articles for *Wild West*, *American Cinematographer*, *True West*, *Roundup*, and the *Los Angeles Times*. Western Writers of America awarded him their Stirrup Award for his articles about the making of *The Searchers* in 2017, and in 2020, about Theodore Roosevelt's efforts to preserve the Grand Canyon.

Michael lives in Arizona with his wife, Linda, and their two dogs.